The Politics and
Economics of
ization

The Politics and Economics of Privatization

The Case of Wastewater Treatment

John G. Heilman and Gerald W. Johnson

THE UNIVERSITY OF ALABAMA PRESS

Tuscaloosa and London

∞

The paper on which this book is printed meets the minimum requirements of American
National Standard for Information Science-Permanence of Paper for Printed Library Materials, ANSI A39.48-1984.

Library of Congress Cataloging-in-Publication Data

Heilman, John G.
    The politics and economics of privatization : the case of
wastewater treatment / John G. Heilman and Gerald W. Johnson
        p.   cm.
    Includes bibliographical references (p.   ) and index.
    ISBN 0-8173-0569-6 (alk. paper)
    1. Sewage disposal—United States—Case studies.
    2. Privatization—United States—Case studies.   I. Johnson, Gerald
W.   II. Title.
HD4477.H45   1992
338.973—dc20   91-43291
                                                                    CIP

British Library Cataloguing-in-Publication Data available

For
Ursula Jung Heilman
and
Nadine Maynard Johnson

Privatization . . . is much more than a set of specific changes in who performs an activity and how. It is part of a fundamental political and economic rethinking that today is reassessing the roles of government and the private sector in the modern welfare state—a rethinking that is having an influence on all segments of American opinion.

Report of the President's Commission on Privatization

Contents

Figures

Tables

Acknowledgments

The Politics and Economics of Privatization is the result of eight years of research—in the library, in the field, in the office, through mail and telephone interviews, published articles and presented papers, and countless hours of office discussion, often lively, between the authors. To acknowledge appropriately all of the individuals, agencies, and organizations that contributed to this lengthy research project would require an extended statement. We thank them each and all and limit ourselves here to explicit mention of just a few of the many who have helped us so much.

Our initial interest in the topic of privatization began with a personal and professional relationship with Douglas J. Watson, City Manager of Auburn, Alabama. In 1983, Auburn was one of the first cities in the United States to make a decision to privatize its wastewater treatment facilities. Douglas Watson involved us in the decision-making process and throughout the implementation of the project until the facilities went on-line in 1985. We are indebted to him for providing us accessibility to the Auburn project and for his advice and review of our work and ideas.

As a result of our involvement in the Auburn project, we subsequently received access, support, and funding for specific research tasks involving privatization from the U.S. Environmental Protection Agency and from Metcalf & Eddy, Inc. In 1986, we received a grant from the U.S. Geological Survey, U.S. Department of the Interior, Award no. 14-08-0001-G1288, to conduct a two-year national study of the feasibility of the privatization of wastewater treatment facilities. This book presents the results of that study. The contents do not necessarily reflect the views and policies of the

Department of the Interior, nor does mention of trade names or commercial products constitute endorsement or recommendation for use. The grant was matched with support from the Research Division and the Water Resources Research Institute of Auburn University. We thank both of these organizations for their support. The support received does not signify that the contents necessarily reflect the views and policies of either the Department of the Interior or of Auburn University.

We are also indebted to Dr. Laurence J. O'Toole, Jr., Professor of Political Science at Auburn University, who conducted some of the policy implementation analyses, and to Dr. Randall G. Holcombe, Professor of Economics at Florida State University, who conducted some of the economic analyses. In addition, during the research period five graduate students and one undergraduate student participated in the project. They are Jean England, Terry Bowen, Alfred Davis, Scott Sullivan, Robert Gottesman, and James Hurston.

We extend our appreciation to Virginia Prickett, Administrative Secretary to the Auburn University Public Administration Program, who contributed invaluable typing and clerical services, and to James Warman and Dennis Block of the Water Resources Research Institute who were tireless in providing administrative assistance.

Lastly, we acknowledge with gratitude the thorough, thoughtful, and constructive review of this manuscript by two anonymous readers. Their suggestions helped shape the final work.

While the preceding and scores of interviewees in both the public and the private sectors contributed much to the project, the authors share sole and equal responsibility for the contents of this work.

The Politics and Economics of Privatization

Introduction

In the mid-1980s hundreds of cities and other local authorities across the United States faced a common and relatively expensive problem of infrastructure development: they needed new or expanded wastewater treatment facilities. Some of these authorities proceeded along the well-established route of obtaining a grant from the United States Environmental Protection Agency (EPA) to support design and construction of the plants they needed. However, as construction grants declined in number and size, some authorities considered an innovative approach to infrastructure project development based on the principle of partnership with the private sector. The approach is privatization. It differs from other public-private partnership approaches to service delivery by virtue of its comprehensiveness and its impact on fundamental public and private structures and processes. The privatizing firm actively undertakes and coordinates all major phases of project development and implementation, including design, finance, construction, operations and maintenance, and ownership.

Between 1984 and 1986 the authorities that decided to use this comprehensive partnership approach to meet their wastewater treatment needs were able to take advantage of substantial financial incentives that had become available to the private sector through tax law changes in 1981 and 1982. At the same time, these authorities accepted—and tried to manage as best they could—multiple financial and political risks associated with privatization. Wastewater treatment projects typically involved some of the largest investments these cities would make. And while this comprehensive partnership approach had been used in solid-waste facilities, its application to wastewater treatment was an innovation.[1] The long-term financial soundness of these deals was open to question, as was accountability, both public and private. In addition, privatization efforts confronted a number of legal, administrative, technical, and political hurdles.

By 1986, it appeared that privatization of wastewater treatment facilities would spread rapidly across the country through adoption by cities needing to upgrade their treatment capacity. The tax reform of 1986, however, removed many of the tax incentives that had generated the first deals (Birnbaum and Murray 1987). The impending rush of privatization deals slowed to a trickle.

Notwithstanding the effects of the 1986 tax law, the comprehensive privatization approach to infrastructure development—and infrastructure policy implementation—remains a viable option for meeting some major infrastructure needs.[2] However, it represents a complex, costly, and risky undertaking, based on concepts that are as yet little understood. The literature of policy and administration has, to date, treated it largely as terra incognita: it is not unlike distant reaches of the globe, shown in ancient navigators' maps to be inhabited by mermaids and monsters. The policy framework needed for its development and implementation remains to be elaborated.

This book[3] explores privatization in the field of wastewater treatment policy and its implementation with attention to the following issues and purposes. What is it? How does it work? What advantages and disadvantages attach to it? Can it be effectively managed, and if so, how? What promise and risk does it hold? And what can we learn from it concerning the role of the private sector in policy and administration more broadly? These issues are subsumed under the more general notion of the politics and economics of privatization.

During eight years invested in the study of national wastewater policy and privatization, the authors have received frequent invitations to explain why this area warrants detailed investigation. If one is going to do a study of public-private sector relationships, why focus on privatization, one form of partnership, and why wastewater treatment? We selected and stayed with this subject for three main reasons.

Why Study Privatization of Wastewater Treatment

"The Future Is Sludge"

One motivation for studying wastewater treatment derives from our conviction that policies and options affecting water quality, including wastewater treatment, are highly important both nationally and locally and merit attention from policy scientists. Many reasons exist for taking this view.

Health. Wastewater treatment is an important environmental policy in terms of quality of life factors—physical, biological, and aesthetic. It is a prerequisite for maintaining the public supply of potable water. Sewage, whether treated or not, flows into surface and groundwater supplies and becomes part of the supply of drinking water. This relationship is especially clear (or cloudy) where sewage plants discharge directly into drinking water reservoirs or where septic tanks in an area pollute the groundwater supply. Poorly treated wastewater becomes poor-quality drinking water. As one presenter at a recent international conference on infrastructure policy commented (Wartemberg 1989), if people don't have safe water to drink, they lose the health needed to employ and enjoy other aspects of the infrastructure. Or, as Philip Giantris stated (1989:47): "Effective management of the environmental infrastructure of a society is critical, as life support, to the very existence of that society. The issues of adequate, safe water supply, and effective, sanitary wastewater treatment and disposal have challenged humankind throughout time."

Cost and Need. Wastewater treatment policy will continue to be a large item in governmental budgets. The Clean Water Act of 1972 provided more than $40 billion in grant funding for the construction of thousands of municipal treatment works during the 1970s and 1980s. However, much of our water is still badly contaminated, and some of the problems result directly from inadequate treatment of point and nonpoint source pollution. The United States Environmental Protection Agency's *1988 Needs Survey Report to Congress* (EPA 1989a) estimates that at least $75 billion is needed simply to provide sufficient treatment facilities to bring communities across the United States up to national treatment standards. We can expect the size and cost of the problem to increase as population increases. As one engineering company executive suggested with respect to the growing problem of disposing of the solid waste left over from treatment, "the future is sludge."

More generally, the need for infrastructure renewal and development is widely recognized to be large and pressing (Pagano and Moore 1985:126). Privatization, properly developed and managed, can help to meet this need. However, proper organization and management will depend in part on a thorough understanding of the privatization option. One purpose of this book is to contribute to such an understanding.

Equity. Equity issues arise as well. The proliferation of bottled water products, ranging from distilled water to Perrier, on store shelves and in dispensing machines, sends a clear message about social stratification. Access to palatable water is coming to depend on ability to pay. The growing business in water filters and treatment systems confirms this message. Water pollution and its treatment increasingly involve policies having differential effects across social class.

Timing and Access

A second reason we did this study had to do with timing and access. The first completed privatized wastewater projects were in Auburn, Alabama, our own backyard. Our early involvement with this initial, path-breaking effort to develop projects of this kind provided a unique opportunity and vantage point from which to explore the development, adoption, and implementation of this policy innovation. Based on our involvement in this frontier effort we were able to secure funding for a national study. This book presents the results of that study.

A Window on Public-Private Partnerships

The third and perhaps most important reason for this study is that privatization as we define it is one form—an important form—of public-private partnership. The worldwide movement to rely on and exploit such partnerships invokes a mixing of political and economic strategies that is innovative and promising but also risky. The form of partnership that we term privatization brings into especially sharp relief this interplay of political and economic factors.

Similarly, the specific field of wastewater treatment is well-suited to the study of this mix of economics and politics. Privatization emerged as a result of broad changes in attitudes and metapolicy, meaning the direction and content of national policy (Johnson and Heilman 1987b).

These changes included tax reform, budgetary constraints, and devolution of policy and programs from the federal level to state and local governments and to the private sector. As discussed in detail in Chapter 2, wastewater treatment policy illustrates quite readily how these political and economic forces can interact to create partnership opportunities.

Debate over public-private partnerships plays out in terms of ideological interpretation as well as in terms of policy formation and implementation. At the level of ideology, the partnership movement appears variously as a revolution, a reform, or a regression. To some it is the answer to increased international economic competition, to the desire to reduce the size of government, and to the demand to do more with less. To others partnerships pose a threat to fundamental political and social values. They are perceived as a return to turn-of-the-century laissez-faire capitalism and economic Darwinism.

As we shall see in more detail in Chapter 1, perspectives differ also on public-private partnerships at the level of policy analysis. One method of analyzing partnerships (see especially Savas 1987) focuses on goods and services to be produced and evaluates their responsiveness to the forces of the private market. In this approach, goods that are responsive to market forces are seen as appropriate for production and delivery by the market.

A different approach suggests that the nature of the good or the market does not directly determine whether production or delivery will be better done in the private sector than in the public sector. Rather, partnerships are evaluated in terms of the processes of management and administration they bring to bear on production and delivery (see especially Kettl 1988 and Wise 1990). This approach invokes a style of administration and management based on common goals derived from negotiations across sectors as well as on a continuing oversight role for the public sector while production and delivery take place in the private sector. The nature of goods and services remains important in this approach to the extent that some goods and services will accommodate this style of administration and management more readily than others.

This book is intended neither to advocate nor to discourage interest in or reliance on the privatization option. Rather, it is intended to provide a conceptual and empirical foundation that not only academic researchers but also decision makers in both the public and the private sectors can draw on usefully if and as they address privatization. In this context, this study concludes that under the style or model of management proposed by Kettl, privatization *can be* conceptually and practically sound for both public and private sectors. It is a highly complex arrangement that capitalizes on the fundamental dynamics inherent in each sector. It differs in multiple ways from the well-established practice of contracting out for services, and to work well it must be understood for what it is and for what it is not.

Audiences and Organization

This book addresses two audiences. The primary audience includes students of political science, public administration, public policy, urban politics and planning, and related areas in public finance and economics. The second audience includes practicing public administrators and policymakers as well as private sector industry, business, and finance personnel who work with or for the public sector. The decision to include practitioners in our audience reflects our belief that privatization has a direct impact on public management as well as on political and economic processes and outcomes. As observed by the National Academy of Public Administration's Panel on the Management of Privatization (1989:ix), "privatization changes the role of the public manager" and "rather than deny this reality students of administration, along with their public administration counterparts, must begin to recognize it explicitly and alter training and inquiry accordingly." As Sundquist has observed even more succinctly (1984:310), "Privatization calls for special talents on the part of the public administrators responsible . . . , because their authority is not commensurate with their responsibility."

We developed a sensitivity to this perspective while conducting our research. In traveling the country to conduct on-site case studies, we were repeatedly impressed by the implications of privatization for the study and practice of public administration. Our experience on this and related projects has led to the development in our M.P.A. and Ph.D. programs of curricular specializations in public-private administration and policy. This background and experience has led us to conclude that a systematic report on privatization, or any form of partnership, can and should address both theoretical and practical issues and audiences who care about them.

The book consists of eleven chapters. The opening chapters consider the emergence, nature, and functioning of privatization. Chapter 1 develops context. It describes how the partnership movement resulted in part from the demand to do more with less, at least less government and resources. It summarizes the arguments raised by advocates and critics of the approach and provides a theory-sketch and research questions that guide the analysis in the rest of the book.

Chapter 2 provides the historical background of the development of national water policy and specifically of wastewater treatment privatization. It describes how privatization developed in this sector in relation to changes in national water policy and tax policy in the 1980s. Chapter 3 presents the first of the book's three major case studies. The case of Auburn, Alabama, provides a classic example of how privatization was developed in a model form.

Chapter 4 explores how privatization works in practice and analyzes how the structure, system, and process of privatization relate to issues of efficiency and costs, both political and economic. It reports the results of extensive field studies designed to respond to the theoretical issues raised in Chapter 1.

In the following chapters the investigation shifts focus from privatization itself, and how it works, to the broader context in which it works. Privatization is, as we shall see, heavily dependent on the legal, economic, and political frameworks within which it operates. As these systems vary, so too do many, if not all, of the factors and relationships identified in the theory-sketch in Chapter 1. Chapter 5 turns to the national and state legal and policy context in which privatization takes place. It describes and analyzes the approaches represented by five different state laws.

The discussion next turns to some of the most important economic questions concerning privatization. Chapter 6 compares the costs of privatized and nonprivatized projects and then assesses the cost of privatization to the U.S. Treasury under different tax scenarios. Chapter 7 considers privatization costs to local communities under different contractual arrangements with the privatizer. A second case study is presented in Chapter 8 and deals with Mount Vernon, Illinois, a post-1986 tax reform privatization project that includes all of the essential elements for successful privatization absent tax incentives.

Chapter 9 examines the broader political and institutional setting in which privatization takes place. It reviews the politics of privatization at the national, state, and local levels of government. It reports on surveys of industry executives and state regulatory agency officials and assesses the implications of the role of each for privatization as a policy strategy. Chapter 10, the third major case study, reviews the experience of the Western Carolina Regional Sewer Authority. The case illustrates how some of the problems in privatization resulted in the eventual de-privatization of a pre-1986 tax reform project.

Chapter 11 presents conclusions. It analyzes privatization in terms of its economic and political conditions, consequences, and implications. Is privatization a revolution, a reform, or a regression? Our overall conclusion is that privatization can be a productive policy and strategy to help meet infrastructure needs. It has the potential to be both economically efficient and politically acceptable in terms of public accountability and responsibility. However, privatization is not without both economic and political costs that must be addressed, through appropriate policy, organization, and management, if it is to serve usefully as a structure and option for meeting increasing public service needs. In agreement with James L. Sundquist (1984) and Charles R. Wise (1990), we conclude that neither the ideological arguments of the opponents of government nor those of the avid proponents of a market solution to all public service problems provide an adequate or sound basis for partnership approaches such as privatization. Rather, privatization requires a changed but essential role for both sectors in the provision, production, and delivery of public services.

1

Public-Private Partnerships

The Partnership Movement

The United States and, in fact, the world's community of nations face a set of political and economic realities that, taken together, are new and pose fundamental challenges to the nature of the state, whether democratic or nondemocratic in form of government. There is, first of all, a growing collective realization that resources are limited (Colman 1989:61–65). Second, citizens are reluctant to pay more for public services (Colman 1989:73–81). Third, needs and demands for public services continue to increase (Sharp 1990:286–89). How is the gap between decreasing resources and increasing needs to be closed?

One approach or strategy being considered in various forms around the world reflects renewed interest in reliance on the private market. This approach is often referred to as "privatization" or as "public-private partnership." It has developed in different ways and with different emphases in different countries. (For multiple perspectives and experiences in the United States, see Finley 1989 and Brooks, Liebman, and Schelling 1984.)

In this book the term *public-private partnership* is used to describe the general movement, and the term *privatization* is reserved for a specific approach or type of partnership. Therefore we speak of the *partnership movement*. In most if not all of its forms, this movement involves restructuring relationships between the public and the private sectors. It involves economic adaptation as well as an altering of the political landscape (Henig, Hamnett, and Feigenbaum 1988). Both implications need to be understood and appreciated because one cannot take place without the other.

To date, the partnership movement has been driven in large part by the nee⸍ ᴐ make economic adaptations. Its foundation thus consists, to an impoɾʟant extent, of assumptions about the efficiency and productivity of a private market based on competition. In the current context of intense competition for limited federal resources in the United States, the call for increased efficiency and productivity is widespread and powerful. However, its reliance on economic values can mask its implications for political values. The premise here is that it is important to understand both the political and the economic consequences of this movement before we "elect" or "buy into" it. The values of efficiency are not the same as the values of democracy. As R. H. Tawney observed in *Religion and the Rise of Capitalism*: "Economic efficiency is a necessary element in the life of any sane and vigorous society, and only the incorrigible senᴛimentalist will depreciate its significance. But to convert efficiency from an instrument into a primary object is to destroy efficiency itself" (1926:232).

The Politics and Economics of Privatization defines and analyzes the stress points that develop as economic and democratic values are meshed in privatization as one form of public-private partnership. Knowledge on these matters serves both theoretical and practical purposes. It can add to our understanding of the nature of the state as well as suggest strategies for strengthening government and administration so that the partnership approach can be politically as well as economically productive. Private market values pursued at the expense of public market values (that is, public goods and public processes) impact the nature of the state.[4] The implications of such for public policy processes may be substantial. As Henig, Hamnett, and Feigenbaum (1988:443) have noted, "enthusiasts liken this policy [privatization movement] to a kind of world revolution. Like all revolutions, we argue, this one is best understood in political terms."

Partnerships and Privatization: Nature and Definition

The partnership movement has developed in the United States over the past three decades and has taken many forms. Its influence and reach were most readily apparent in the 1980s when "President Reagan was the first to redefine the federal government's role as limited, wherever possible, to providing services without producing them" (Seidman and Gilmour 1986:119). Reagan promoted tax policies (Anderson

1984:57–60; Palmer and Sawhill 1984; Wittl 1985) that strongly encouraged private investment in a range of public projects. He also called for the federal level of government to make greater use of the private sector through implementation of Circular A-76 (Executive Order 12615, 1987), established an Office of Privatization in the Office of Management and Budget, and appointed a Commission on Privatization (Report 1988). At the state level, many states adopted comprehensive privatization legislation (Feldman 1989a; Privatization Council 1987). Local-level governments contracted increasingly with private firms for services ranging from airport operation to zoning and subdivision control (Rehfuss 1989) and experimented with a form of local-level denationalization called privatization (Johnson and Heilman 1987b; see generally Colman 1989).

It is important to note, however, that the partnership movement so evident in the 1980s was "not so much the beginning as the culmination of a trend in federal administration and management of domestic programs" (Seidman and Gilmour, 1986:120, for all quoted material in this paragraph). In "a shift from direct to what Salamon [1981] calls 'indirect or "third party" government,'" the "preferred means for carrying out federal programs" came to include "contracts, loan guarantees, tax subsidies," each of which tends to shift important responsibilities or powers over services from the public to the private sector. While the overall size, pace, and intensity of the shift can be argued, Seidman and Gilmour cite evidence, provided by Mosher (1980:12), that strongly suggests that the shift was unmistakably under way prior to 1980: "From 1970 to 1980, the size of the civilian executive branch workforce decreased by 120,000 employees, as total federal expenditures increased by about 195 percent. In the same period expenditures for service contracts increased 28 percent."

These shifts in administration and management were paralleled in the field of public administration theory by the development of the public choice paradigm (Ostrom and Ostrom 1971). Louis Wechsler (1982:289) identifies several works published in the 1960s and 1970s that applied "rational individual choice to rule making, organizational design, and administrative behavior." These works include Buchanan and Tullock, *The Calculus of Consent* (1962); Tullock, *The Politics of Bureaucracy* (1965); Downs, *Inside Bureaucracy* (1967); Niskanen, *Bureaucracy and Representative Government* (1971); and Ostrom, *The Intellectual Crisis in American Public Administration* (1974). Wechsler states that these books "form the core of what might be called 'classic public choice' for public administration. . . . The[y] apply models of rational individual choice to rule making, organizational design, and administrative behavior."

The trends in administration and policy cited by Seidman and Gilmour, together with the intellectual developments Wechsler describes, laid a foundation for the growth of the partnership movement during the 1980s. The gain of momentum in this decade occurred not just in the United States but worldwide.

In Great Britain, Prime Minister Margaret Thatcher presided over extensive denationalization, meaning the selling off of British industry to the private sector (Fraser 1988; Kay, Mayer, and Thompson 1986). Publicly owned industries were also denationalized in countries ranging from Japan to Mexico and Brazil. In China, "farming communes were disbanded and most farmland was returned to private ownership, with the result that food production rocketed" (Savas 1987:169–70). And, a central theme in President Mikhail Gorbachev's conception of "perestroika," or restructuring, was to legitimize and to expand the role of the private sector in the Soviet Union. The tenuous nature of this restructuring in the early 1990s, incidentally, provides comparative evidence on a point made repeatedly later in this book: moves toward greater private sector participation in public service production can be reversed, and both public and private sector players need to plan with that possibility in mind.

In general, the movement seems likely to maintain its momentum, not because public-private partnerships are inherently good or desirable but because the pressures to refine and rely on them will prove ineluctable (Salamon 1989). This prediction is controversial: more than one rationale has been advanced to explain why the partnership movement will slow or even wither. For example, Elaine B. Sharp (1990:285–86) suggests that, viewed as an innovation, privatization will reach a peak of adoptions and then level off. She also suggests that the idea of privatization is no longer in as "good currency" as it was during the 1980s. Also, Charles R. Wise (1990:146) forecasts "a limited, rather than comprehensive, role for privatization . . . because it is not even a theory of organization—it is a reaction or a series of counterproposals to traditional bureaucracies. Privatization is not a single set of measures that logically or practically entail one another."

The partnership movement is more likely to thrive than they suggest. As Seidman and Gilmour's work indicates, this movement is already deeply woven into the fabric of American public policy and administration. Hints of its sociopolitical richness appear in the different labels that have been applied to it: each suggests a different emphasis. The reference to government by proxies calls attention to our pluralist nature—to the "third parties that ultimately administer . . . programs" (Kettl 1988:5). The term *privatization* emphasizes the location of those third parties in the private sector (Beard 1913 suggests the constitutional relevance). And the notion of partnerships calls attention to the organizational structures and management processes through which public and private sector players interact (for an exposition of relevant issues, see Wise 1990).

Whatever labels are applied to them, strategies for public-private partnership involve a reconfiguration of organizational structures and relationships between the sectors so as to provide, produce, or deliver a service (Kolderie 1984, 1986). Many options exist, and they differ in terms of organizational arrangements and the extent of reliance on the private sector.

Savas (1987:62−88) describes many of the principal arrangements. As drawn largely from his discussion, the following options reflect the variety involved:

Contracting. The government unit pays a private firm to produce or deliver a service. A common example is solid-waste collection.

Denationalization. This option involves the transfer to the private sector or to workers, through sale or otherwise, of a government-owned arrangement for service production. The sale of Conrail to the public in 1987 is an example.

Tax expenditures. Federal or state tax code provisions offer incentives to private organizations and individuals to produce a public service. The comprehensive privatization of certain infrastructure projects in the 1980s, as described in this book, makes use of such incentives. Savas (1987:77) appears to classify tax exemptions as grants. They are listed here separately on the grounds that in some cases, such as financing for infrastructure projects, grants may involve so much more regulation than tax expenditures that they tend to result in higher production costs.

Grants and *vouchers*. These are arrangements through which government subsidizes the production of a good or service. Grants typically involve government subsidy of the producer, though the grant money may flow to the producer through the consumer (Savas 1987:77). As described later in this book, federal grants were commonly used to finance municipal wastewater treatment plants. Vouchers provide a subsidy to consumers, allowing them relatively complete freedom of choice in the marketplace. Food stamps provide one example. Another is the perhaps more controversial proposal to provide parents with vouchers they can use to pay for the schooling of their children.

While the forms and names of public-private partnerships vary, they typically share a common objective. They are intended to create or enhance a market opportunity for the efficient production or delivery of a public service. Opportunities for successfully increasing the role of the private sector depend on time and place. What is traditionally public service in one setting may not be so in another; and new partnership configurations do not necessarily travel well from one setting or function to another. Thus, prospects for developing a very general theory to explain partnership outcomes are necessarily limited. Nevertheless, the partnership movement has a political and intellectual history broad and deep enough to offer a common foundation for the different strategies or options discussed above.

The partnership movement is hardly new. In the United States, it draws on conceptions of efficiency and nonpartisanship linked to the intellectual tradition of the Progressive movement of the early 1900s (see generally Wiebe 1962). More recently, the partnership movement derives from a line of political ideology that draws together three normative strands. The first of these is an emphasis on government failures in the economic, social, and international arenas. The second is faith in the perceived inherent efficiencies of the market economy (for extended discussion of both market and government failures, see Weimer and Vining 1989:29–173). The third element is a call for a general reduction of the bureaucratic and financial size and role of the public sector (see publications of the Adam Smith Institute, the Reason Foundation, the Heritage Foundation, and the "public choice" school generally).

These political and economic developments raise fundamental issues of public life and the nature of the state. The Report of the President's Commission on Privatization (Report 1988) suggests some of the principal issues when it states that "Privatization . . . is much more than a set of specific changes in who performs an activity and how. It is part of a fundamental political and economic rethinking that today is reassessing the roles of government and the private sector in the modern welfare state—a rethinking that is having an influence on all segments of American opinion" (xii). Again, to cite the report of the commission:

> The United States is experiencing a renewed interest in the systematic examination of the boundary between public and private delivery of goods and services. The interest has been stimulated in part by concerns that the

federal government has become too large, too expensive, and too intrusive in our lives. The interest also reflects the belief that new arrangements between the public and the private sector might improve efficiency while offering new opportunities and greater satisfaction for the people served. (1)

More importantly, however, the report provides an instructive insight into the intended impact that the movement will have on government if it is fully implemented as envisioned and supported by the report. In essence, the report calls for a withering away of the state. To illustrate:

Government is facing a major challenge, because the political and economic concepts that have traditionally given legitimacy to government actions have come under growing criticism. The potential influence of the privatization movement has only begun to be felt. Current political and economic trends will make privatization a policy direction of fundamental social significance for the future. (229)

As American politics becomes more ideologically and religiously pluralistic, it becomes more and more difficult to see government as the valid expression of any single national community of common values. (239)

Yet, in a pluralistic American society where in some key areas there is little social agreement on values, who is to say what values are to be asserted throughout the process of governing? Indeed, does it make any sense to favor one set of values over another? If not, then a reduction in the scope of national government may be the only answer. (250)

If privatization consists simply of eliminating government programs and cutting off benefits, change may come at a slow pace. If privatization consists, however, of forming and recognizing new private rights for the beneficiaries of existing programs, the pace of privatization could accelerate. In fact, privatization in this form might even be an inevitable long-run result of the dynamics of interest-group politics. (249)

The implications of the report are quite clear. Government no longer has a valid claim to determine values and set priorities for society. The private market can and should undertake this function. These radical claims are far removed from arguments over simple efficiency or who does what. They imply a pressing need for careful analysis of both the economics and the politics of the movement toward greater reliance on the private market.

This book has as its immediate subject a particular form of partnership that is capital intensive. It is referred to simply as privatization. This usage represents a departure from general practice and from our own usage in earlier publications (Johnson and Heilman 1987b; Heilman and Johnson 1989). Many works (for example, Savas 1987 and Report 1988) use the term privatization as an umbrella covering a range of public-private partnership approaches. A review of the existing privatization literature, however, reveals that this term has been used in such a variety of ways that it has lost its power to define any reasonably precise pattern or structure of activity. In addition, the term has taken on ideological connotations. Therefore, it is appropriate to assign a narrow meaning to the term *privatization* and treat it as one of several forms of public-private partnership. In this book the term *public-private partnership* serves as an umbrella, covering multiple strategies for service production and delivery, including privatization and other forms of government by proxy.

Under the restricted definition used here, privatization is a capital-intensive form of public-private partnership in which the private sector may build, own, operate, and partially or totally finance a facility.[5] It can be interpreted as a local equivalent of denationalization. The private sector produces and delivers a service and, to some extent, provides it. This relatively narrow definition allows increased control over the analysis of the issues that arise and problems that appear in one particular partnership form.

A Problem for Public Policy

Public-private partnerships pose a prickly policy problem: they can provide both very attractive and very risky strategies and structures for serving public needs. On the one hand, ample (although mixed) evidence exists to show that public officials can successfully use these strategies to respond to economic pressures for cost cutting and efficiency, to answer public demands for quality and accountable service, and to meet national, state, and local compliance standards (Savas 1987; see also Weimer and Vining 1989:174–78). For some, the ideological benefit of less government provides added appeal (Heritage Foundation 1987). Thus, powerful arguments favor increased reliance by the public sector on partners in the private sector.

On the other hand, such partnerships can pose threats to political values and result in loss of jobs, loss of public accountability, inefficiencies, fraud, mismanagement, and corruption in various forms (American Federation of Government Employees 1987; Squires 1989). Three of the most prominent cases from the 1980s include abuses in Pentagon contracting, scandals in the Department of Housing and Urban Development (HUD), and the savings and loan (S&L) bailout. These examples and many others fuel arguments against overreliance on the private sector to serve public purposes. Thus, the movement has ardent advocates (Butler 1985a, 1985b; Savas 1989) as well as opponents (AFSCME 1983; Kuttner 1989).

The policymaker who enters into a partnership faces the problem of how to organize and manage it so as to maximize its advantages while minimizing the risks, in effect combining economic efficiency and political accountability. In this context, the challenge for policy science is in part to define, assess, and respond to the tensions, risks, and conflicts of values inherent in public-private partnerships. The issues involved are both theoretical and practical. A theoretical concern is the impact of public-private partnerships on the constitutional and political fabric of our system of governance (and vice versa).

At a practical level, what strategies might public managers adopt to balance economic and political values in these partnerships? Specifically, how can a public-private partnership balance or join the different values inherent in the private and public markets? The fundamental private market value is profit. Profit is driven in part by the efficiency that competition imposes on the market. Pure competition is characterized by processes of information sharing and decision making that are in important ways closed and noncooperative, for instance, with respect to production techniques. In Adam Smith's (1937) view, the market penalizes such cooperative behavior. By contrast, the public market is based on the values of representativeness and public accountability. Public accountability results, in part, from open and cooperative processes of information sharing and decision making. For instance, such processes include public notice, public meetings, and voting.

Thus, the fundamental dynamic of each type of market is in conflict with the other. The problem for public-private partnerships is how to resolve, or accommodate, this conflict. The concepts of accommodation and balance are central to the working out of this problem. If the private sector attempts to provide a basic public service (such as solid-waste disposal or wastewater treatment) in a strictly private market context (such as through a merchant facility), the absence of public accountability will tend to force the service back into the public sector or into a public service commission regulatory structure.[6] Neither of these results serves the objectives of both markets. A true partnership structure, however, can.

From this perspective, the problem becomes one of what a true partnership means and how to provide the policy context in which it can be developed and implemented. To address this problem it is not sufficient to distinguish appropriate markets on the basis of the nature of the good (Brooks 1984; Savas 1987). Nor is it adequate to allocate to one of the markets a particular function or service on the basis of the role or nature of the market (Kolderie 1984). Rather, it is a question of configuring public-private structures so that goods or services are adequately subject to the dynamics of both markets.

The allocation of goods or services to the public market or the private market is not fixed in political or economic terms or even in legal ones. The U.S. Supreme Court has held that

> There is not, and there cannot be, any unchanging line of demarcation between essential and non-essential govermental functions. Many governmental functions of today have at some time in the past been non-governmental. The genius of our government provides that, within the sphere of constitutional action, the people—acting not through the courts but through their elected legislative representatives—have the power to determine, as conditions demand, what services and functions the public welfare requires.[7]

That is, each generation must determine the appropriate allocation and mix of functions between the public and private markets.

The theoretical framework used to analyze these issues is presented later in this chapter. The book proceeds from the premise that a review of the issues just discussed is highly important for the development of sound public policy in the 1990s. The National Academy of Public Administration, in its report on the management of privatization (1989:vii), noted that, to date, these partnerships, at least in some of their forms (for instance, privatization), "remain poorly understood. Much of the recent debate has proceeded in philosophical terms that rarely get down to the nuts and bolts of actual operations."

Privatization

In privatization, as defined here, a private sector firm acquires or builds a facility to produce a service identified, at a particular time, with the public sector. In the most extended form of privatization, the private sector is responsible for all elements of service production. If new facilities are involved, these elements include project design, construction, finance, ownership, operation, and maintenance. This strategy is suited to high-cost capital-intensive infrastructure projects, such as prisons, roads, solid-waste combustion facilities, wastewater treatment works, housing, and airports. It typically can involve equity contributions from the private firm to defray project costs and can result in service costs substantially lower than the public sector could otherwise obtain.

In an era of increased competition for limited resources, this partnership strategy provides an alternative approach to providing high-cost and high-demand services. Its appeal grows in part out of the nation's needs for infrastructure renewal. We know that the bill for this renewal will be enormous and that units of local government are increasingly called on to meet these costs. We also know that in an era of deficit reduction, traditional public funding for projects of this type will not be available to meet more than a modest fraction of the needs. Chapter 2 reviews this situation in the setting of wastewater treatment policy. Privatization offers an alternative strategy for addressing some of these pressing needs. Because it represents the most extended form of public-private partnership, it bears with unusual directness on fundamental public sector values of representativeness and accountability.

Despite its distinctive nature and potential utility, privatization is practically unaddressed in the public policy literature.[8] An industry literature on the subject exists, but it is clearly self-interested.[9] At least one federal agency has addressed privatization, as well as other public-private partnership forms, but these efforts have been late in coming and their future is uncertain (EPA 1989b). Thus, a need exists for systematic information. The present study responds to this need by describing, analyzing, and assessing in detail the application of this approach in a single service area: the design, construction, and operation of local wastewater treatment works (WTWs).

The rationale for focusing on a single type of project is that to understand privatization means in part to understand how it works in particular forms and settings. Through a national study involving case studies, surveys, and on-site interview data, the functioning of privatization in one service area is documented thoroughly. The study includes, first of all, a careful examination of the broad system of political and economic actors involved. Among these actors are private sector firms as well as state legislatures, state regulatory agencies, national interest groups, and federal agencies and committees in Congress. Thorough assessment also involves multiple case studies. Privatized projects are so large and complex that no single case can provide access to all the main issues.

A further reason to concentrate on WTW privatization is that success or failure in privatization is heavily dependent on the specifics of local setting, the service involved, and the kind of privatization involved (Hatry 1987). In this same vein, Roger Feldman, among others, has warned against assuming that a privatization strategy that works well for one kind of service or government entity will travel well. As Feldman puts it, "you can't necessarily mix and match" privatization strategies across service functions or governmental settings (Feldman 1989b). Some projects will work better than others, and the reasons why they do so will vary across projects. Knowledge of these variations is essential to an understanding of the complex risks the privatizing community or authority faces.

Once this understanding is developed in a given service area, the results permit some careful generalization. Evidence exists to suggest that capital-intensive privatization raises a fairly stable set of issues across service areas.[10] These issues can be identified and clarified. Certainly variation occurs. For instance, solid-waste facilities offer revenue streams not present in wastewater projects. And prison privatization raises difficult constitutional issues that are not prominent in other service areas (Fitzgerald and Lyons 1986). However, the results of detailed study in one area can plausibly suggest relationships and issues that apply in other areas.

Political and Economic Consequences

While little has been published concerning privatization, a substantial and growing literature exists on public-private partnerships.[11] Much of this literature focuses on three issues: efficiency and competition, accountability and redistribution, and the compatibility of public-private partnerships with the nature of the state. Much that has been written about public-private partnerships concerns the tradeoff between political values, including accountability and sovereignty, against the economically driven benefits of efficiency and cost-effectiveness. That is, the posture of local government within the political economy of partnerships is typically interpreted as reactive rather than proactive. The calculations are implicitly framed in terms of the extent to which political accountability must or should yield to economic efficiency.

Efficiency and Competition

The argument for reliance on the private sector to produce public services rests centrally on notions of efficiency and competition (Goldman and Mokuvos 1984). The case is made in terms of the differing norms around which the public and private sectors respectively are organized and the differing institutional arrangements that give expression to these norms. As stated, the energizing force for private sector activity is the norm or incentive of profit (Hanke 1985, 1987). The institutional vehicle is the competitive market (for the classic statement, see Adam Smith 1937). Competition leads to efficiency and in turn to profits (Savas 1987:262; Armington and Ellis 1984).

By contrast, the public sector is organized around political norms including representation and accountability. They shape the institutions of policymaking and administration to be responsive to the multiple and conflicting preferences of individuals and groups in a pluralistic society. The outcome is evaluated by those standards and not necessarily on the basis of efficiency or profit (Savas 1987:5–32; Chandler 1986:643–44). The alleged result is that policy formation reflects satisficing and suboptimization; implementation becomes mired in the efforts of bureaucrats to preserve and extend their personal and organizational interests. The expected result is growth in regulation, paperwork, staffs, programs, and budgets.

Some observers, however, question the general argument of greater private sector efficiency and competitiveness. They reject at various levels the notion that the two sectors are fundamentally dissimilar. At the level of personnel, some critics deny that the sectors select, or shape those who work in them to be, two different kinds of people. Thus Chandler (1986:650, drawing on Goodsell 1983) argues against the "myth" that "public sector managers are lazy, incompetent, and wasteful while their private sector counterparts are intelligent, industrious, and efficient." This counterargument is supported by the common case of career professionals who move back and forth between the public and the private sectors and academia as well (Holcombe 1988c). The suggestion here is that if differences are observed, it is likely that institutional system and process rather than individuals may account for them.

At the level of organizations, critics of public-private partnerships reject the view that the public and private sectors are dissimilar with regard to the elements of efficiency (Hula 1986:5). Jackson (1988:2) observes that the efforts of organizations "to protect and enhance their revenue sources" will be the same "whether the revenues come from market sales or public budgets. Competition controls this behavior. In the private sector, the competition is between firms. In the public sector, the competition is between political parties; the legislative, executive, and political branches; and between different levels of government." Thus, good reasons exist to expect efficiency in the public sector.

At the level of market structure, DeHoog (1984) questions whether the market conditions alleged to produce efficiency are always present. She asserts that markets can be less than perfect in terms of competition and information, in part because competent watchdogs are not always present to encourage or enforce these conditions. In this regard, Clark (1984) argues that the role of government is to correct these market failures.

Accountability and Redistribution

The notion of the watchdog as preserver of market efficiencies and competition puts on the table the issue of accountability: do the "public or program recipients" (DeHoog 1984:14) have institutionally firm opportunities "to hold contractors responsible . . . when service proves to be unsatisfactory?" And, how does access to redress and also to the public goods the plant represents, such as employment opportunities, vary across social groups? Sullivan (1987) suggests that partnerships may constrain the constitutional rights of service recipients, who will have less protection when dealing with a private service provider than with a public provider. Palumbo and Maupin (1987:9–13) raise distributional issues while discussing the "Political Consequences of Privatization." They suggest privatization "will reduce the amount of mobility for several groups," and they conclude that it places profit-making firms "in a position of making decisions about the public realm of activity which are neither responsive nor accountable to the institutions of democracy."

Rosenbloom (1983:221) suggests that the public sector's alleged efficiency can be directly at odds with the goal of accountability. He, too, casts the conflict in terms of economic versus political concerns: "the values sought by the political approach to public administration are frequently in tension with those of the managerial approach." For example, the values of the political approach ("representativeness, responsibility, and accountability" in a pluralist setting) "can dissuade public administrators from taking some courses of action, though they may be most efficient, and can divert time and resources from program implementation." For example, in the case of wastewater treatment project construction, a simple accountability question is who responds when citizens complain because yards and streets are torn up during construction? Additional immediate questions have to do with wage rates on construction sites (do privatizers pay less?) and opportunities for minority firms to gain contracts (are privatizers less likely to subcontract with such firms?).[12] A less obvious accountability issue, which has long-term ramifications, is who monitors progress and has the power to require that work conform to specifications?

The standard answer to these questions (Goldman and Mokuvos 1984; Bynum 1983; Tieder and Cox 1983) is that the private firm will act to satisfy these concerns if a well-drawn contract requires it to do so. For instance, Fitzgerald and Lyons (1986:610) show how one private contractor of sanitation services agreed to establish an office and procedures for resolving citizen complaints "within 24 hours." Self-interest will motivate the private firm in this direction as well. The privatizing firm not only builds a facility but also is responsible for operations and maintenance, which typically consume more than half of a plant's life-cycle costs. One element of long-term operating efficiency is good construction. Therefore, the privatizer will want to ensure that design is good and that construction conforms to it. In sum, the propartnership literature asserts that safeguards for accountability are built into the structure of the partnership arrangement.

Compatibility

Issues of efficiency, competition, accountability, and redistribution, and of the tradeoffs among them, play prominently in the debate over partnerships. A less obvious but equally important theme has to do with what Rogers (1983:223) terms compatibility. The question here is both philosophical and practical. Is the transfer of given services from one sector to the other compatible with the basic values and functions of both sectors? Supporters of privatization tend not to see this as an issue. Butler (1987:1) refers to the view that there can be an "appropriate division of labor between policymakers and the private sector, allowing the former to concentrate on their central role, delegating to the latter the mechanical features of government."

This premise is controversial. Some observers are willing to grant, at least implicitly, that the private sector often offers greater efficiency than the public sector. However, they argue that, even if this is so, transfer of functions to the private sector is in at least some cases incompatible with the nature of well-being of the state. For instance, Goodsell's response to the "appropriate division" thesis is to assert (1984:200) that "a clear borderline between policy and its implementation does not exist." He argues that it is not possible to tighten up management "without altering public policy." In other words, one limit on the transferability of functions is that privatization will change policy rather than just implementing it more efficiently. Put differently, the argument for partnerships is based in part on a long-since discredited politics-administration dichotomy (see especially Waldo 1987 on this subject).

A related argument is that partnerships can change the nature of the state itself. Moe (1987:456–57) calls attention to the "concept of sovereignty" as the single most important characteristic that separates the public and the private sectors. He goes on to observe: "In any serious proposal to assign the performance of a function to the private sector, the first question should be: does the performance of this function necessarily involve the powers properly reserved to the sovereign? Or, is the function largely private in character, requiring none of the coercive powers of the sovereign?" If we leave aside the efficiency argument and even the straightforward accountability argument, public-private partnerships pose a deeper problem, which is the diminution of the sovereignty of the state.

This argument may seem abstract, but Sundquist (1984:317) suggests a not-unrelated practical outcome: the weakening of the organizational mass and administrative competence of the state. After exploring the development of the civil service in this country, he observes: "By definition, government bureaucracies operate in a political environment, which means they must satisfy political constituencies, even if sometimes that must be done at a cost to efficiency." He concludes that the issue underlying all of this is that "Government must be made as competent as possible as an end in itself, whatever level of privatization may be desirable or attainable, simply because government will remain an indispensable institution."

A growing number of voices speak to this view. Nelson (1987:544, quoted by Wise 1990:151) states: "Government is not there so much because other institutions occasionally fail, but to set the stage so that they can work decently well in their assigned areas of action, or as an instrumentality in its own right for getting a job done." Another example is Palumbo and Maupin's (1987:9) suggestion that privatization will "weaken the structure of government and lower the status of public employment." Also, Wise (1990:142) refers to the "new realization . . . that formal government (i.e., the state and its institutions, not just political attitudes, interest groups, and demographic and economic trends) . . . matters for policy outcomes and for the well being of the society of which it is a part."

While theoretically grounded, these concerns are also eminently practical. For instance, both the S&L bailout and the HUD insurance scandal may be read as examples of precisely the problems referred to here. In demeaning the core governmental function of regulation, and cutting back on federal agency auditing staffs and administrative purview, President Reagan contributed to an invidious weakening of government to a point at which enormous losses resulted.

In summary, the literature on public-private partnerships tends to define the partnership problem in terms of sacrificing political values in return for economic benefits. The arguments that make up this literature were developed, for the most part, in relation to partnerships such as contracting for services. However, they apply, perhaps more forcefully, to privatization. The privatizer not only produces the service in question but also contributes investment capital and builds the facility through which the service is produced. Thus it is appropriate to consider privatization as a particular type of partnership meriting attention to the issues of efficiency and competition, accountability and redistribution, and compatibility.

Political and Economic Conditions

This book is based on a rejection (Wise 1990:149) of the notion that skillful management of partnerships consists in recognizing how to allocate functions between sectors. Rather, the premise is that a public-private partnership "is . . . fundamentally a process of bringing different systems together to produce cooperatively some publicly defined end" (Kettl 1988:17).[13] This premise implies a more proactive role for public management in the partnership context than much of the literature suggests. Questions flow immediately concerning this proactive role: How are the two systems brought together? How do they cooperate? How is the end defined and by whom? The polity or the market? Both?

The ideas of Donald Kettl (1988) and E. S. Savas (1987) concerning the dynamics of public-private partnerships support a conceptual framework for analyzing and responding to these questions. As developed in the following sections, the framework serves to guide an assessment of what happens both politically and economically in privatization and what factors contribute to these outcomes.

Political Conditions for Successful Partnership

Donald Kettl's study of government by proxy addresses both the political factors that fuel partnerships and the political conditions on which they depend. The political factors, as already discussed, include ideology, increased service demands, and decreased public willingness to provide resources. Given the political origins of the growth in public-private partnerships, it is hardly surprising that success in these efforts depends on political conditions as well. Kettl identifies two such conditions: negotiated agreement on goals and continuing feedback in operation (i.e., oversight). These conditions grow out of his conclusion that "government by proxy is neither necessarily better or worse than direct government management of public services. Rather, it is fundamentally different" (Kettl 1988:14). These differences, he concludes, have to do with authority, values, and management. Public-private partnerships, to succeed, must recognize the differences and deal with them.

Kettl suggests that in the partnership framework the goals of the public and private sectors can readily be joined. The public sector has a service responsibility that must be met efficiently and productively. However, public accountability must be maintained. The private sector seeks a market opportunity. These three elements intersect in a "true" public-private partnership when all three requirements are met. Means for satisfying these requirements are available. For instance, goals can be synchronized through negotiation. Public accountability can be maintained through positive educational activities and long-term contracts that include provisions for feedback and resultant oversight. To use

Kettl's terms, such strategies strengthen "the performance of government programs" by establishing a formal framework of "interdependence between government and its proxies" (1988:14).

Economic Conditions for Successful Partnership

E. S. Savas provides a different set of requirements for successful public-private partnerships.[14] He accepts the arguments of inherent efficiency and productivity in the market, and he examines privatization opportunities in terms of the nature of the goods (or services) involved. He categorizes goods in two ways. First, can individuals feasibly be excluded from using the good if it exists? For instance, it is easy to exclude individuals from an electrical distribution system but difficult to prevent them from breathing air. Second, can the good be used or consumed simultaneously (jointly) by more than one user? Some goods, such as city streets or network television, can be used simultaneously by many people without diminishing their quality or availability. Others, such as hats and ice cream cones, tend to have single individual users.

Employing these distinctions, Savas develops a typology of goods and services. Two types permit exclusion of users: "private" goods, such as clothing and bicycles, are individually used; "toll" goods, such as electric power and phone systems, are subject to joint usership. The ease with which potential users can be excluded from access to these types of goods makes them relatively amenable to market provision and production. For example, a municipality or other authority can address wastewater treatment as a toll good. Residents choose, or can be required by ordinance, to discharge wastewater into the treatment system. They use the system jointly, but can be excluded from it, and thus can be required to pay for it through taxes or user fees.

Two additional types of goods do not readily allow exclusion and are less amenable to market provision. "Common-pool" goods, such as fresh air or grazing fields, are individually consumed. On the other hand, "collective" goods, such as national defense and street lighting, are jointly consumable. Because these two types of goods are accessible to all once they exist, market incentives to produce them are limited at best. Thus their provision and production often bring the public sector into play.

The public sector enters in two related ways. First, some collective goods, such as national defense, must be collectively provided if they are to exist at all. Second, collective action is often needed to preserve the supply of common-pool goods, such as underground water supplies. This outcome occurs because individuals tend to consume these goods to their own advantage until they are degraded in quality or exhausted in quantity. This is often referred to as the tragedy of the commons (Hardin 1968).

As Savas notes, most goods do not fall purely and neatly into one of these categories. Rather, they fall onto continua anchored by these ideal types. Further, the nature of a good or service is subject to change. For example, private actions such as neighborhood watches can serve as "partial substitutes" for the collective good of police protection. Also, the nature of a good or service can be the object of policy. For instance, New York City originally operated Central Park as a toll good (by charging admission at gates) but then opened the gates, abandoned exclusion, and allowed the park to be "used—and abused—as a collective good." Government in many cases acts to supply goods. For instance, government can act to preserve a common-pool good or empower a specific owner to manage consumption. In many countries, government supplies toll goods by establishing user fees. Further, collective goods are typically provided by government and paid for through user fees or taxes (Savas 1987:42, 46, 47).

According to Savas, the largest cause of government growth has been the societal decision that certain private and toll goods, such as food, education, and mass transit, are so "worthy" that their production and consumption should be encouraged regardless of the consumer's ability to pay. As a result, these worthy goods have either been subsidized by government or produced directly by government and supplied to those deemed to require or merit consumption. If no use is made of the exclusion property of private and toll goods—that is, if there is little or no charge for their use—then in effect the good is being treated as a common-pool or collective good.

Government has elected to provide certain private and toll goods completely or partly as if they were collective goods. The services provided could, according to Savas, be provided more efficiently and productively by the market through public-private partnerships. Policies reclassifying goods in this way would enable the private sector to correct the failures of government. While Savas (1987:95–107) evaluates partnership strategies in terms of some political variables, such as equity, his evaluation is basically economic and not political.

Political and Economic Conditions: A Summary

The Kettl and Savas models provide criteria for evaluating a partnership arrangement as well as hypotheses to be tested in the study of that arrangement. Savas looks at the arena of partnerships and focuses on the nature of goods and the market setting. Kettl looks at the same arena and sees two markets that are fundamentally different but related in many ways. He also sees a potential set of structures, linking the two sectors, that differs from what is at the core of either of them. Goods generated through these linking structures must pass different tests from those we apply to goods produced in either the public or the private sector exclusively. First, the goods that are suitable to this model are those based on common goals derived from negotiation between the two sectors. Second, they must be goods that allow for a feedback mechanism between the sectors sufficient to allow public oversight. Third, because these structures are different, they call for a new kind of management (compare National Academy of Public Administration 1989).

Kash (1989:217) makes the same argument, here broadly paraphrased, in the call for new policy instruments (linking structures and mechanisms).

> The ability of the public-private policy system to build and sustain an interorganizational complex, capable of delivering public services efficiently and accountably, requires appropriate policy instruments. Specifically, the policy system needs the ability to: (1) provide up-front funding; (2) link the diverse organizations (. . . government agencies and industry) needed to carry out accountable service delivery; and (3) provide incentives for identifying and refining effective public-private arrangements for doing so.

The evaluation of existing linking structures is already under way (see, for example, Moe and Stanton 1989). So too is the search for new models (see, for instance, the "heuristic models" that Morgan and England [1988] propose in the general area of coproduction). The present study proceeds from the view that the Savas model offers a necessary but insufficient test of the feasibility of public-private partnership structures. A broader framework is needed along lines suggested by Kettl and Wise. The concluding section of this chapter sketches a theoretical framework (model) for privatization.

A Theory-Sketch of Privatization

The theory-sketch is drawn in relation to the prominent features of privatization as one form of public-private partnership.[15] However, at least some elements of the sketch can apply to partnership approaches more generally. The purpose of the sketch is to posit several important and interrelated ideas about how privatization works. It begins at the level of the individual project and then moves to the level of the political and economic context. The propositions that make up the sketch are written in positive terms: they refer to a system of relationships that is reasonably able to satisfy both economic requirements of efficiency and political requirements of accountability. They assume innovative mechanisms are needed, and can be developed, to mesh political and economic requirements successfully. The propositions lead in turn to empirical questions, testable through hypotheses.

A Theory-Sketch

Privatized projects will be built faster and more economically, and will be operated more efficiently, than publicly owned and operated projects. This result will take place for two kinds of reasons. First, the privatizing firm has more latitude to coordinate project development and is less subject to regulatory intrusion than the public authority would be. Second, the privatizing firm is more subject than the public authority would be to certain economic and legal-contractual constraints: the competition of the marketplace will force the firm to be economically efficient and politically responsive and accountable to the authority with which it contracts. The contract, as drawn to reflect goals negotiated by the parties in the context of the competitive market, will provide cooperative mechanisms for ongoing public monitoring of private operations and negotiated resolution of problems.

Shifting to the level of economic and political systems, the theory addresses the linking of public and private sectors, or markets, through privatization. Each sector has its own distinctive dynamic. The driving forces for the private sector are competition, efficiency, profit, and the control of information that is central to maintaining competitive position. The driving forces in the public sector are representativeness and accountability and the openness of information on which they depend. Privatization engages and meshes these two different dynamics to capitalize on the positive aspects of each. The way this meshing occurs depends on several contextual features, one of which is the nature of the good or service being produced. The nature of the good or service also affects the issues privatization raises and the extent to which it can improve upon public production. More broadly, privatization affects, is affected by, and at times must adapt to changes in multiple elements in the broader social system of economic and political activity. These elements include state and national law, industry structure, and regulatory processes.

In this broader context, the individual project contract can provide part of the institutionalized structure of rights, obligations, processes, and expectations that privatization—or any approach to service delivery and policy implementation—requires. But the contract cannot supply all of the framework because it is mainly concerned with allocating risks that order the economic interest of individual parties. It responds to, but cannot itself adjust, the elements of the broader context, including law, regulation, industry, and even the nature of the good involved. Rather, public policy must structure these elements appropriately for privatization to function effectively. In order to function effectively (efficiently and accountably), privatization also requires mechanisms that link the public and private sectors, accommodating their changed roles in the privatized setting.

Hypotheses

The propositions of the theory lead to the following hypotheses (and potentially to others as well). The hypotheses are phrased for the most part in general and positive terms.[16] Some are purely descriptive (privatizers are subject to competition), while others posit relationships between variables (such as the relationship between competition and economic efficiency). The individual chapters of this book address some of the major hypotheses and test them empirically.

1. *Time.* Project development proceeds faster under privatization than under other means of project development.
2. *Economy.*
   a. Project development costs will be lower under privatization than under other approaches.
   b. Project development will be relatively more cost-effective under privatization than under other approaches.

3. *Efficiency.* Project development and operation will be more efficient under privatization than under other approaches.
4. *Coordination.* The privatizer has greater latitude to coordinate project activities than any single actor would have under other approaches.
5. *Regulatory involvement.*
   a. State and federal regulatory agencies will be less involved in the development of privatized projects than they are in other kinds of projects.
   b. Delays due to regulatory processes and requirements will be fewer under privatization than under other approaches.
6. *Competition.* The privatizer will be more subject to competitive pressure than the public authority.
7. *Accountability.* The privatizer will behave accountably, responsibly, and responsively (if negotiated goals and cooperative ongoing management structures are fixed in the contract).
8. *Contract.* The contract will reflect agreed-upon goals of the parties, negotiated openly and cooperatively by the parties in a context of market competition.
9. *Changed roles.* Privatization changes the roles of the public and private sector organizations directly and indirectly involved in it.
10. *Cooperative linking structures.* The contract will provide for, or at least accommodate, a cooperative linking structure—which may be an interorganizational configuration—for ongoing management. Under this structure the public authority will routinely monitor ongoing operations, and methods of negotiation on issues and problems will be effectively set up. The structure will reflect and mesh the changed roles of the sectors in privatization, capitalizing on the inherent dynamic of each sector.
11. *The nature of the good.* How privatization is applied, how it changes the roles of the sectors, the issues it raises, and its relative utility, compared with other approaches to service delivery and policy implementation, all depend to some extent on the nature of the good or service involved.
12. *The political context.* Privatization affects, is affected by, and adapts to:
    a. National politics and policy, expressed in part through law.
    b. State politics and policy, expressed in part through law.
    c. Local politics and policy, expressed in part in the privatization decision.

    d. Industry structure.
    e. Regulatory processes.

   This sketch of theory, together with the hypotheses derived from it, both reflects and attempts to extend an emerging perspective on public-private partnerships. This perspective looks beyond the economic aspects of goods and processes in two ways. First, it emphasizes configurations of organization and management at the level of individual cases. Second, it emphasizes the interactive relationship between privatization efforts and the broad context of law, regulation, and industry. *The Politics and Economics of Privatization* applies this theory-sketch to the case of wastewater treatment.

2

National Water Policy and Wastewater Treatment Privatization

In the United States, the national government has been involved in the water pollution control effort in a direct way since the Water Pollution Control Act of 1948 (PL 80-845).[17] However, a clear assumption of national-level responsibility for clean water did not occur until 1972. Like other national-level assumptions of program responsibilities that occurred in the 1960s and 1970s, the intent, at least from the perspective of some, was for a temporary federal role. To a considerable degree, the attempt of the federal government to reduce its role in this area is the story of the privatization of wastewater treatment works (WTWs).

While the case of national water policy is only one element in the larger story of the devolution of federalism in the United States, it provides the most significant example of the application of privatization to meet this objective. This chapter provides the historical and policy context for the emergence of privatization. From this context, two important conclusions emerge for the current and future status of privatization. One: privatization was an opportunistic consequence of changes in other national policies. That is, no national privatization policy was ever adopted. Two: the WTW privatization effort that took place in the 1980s did so without a developed theory of public-private organizational relationships. Rather, old or existing public-private sector concepts were applied to privatization efforts. The result of the failure to address both policy and theory has been a slow and uneven development of privatization as a general model and option for federal devolution and public-private partnerships.

National Water Policy History

Prior to 1972, state and local governments and private sector industries or developers were primarily responsible for wastewater treatment.[18] The Water Pollution Control Act of 1948 (PL 80-845) was the first federal program enacted to provide assistance to state and local governments to construct WTWs. The act provided $22.5 million annually for five years for loans to construct wastewater facilities. Loans were limited to $250,000 or one-third of the total cost. Grants were also provided for partial support of planning and design work.

In 1956 a second Water Pollution Control Act (WPCA) was adopted that authorized $50 million a year for ten years. Again loans were limited to $250,000. The WPCA was amended in 1961 (PL 87-88) and 1965 (PL 89-234). In 1966, the Clean Water Restoration Act removed the dollar limit, increased the project grant share to 40 percent, and increased the authorization to $3.5 billion for the period 1967–71 (Dilger 1986:251). Federal involvement in and funding for wastewater facility construction increased with each of these acts. Annual appropriations increased from $50 million in fiscal year (FY) 1961 to $1.25 billion in FY 1971. The federal share of project costs increased from 30 percent to 55 percent. By 1972 more than 13,000 grants were awarded to some 10,000 state and local public water authorities (Illinois EPA 1987:1). Thus, the federal government was substantially involved in addressing local wastewater needs. However, the need was far greater than the resources available at either the federal or state and local levels of government. In 1972 the Federal Water Pollution Control Act Amendments (PL 92-500)— known as the Clean Water Act (CWA)—were adopted to provide an increase in federal funding and a larger federal share of total project costs. The initial intention was to provide a large amount of federal funds over a fixed period of time to enable local authorities to meet the backlog of needs. However, the amendments were based on the premise that WTW construction was a state and local responsibility. The amendments authorized $18 billion for FY 1973–75 to meet a backlog of $24 billion in needs (EPA 1984:1-1) and thus constituted a significant increase in the federal role in national water policy. New and stricter discharge requirements were adopted; 75 percent grants were provided for planning, design, and construction; eligibility requirements were expanded; and the amendments called for compliance with effluent standards by 1977, the achievement of interim goals by 1983, and the elimination of the discharge of pollutants into navigable water by 1985. Noncompliance was to be enforced by fines and imprisonment.

In 1977, federal funds were authorized for an additional five years at a level of $5 billion annually. The 1977 reauthorization of the CWA was revised to allow for funding of innovative and alternative technology projects, a 2 percent or $400,000 allotment to delegated states for administration of the construction grants program, and extension of the deadline for compliance to 1983. By 1977 it was generally recognized that wastewater treatment needs had been underestimated and that implementation of the national policy was going to be more difficult than expected. Added to these problems was growing concern on the part of the administration about the total cost of the program. The 1977 amendments attempted to strengthen the role of the states in water programs by placing primary responsibility for management and implementation of water programs at the state level. But by 1977 the WTW construction grant program had become the second largest federal domestic public works program.

While the original intent of the program may have been to address only backlog needs with federal funding, concerns began to increase that state and local authorities were looking more and more to the federal government as the major, if not the total, source of WTW construction funding. However, federal funding (appropriations) was inconsistent over the FY 1977–80 period, with an actual rescission of $1.7 billion in 1981. In addition, by 1977 the needs estimates themselves were being challenged. As a result, Congress was unable to adopt a needs-based formula for the distribution of funds (Dilger 1986:253).

From 1972 to 1984 Congress authorized more than $40 billion to assist local authorities in the construction of WTWs. Some 17,000 grants were made over this period. However, criticism of the program increased. Congress and the administration wanted the states and local authorities to assume major responsibility for funding and management. Results of the program have been disputed. Evidence exists that the federal program has resulted in local authorities reducing WTW construction funding and that, in fact, the federal government has subsidized the states and municipalities and thereby kept wastewater fee structures artificially low. In addition, the charge is made that WTWs have been overbuilt and are, in part, pork barrel projects. At the same time, the 1980 U.S. EPA Needs Survey projected $120 billion in needs through the year 2000. Finally, in the context of poor economic conditions and a huge and growing budget deficit, a general call for reduction of the federal role in this area was sounded (Dilger 1986:253–55).

In 1980 these efforts resulted in proposals for specific reforms in the Clean Water Act. The reforms were designed to move the program back to the state and local governments. The 1981 Amendments to the Clean Water Act (PL 97-117) reduced eligibility, lowered the federal share from 75 to 55 percent, eliminated planning and design grants, extended the deadline for compliance to 1988, increased the administration set-aside to 4 percent, and reduced annual authorization to $2.4 billion (EPA 1984:1-2). Clearly the intent was to reduce the federal role in the funding and management of national wastewater treatment policy and programs. The 1981 amendments, however, represented only a transitional stage leading toward even greater state and local assumption of responsibility.

In 1984, EPA initiated a study on the future federal, state, and local roles for municipal wastewater treatment. The study had two major goals:

1. Build a national consensus on the shape of alternatives for future federal financing of municipal wastewater treatment.
2. Develop a set of policy and legislative recommendations regarding alternative program strategies that will best promote both the intent of the Clean Water Act—long-term state and local self-sufficiency—and the goal of the act—long-term municipal compliance (EPA 1984:1-3).

The study produced eight areas of consensus:

1. A gradual transition from federal responsibility to state and local self-sufficiency should be pursued.
2. While federal aid continues, its level should be certain and states should be able to deploy funds flexibly.
3. Continuing and future wastewater treatment needs must be made an element of any new funding scenario.
4. Delegation of construction grant program responsibilities to the state has been successful and should continue.
5. Major changes in standards and compliance deadlines efforts are counterproductive.
6. Federal funding strategies must promote compliance and be supplemented by strong enforcement actions.
7. Funds should be distributed equitably to meet core treatment

Figure 2.1 Federal, State, and Local Funding of Wastewater Treatment Works

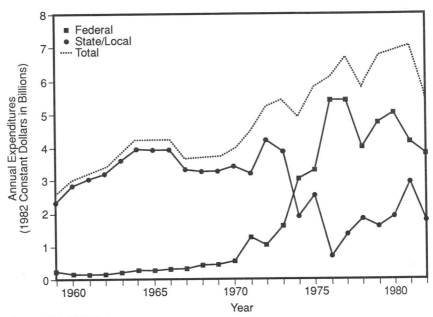

Source: EPA 1984:3-2.

needs first, and states should be given the flexibility to address project affordability issues.

8. The funding mechanism chosen must provide for both short- and long-term financial "leveraging" of available funds. That is, the earning power of each funding dollar must be maximized (EPA 1984:ix).

A major conclusion of the study that shaped the consensus statement was that the federal government role in WTW construction funding had, in fact, subsidized and undermined the state and local role. Figure 2.1 shows quite clearly that total state and local expenditures for WTW construction dropped sharply following passage of the 1972 Clean Water Act, which established the 75–25 percent federal construction grant program.

The study laid the foundation for the Water Quality Act of 1987 (PL 100-4). The Clean Water Act of 1981 expired in September 1985. Revisions to the act were passed unanimously by Congress in 1986 but were vetoed by President Reagan. Among the first acts passed in 1987 was the

Figure 2.2   Federal, State, Local, and Private Sector Roles in Wastewater Treatment Financing

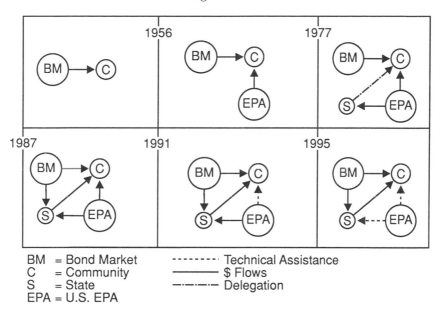

BM = Bond Market
C   = Community
S   = State
EPA = U.S. EPA

-------- Technical Assistance
———— $ Flows
—·—·— Delegation

Source: Peat Marwick Main and Co. 1987:VI -1.

Water Quality Act, which established a specific schedule and mechanism (state revolving fund) for the transition to state financial self-sufficiency (Savage 1987). Over a period of five years the federal government provides 80–20 matching grants to states to establish state revolving loan funds to be used to meet state and local water needs. At the end of the five-year period, 1994, the federal government will have terminated all funding of wastewater construction grants. The act authorizes $1.2 billion annually for FY 1989–90 and a decreasing amount to $600 million for FY 1994. Through a complex combination of grant and loan fund provisions, the act will effectively end the major role that the federal government has played in this area since 1972.

The shifts in federal, state, local, and private sector roles in funding construction of wastewater treatment facilities are presented in figure 2.2. In brief, the changes were and will be as follows:

- Prior to 1956, money for wastewater treatment facilities flowed directly from the bond market to the community.

- From 1956 to 1977, money flowed from the federal government as well as the bond market to the community.
- From 1977 to 1987, money flowed from the U.S. EPA to the community and to delegated states. Money also flowed from the bond market to the community.
- From 1987 to 1991, the process became more complex as the money flowed from the U.S. EPA, the state, and the bond market to the community. Money also flowed from EPA and the bond market to the state.
- From 1991 to 1995, money will continue to flow from the U.S. EPA to the state and from the state to the community. EPA will provide technical assistance rather than money to a community. Money flows from the bond market remain the same.
- From 1995 on, EPA will provide technical assistance to the state as well as the community. Money will continue to flow from the state to the community, and the bond market money flows remain the same. (Peat Marwick Main and Co. 1987:III-2).

As these shifts occurred, particularly after the reductions in federal funding in 1981, state and local authorities were forced to seek alternate funding sources. After 1981, privatization was one option that developed to meet funding needs. However, before addressing the development of the privatization option, the following provides a brief picture of the status of wastewater treatment in the United States in the 1980s.

Status of Wastewater Treatment in the United States

The status of water quality needs in the United States in the 1980s indicates a substantial and continuing need for WTW construction and for funding to support that activity.

Wastewater Treatment Works (WTWs)

The total number of publicly owned wastewater treatment works in the United States, including U.S. territories and commonwealths, is 15,438 (EPA 1987). This number increased from 13,200 to 15,400 (17 percent) from 1976 to 1986, with the largest increase (15 percent) occurring between 1976 and 1980, the period of highest federal expenditure for WTW construction grants (National Council on Public Works Improvement 1988:164). The council reported that the total capacity of public WTWs increased from 32.1 million gallons per day to 36.7 million (a 14 percent increase) between 1978 and 1986. Half of that growth (7 percent) came in a two-year period between 1978 and 1980. Since 1980, growth in capacity has averaged about 1.1 percent a year. From 1976 to 1986 the volume of wastewater treated increased from 25.5 million gallons per day to 27.7 million, an 8 percent increase, for an average growth rate of .8 percent annually, compared to population growth of 1 percent annually over the same period. The population served during the same period increased from 158.6 million to 185.6 million, a 17 percent increase, and the percentage of the U.S. population served by centralized WTW facilities increased from 66.7 percent in 1976 to 74.9 percent in 1986 (National Council on Public Works Improvement 1988:164).

The data show that the greatest growth in WTWs in all categories took place between 1976 and 1980, the period of maximum EPA participation in the WTW construction grant program. However, as the following shows, the need for WTWs has been and continues to be substantially greater than available resources. For this reason, in part, the privatization of WTWs emerged as an option in the early 1980s, the point at which federal resources for WTW financing began to decline.

Public Spending for WTWs

Total public spending, capital and operating, for wastewater treatment increased from around $4 billion in 1960 to more than $14 billion in 1981. The greatest increases during this period came in federal spending after 1972 in response to EPA's WTW construction grant program authorized by the 1972 Water Pollution Control Act referred to as the Clean Water Act (CWA). Since 1972 Congress has authorized more than $40 billion for construction of publicly owned WTWs. However, during the period 1981–84 total spending in constant dollars declined to $11 billion a year and federal WTW construction grant authorizations declined from $4.2 billion in 1981 to $2.4 billion in 1987.

During the peak period of federal funding for WTW construction, state and local capital expenditures were inversely related to federal capital outlays and decreased from a high of about $5 billion to a low of $2 billion. While capital spending decreased, state and local operating expenditures increased steadily from 1960 to 1974. Local operating cost per person served by a central sewer system increased from $15.80 a year in 1960 (in 1984 dollars) to $47.20 per person in 1972, the beginning of the federal construction grant program. While construction costs have increased more slowly than inflation since 1982, operating and maintenance costs have increased about 1 to 2 percent a year above inflation.

Water Quality

The impact on water quality of the 1972 CWA, specifically the WTW construction grant program, is a highly complex issue. While that issue is not addressed in this report, the issue of water quality is very briefly reviewed to show national water policy objectives had not been met by the 1980s, thus requiring continuing resources to meet compliance standards in addition to expansion needs.

The U.S. Geological Survey operates two nationwide sampling networks designed to provide data on national water quality trends. They are the National Stream Quality Accounting Network and the National Water Quality Surveillance System. Data from these networks for the period 1944–81, as reported by the National Council on Public Works Improvement, show some, but limited, improvement in the nation's water quality, at least as directly related to municipal wastewater treatment plants. In 1986, 12.1 percent of the major municipal WTWs (capacity of at least one million gallons per day [mgd]) were still in significant noncompliance. The percentage range of noncompliance across states was from 0 to 33 percent and varied substantially by region, from a low of 8.25 percent in the east-south-central region to a high of 22 percent in the west-south-central region (Fund for Renewable Energy and the Environment 1988).

By 1988, 87 percent of all major and minor publicly owned treatment works were in compliance. Most of the majors not in compliance were either on schedules to reach compliance standards or were the subject of federal or state civil actions (EPA 1988). However, these data refer to existing WTWs and do not indicate expansion needs. In addition, the data reflect WTW unit compliance and not percentage of water treated relative to compliance.

The status of wastewater treatment in the United States in the early 1980s provides the broad context of public policy within which the privatization of WTWs can be analyzed and evaluated. In summary, the 1972 CWA initiated a national effort to address point source water pollution. The objective was to make the nation's water swimmable and fishable. National standards were established, and publicly owned WTWs were required to comply, whether or not federal funds were available. However, federal funding of the construction of WTWs from 1972 to the mid-1980s constituted a major element in this effort. While WTW needs remain substantial, and while evaluations of the ultimate success of the EPA construction grant program vary, current national policy calls for a phasing out of the grant program and a transition of program responsibility from the federal government to the states. These changes in national policy resulted in the emergence of WTW privatization during the 1980s.

Metapolicy Transition and the Emergence of Privatization

In the early and mid-1980s, privatization of WTWs emerged rapidly and then underwent major changes as a result of several uncoordinated changes in national policies and the laws that reflected those policies. Private sector firms played the major role in developing privatization within the shifting, and at times chaotic, framework of national law. Two related developments are central elements of the national policy context: New Federalism and tax law changes.

Beginning in 1981, national clean water policy became subject to the metapolicy of New Federalism. The term *metapolicy* means policy about how policy shall be made (Dror 1968). The notion of metapolicy is useful because it identifies the level of policy changes that created the conditions for privatization. The New Federalism metapolicy involved the general positions that the federal goverment should do less and that state and local governments and the private sector should do more to provide public services. The initial impact of the New Federalism on clean water policy was to reduce the level of U.S. EPA grant support for WTW projects while maintaining compliance requirements.

A second set of consequences of the New Federalism metapolicy included the Economic Recovery Tax Act of 1981 and the Tax Equity and Fiscal Responsibility Act of 1982. These laws provided tax incentives for private investors to enter the field of capital-intensive public works projects, including WTW construction. The incentives included a 10 percent investment tax credit, tax-exempt municipal bonds, arbitrage, and accelerated depreciation schedules. At one point, WTWs could be depreciated over five years, even though a plant is typically designed to operate for up to twenty-five years. For the most part, these incentives required that the privatizer own the facility. The Deficit Reduction Act of 1984 further defined this area of activity by effectively limiting such arrangements to long-term contractual agreements and by making special arrangements for WTWs.

Thus, national policy in the mid-1980s offered the possibility of privatization as a new option for WTW funding in addition to conventional bond financing and continuing, though reduced, U.S. EPA project grants. Private sector engineering and accounting firms perceived the opportunity and began to promote, develop, and implement privatization deals in the WTW field. Seminars were held in several cities. A trade literature appeared. Articles, books, and presentations by industry experts (Goldman and Mokuvos 1984) and some supportive government officials (Longest 1983) made the case for the economic advantages of privatization.

By early 1986 the first two privatized WTWs had gone on-line, one in the Southeast and one in the Southwest. An increasing number of cities actively considered privatization (Johnson and Heilman 1987b). In late 1986, however, Congress passed the Tax Reform Act, which reduced or eliminated most of the incentives that had played a major role in the initial privatization deals (see Zimmerman 1987:512–13 for an overview of the act and congressional purposes underlying it). The immediate effects of these changes were to reduce the financial attractiveness of privatization deals to cities, to reduce the importance of structuring deals to include private ownership of facilities (as a basis for tax benefits), to sharpen debate over the inherent advantages of privatization, and to raise questions about the potential role of privatization under the Water Quality Act of 1987.

The point is that privatization emerged from and was buffeted by high-level shifts in national policy that in themselves had little to do directly with wastewater treatment policy. Figure 2.3 shows these developments in terms of a shift in metapolicy from the 1960s to the 1980s, with attendant changes in substantive policies and implementation options. In the 1960s the dominant metapolicy was to promote active federal involvement in solving problems with national policies, programs, and resources. The 1980s witnessed a shift of metapolicy toward reduced federal involvement in many areas of policy, programs, and resources, primarily through deregulation and reduced resources.

Figure 2.3 The Clean Water Policy Arena: Metapolicies, Substantive Policies, and Implementation Options

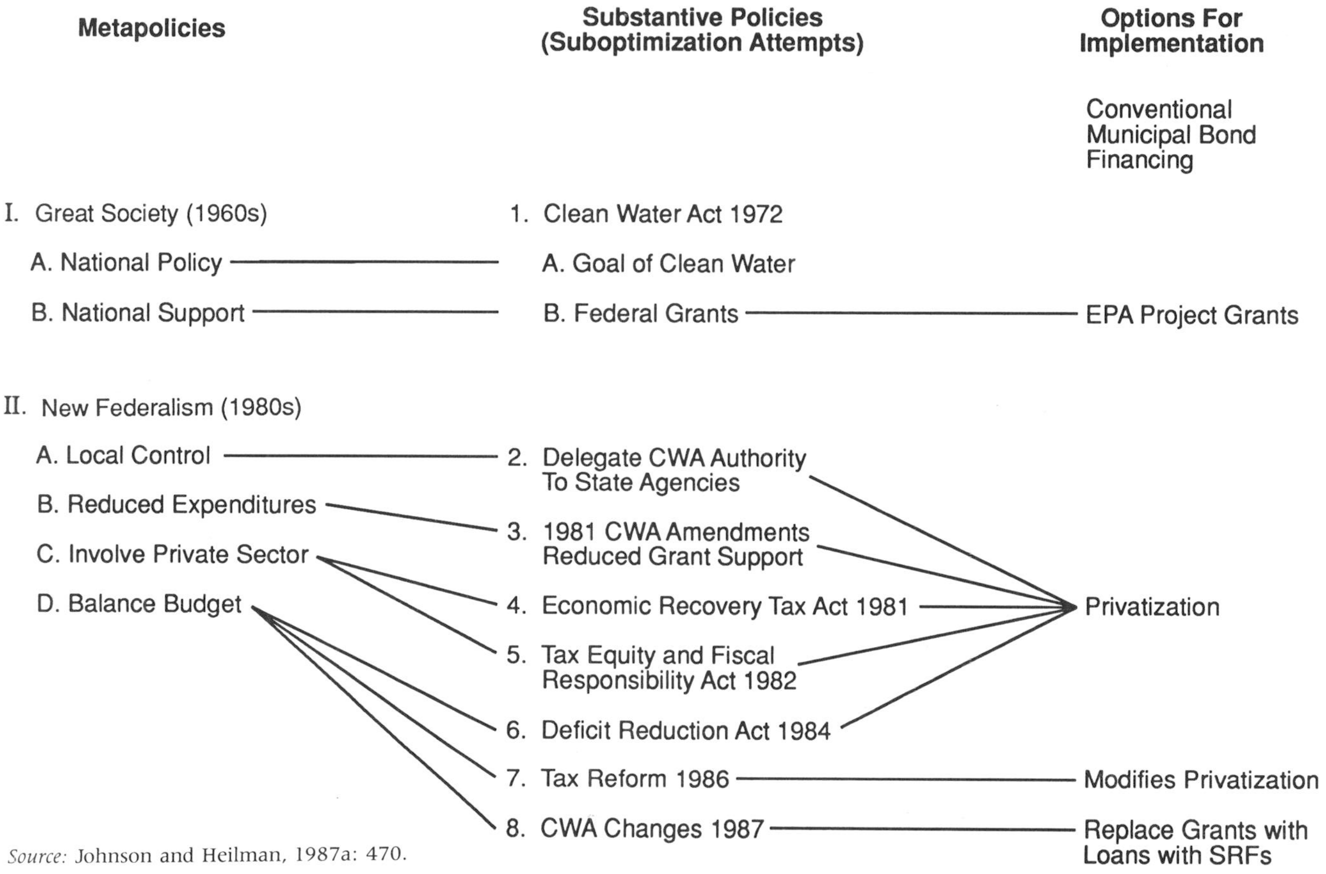

Metapolicies	Substantive Policies (Suboptimization Attempts)	Options For Implementation

Metapolicies

I. Great Society (1960s)

A. National Policy

B. National Support

II. New Federalism (1980s)

A. Local Control

B. Reduced Expenditures

C. Involve Private Sector

D. Balance Budget

Substantive Policies (Suboptimization Attempts)

1. Clean Water Act 1972

A. Goal of Clean Water

B. Federal Grants

2. Delegate CWA Authority To State Agencies

3. 1981 CWA Amendments Reduced Grant Support

4. Economic Recovery Tax Act 1981

5. Tax Equity and Fiscal Responsibility Act 1982

6. Deficit Reduction Act 1984

7. Tax Reform 1986

8. CWA Changes 1987

Options For Implementation

Conventional Municipal Bond Financing

EPA Project Grants

Privatization

Modifies Privatization

Replace Grants with Loans with SRFs

Source: Johnson and Heilman, 1987a: 470.

As the shift in metapolicy took hold, some corresponding changes in substantive policy occurred. As stated, the reduction in U.S. EPA grants was one result, and the tax law changes of 1981 and 1982 were another. Independently of these two developments in national policy, the U.S. EPA moved to force municipal compliance with national clean water standards under the National Pollutant Discharge Elimination System (NPDES) established by the Clean Water Act of 1972. The Clean Water Act put in place discharge standards that were to be met by the late 1970s. However, the deadline for municipal compliance was delayed more than once, so that by the early 1980s the U.S. EPA's enforcement policy began to lose credibility. At the same time that U.S. EPA project grants were reduced in the 1980s, a firm municipal compliance deadline of July 1, 1988, was established. Municipalities that were not in compliance thus faced the problem of stricter compliance requirements and reduced prospects for federal grant support. Each set of changes affected options for the implementation of the national policy promoting clean water. The changes themselves were uncoordinated at the national level. However, they were coordinated at the implementation level independent of any general national policy. Primarily through the initiative of the private sector, these changes were joined in the privatization of WTWs. In essence, privatization was the opportunistic consequence of changes in national policies.[19]

The Diffusion and Adoption of Privatization

The uncoordinated and opportunistic manner in which privatization emerged fails to meet the requirement of linking mechanisms referred to in the theory-sketch in Chapter 1. Such mechanisms clearly were not present, and they did not develop, at the level of national policy. The setting was much more yeasty, however, at the level of local administration and politics. Privatization was considered in several dozen jurisdictions and was adopted in eight. The process by which decisions were reached in these cases illuminates the mechanisms that did emerge to enable the public authorities and private sector firms to join in the first stage of privatization: the decision to proceed. The story of the diffusion and adoption of privatization is the story of these decisions. It begins with outlines of the steps involved in, and of the industry case for, privatization.

The Privatized Deal: An Outline

The privatized deal is complex and presents many opportunities for engagement between the public and private sectors. Earliest among them is the opportunity the public authority and the private firm have to make the deal itself. Absent a framework of national policy, these opportunities play out at the local level and on the basis of personal interactions between industry on the one hand and public officials and citizens on the other. What the local officials thought the privatization option would entail and how they evaluated and approached this option were central elements in the process of reaching agreement and making a deal. In exploring these matters, it is useful to start with an outline of how a privatized deal proceeds. What did most local officials expect would happen if they considered, and went on to adopt, privatization? While the perspective presented here refers to the pre-1986 environment, the present tense is used because it reflects the officials' focus on what they would see happening step-by-step. Of course, variations occurred in this pattern in individual deals, and some of these variations are elaborated in the case studies.

The privatization transaction involves various parties that take on multiple responsibilities and risks. Typically, the privatizer is an engineering firm affiliated with a financially strong parent corporation and with a company specializing in WTW operations and maintenance. The parent corporation and the municipality create a limited partnership to participate in the deal. The municipality issues bonds through a specially created government utilities service corporation and loans the proceeds to the privatizer. The transfer of funds proceeds through a trustee. The bond issue is tax exempt and does not draw on the full faith and credit of the city. Several methods are used to enhance the bond issue's credit rating, including bond insurance or letters of credit. The parent corporation provides some financial support. In the pre-1986 tax environment the support took the form of equity contributions based on the tax benefits then available. In the post-1986 tax environment the privatizer's contribution may take a variety of forms. The effect of the privatizer's contribution is to reduce the size of the bond issue needed to finance the project. In the first privatized cases, the contribution and credit enhancements, such as bond insurance, resulted in lower total costs to the communities and lower sewer fees to users than could be achieved through other options absent a federal grant. In addition, privatized projects could be completed significantly faster than the norm for federally funded projects, further reducing costs.

Once the parties reach agreement, the privatizer hires a contractor to begin construction. When construction is complete, the operations and maintenance (O&M) firm affiliated with the privatizer takes over operation of the firm. Typically the privatizer or an organization related to it (such as the limited partnership) owns the facility and holds the NPDES discharge permit, meaning it is responsible for plant performance.

The Industry Case for Privatization: Theme and Variations

To understand the context in which the initial privatization decisions were reached, it is helpful to know not only what the local officials thought would happen step-by-step in privatization but also why industry officials felt that privatization could reduce the local authority's costs dramatically. The industry case was in effect the up side of the private sector dynamic that local public sector officials were invited to engage. Privatizers certainly pointed to the public sector–driven tax benefits that they could translate into equity contributions. But they also argued that the inherent private sector dynamics of privatization offered efficiencies and cost savings independent of tax benefits. These efficiencies are related to, and elaborate upon, some of the points developed in the literature review in Chapter 1 dealing with efficiency and competition.

The case for privatization is orchestrated as a theme with variations. The theme is the differing dynamics of the two sectors. Private owner-operators are not subject to regulatory restrictions to the extent grant-funded local authorities are. They are subject, however, to market competition in ways that local authorities cannot be. Thus, competition leads the privatizer to make design choices that are efficient in terms of life-cycle costs and to use the design-build approach to maximum advantage to reduce overall costs. (This theme is developed in Chapter 4.) Some reports suggested the savings resulting from these features of privatization could be sizable. A 1984 EPA study (O'Toole 1985:299) cited evidence that privatization could reduce the capital costs of a facility by up to 40 percent. Moore and Butler (1987:97) reported a finding by the Congressional Budget Office that "when cities were paying only 25 percent of construction costs for federally funded facilities, costs were at least 30 percent higher than when local governments paid for the projects themselves." These assertions are analyzed in Chapter 4.

The first of several variations on the basic theme stresses hypothesized savings through design choices. The general idea is that when cities build facilities with grant support they can afford (and, in fact, the process may require) redundant systems as well as amenities that are unnecessary and inflate project costs. The term *goldplating* is used at times in this regard.

A second variation stresses the absence of regulation. Because no grant support exists for privatized projects, U.S. EPA's regulatory presence is reduced and cost savings result. (However, in this respect, as Chapter 9 reviews, the state regulatory role differs from state to state.)

A third variation addresses life-cycle costs. It suggests that because the engineers who design the plant can work with the O&M firm that will run it (in some cases the same firm) the designers can tailor long-term efficiency into the plant by fitting it to the routines and capabilities of the O&M staff. Because such firms are in the business of running sewage plants, they bring more expertise to bear on this activity than would normally be available in a city that has a single facility. Where technically complex systems can in the long run save costs, the design engineer can choose to use them and know that the operators will treat them competently.

A related point is that because the O&M firm usually serves more than one WTW it offers advantages of economies of scale. It can easily bring its experts to any single plant that encounters difficulty and can readily bring in needed equipment on short notice. Thus the size and expertise of the firm reduce the need for redundancy in the initial design. It is important to note that the municipality can choose to have back-up systems and expensive features built into the system if it chooses to do so. The point is that in the privatization model choices are created.

A fourth variation states that the design/build fast-track approach used on privatized projects saves time through the use of an integrated implementation structure. Plant design, construction, and operation are all under the control of a single entity, the privatizer, and are not subject to intense regulatory scrutiny or, more importantly, to compartmentalized design, construct, and operations procedures. In this setting, design can overlap with construction. The engineering firm completes detailed plans and specifications as the contractor needs them. As developed in Chapter 4, this case stands in contrast to that of the grant-funded setting in which the designer typically must prepare all plans and specifications and have them approved by the relevant regulatory agency before construction can begin.

A fifth and related variation focuses on the way in which the integrated implementation structure saves time and costs. The privatizer exclusively controls and coordinates schedules, personnel, and purchases. Materials can be bulk purchased and be in place when needed. The result is that relationships among the designer, general contractor, and subcontractors are less conflictual, more timely, and more productive than they are when responsibility is divided among the engineer, builder, municipality, and regulatory agency.

These arguments are not self-certifying; indeed, some observers reject them. For instance, Foster (1983:120) suggests that certain problems arise precisely because so many functions are combined in a single overarching organization. Examples include: the ambiguity of scope of work when plans are drafted as construction proceeds; difficulties of allocating the costs of design and construction; and possibilities of "nonconforming work and improper payment." These concerns point to basic questions of accountability for the municipality. Where the privatizer controls and coordinates design and construction and ultimately owns and operates the plant, does the municipality seriously sacrifice its effective control over and accountability for a basic public service and policy objective? AFSCME (1983) raises related questions of the redistributive effects of privatization, arguing that the privatizer is not subject to the same standards of equal opportunity employment and management fairness as a public sector employer is. Thus, the changes in national tax law that have focused attention on the economics of privatization also call attention to its political implications.

Privatization Diffusion and Adoption

During the 1981–87 period in which local authorities were seeking viable options to federal funding to address wastewater needs, some twenty-five authorities formally considered privatization. These cases provided the population for the study of the diffusion and adoption of WTW privatization.[20] The following provides a brief general description of these cases and the factors that influenced the decision to privatize or not to privatize. The discussion section then addresses the implications of these findings for the theory as sketched in Chapter 1.

Two surveys were conducted of the twenty-five municipalities that made a formal privatization decision. The first survey was designed to determine why privatization was considered and what factors accounted for the decision. The second survey was designed to determine how privatization diffused, how the inherent characteristics of privatization were evaluated, and how these characteristics related to the privatization decision.

Table 2.1 presents a list and description of the authorities surveyed in both studies. Through confirmation with privatizers, national waste-water and municipal organizations, and the Privatization Council, the survey population included all local authorities that could be identified that had formally addressed a wastewater privatization decision between 1982 and 1987. The authorities are mostly municipalities, are generally medium sized, have growing populations, and have above-average mean family income levels. The manager form of government or an equivalent is most prevalent. The twenty-five cases are located in all regions of the country, with some concentration in the Southeast and the Southwest and in two states within these regions.

Figure 2.4 shows the key dates (first learned, adopted or rejected, and on-line) of the privatization decisions of twenty-two of the twenty-five cases shown in table 2.1. The data on the three remaining cases were deleted from the analyses because the privatization decisions did not relate to WTW privatization. Three municipalities first learned of it in 1982, nine in 1983, seven in 1984, and the remaining three in 1985 and 1986. The incidence of "first learned" was clearly a function of industry's response to the 1981 and 1982 tax code revisions. All of the decisions to privatize were made prior to 1986, while three of the decisions to reject privatization were made after 1986. One municipality privatized in 1987 and other authorities proceeded with privatization in 1988 and 1989, indicating that privatization has positive attributes beyond those associated initially with the 1981 and 1982 tax code revisions.

In the first study, each of the authorities surveyed had addressed the issue of whether to privatize a wastewater facility. That is, each local decision-making body was faced with a need to build new or additional treatment capacity, and each formally considered privatization as an option. It seemed plausible to suppose that needs to build new facilities would be driven largely by regulatory mandates, given that compliance standards were already in place that provided for an elaborate process of reviews and sanctions for failure to comply. However, in a rank ordering of factors that created the need for new or expanded WTWs, population

Table 2.1 Characteristics of Twenty-Five Municipalities Identified as Having Made a Wastewater Privatization Decision

Location of Municipality[a]	Form of Government[b]	1986 Population	1980–86 Percentage Increase	1986 Mean Family Income	Privatization Decision[c]
SE	MG	32,000	12.3	$19,231	P
SW	MG	63,855	115.2	$26,799	P
NE	MG	8,500	2.4	$18,000	P
NE	MG	7,200	5.9	$24,000	P
SW	MG	18,580	225.0	$29,698	P
SE	SD	339,000	4.9	$17,970	P
SE	MC	10,500	55.3	$15,948	P
SE	MC	60,000	15.3	$16,200	P
SE	(CO	24,800	9.6	$22,947	P)[d]
SE	MC	392,547	7.2	$12,580	NP
SE	MG	9,000	45.2	$15,000	NP
SE	MG	2,230	65.3	$18,562	NP

SE	MG	53,400	11.3	$13,937	NP
MW	MC	9,800	6.0	$23,000	NP
MW	MG	52,000	3.0	$25,000	NP
SE	CO	474,800	4.9	$10,082	NP
W	MG	24,950	30.8	$23,979	NP
SE	MC	135,000	5.2	$16,125	NP
NW	SD	8,500	12.1	$22,000	NP
SW	(MG	19,100	25.0	$17,273	NP)d
NW	MC	5,600	12.1	$22,000	NP
SW	MG	17,091	70.9	$15,484	CP
NW	MC	24,000	4.3	$19,357	CP
SE	MG	12,700	14.4	$12,186	CP
SE	(MC	394,300	8.9	$28,657	CP)d

aSE (Southeast)
SW (Southwest)
NE (Northeast)
NW (Northwest)
MW (Midwest)
W (West)

bMC (mayor/council)
MG (manager/council)
CO (county commission)
SD (special district)

cP (privatized)
NP (did not privatize)
CP (considering)

d( ) survey not completed

Figure 2.4   WTW Privatization Dates

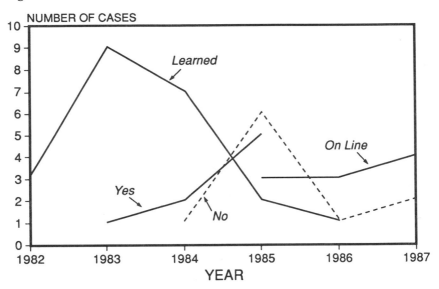

growth, overall, was more influential in this determination than was compliance. Other factors such as public demand were substantially less important in influencing the decision. Interestingly, no respondent directly reported environmental or health-related factors as reasons for needing new or expanded capacity.

Each city had essentially three options to finance and build a treatment work:

1. An EPA project grant or a combination of an EPA project grant and other funds.
2. A self-financing structure involving the issuance of bonds.
3. Privatization.

Each of these alternatives contained problems or barriers to implementation. As noted, the option of EPA project grant construction was limited due to the inadequacy or unavailability of grant funds. In addition, the time-frame requirements for compliance and the need for more immediate attention to a wastewater problem—for compliance, health, or economic development reasons—also restricted use of this option.

The option of self-financing through the issuance of local revenue bonds also encountered two major hurdles. First, local governments have limits on the total amount of bonded indebtedness allowable.

Major capital projects, such as construction of sewage plants, often would extend local bonded indebtedness above this limit. In addition, reservations occur about utilizing bonded indebtedness potential in sizable projects and thereby removing the use of these bonds for other needed projects such as schools, buildings, roads, and industrial development. A second hurdle in the early 1980s was that self-financing bond rates were higher than rates associated with other options.

The third option, privatization, encountered a number of obstacles. Because privatization was not a product of public policy, decisions about it faced additional barriers beyond those normally associated with public policy development and implementation. That is, local decision makers had to overcome an unusually complex array of constraints in order to reach a decision in favor of privatization.

In addition to legal barriers and the obstacle of a massive contract development and execution process, with its associated requirements for highly qualified and specialized personnel, the decision to privatize encountered four specific and major hurdles:

1. The issue of conflicting values and perspectives concerning the private sector role in the production and delivery of a traditionally public service had to be addressed.
2. Multiple specific issues related to policy implementation in an intergovernmental structure (i.e., the roles of U.S. EPA, state environmental agencies, and local units of government) unavoidably complicated the decision.
3. The privatization option faced an especially complex burden of persuasion in terms of its economic viability, precisely because it was innovative and financially intricate and faced an uncertain future in terms of tax law.
4. The relevant national and state-level regulatory agencies provided little or no information or guidance to local authorities on the advisability of privatization or the problems or advantages it might present.

The lack of policy and guidance increased constraints. However, it also increased discretion and opportunity for innovation for those local policymakers who were willing and able to address a privatization decision. The congressional decision to reduce or eliminate, at some future date, the resources required to comply with national water policy, without revision of the compliance standards or the timetable, did in fact increase discretion, even though local decision makers may not have wanted it (Montjoy and O'Toole 1979). Discretion, as in most cases, can range from defiance to innovation. Thus, while some, perhaps many, local authorities made no attempt to address wastewater compliance requirements outside the federal grant process, others sought innovative solutions. The decision to privatize clearly involved the application of innovation in an arena of discretion. The case studies show that the muncipalities that sought nonroutine resources to address the wastewater problem (i.e., privatization) were the ones that had the "forces within the organization" (Montjoy and O'Toole 1979:467) to deal effectively with the complex process of privatization and were able to overcome the substantial legal, political, and economic barriers that characterize privatization. These forces include organizational and managerial elements that integrated the normally divergent public and private sector structures and processes.

In the local authorities' final decision to privatize, the factors that were influential included: economics, time, need for clean water, and unavailability of grants. While economic factors were of major importance, other factors—particularly the immediate need for increased water treatment capacity for community development and the ability of the municipality to deal with a complex set of economic, legal, and political issues—were prominent in the decision to privatize. While it might appear that economic factors were paramount in decisions to privatize and not to privatize, the data suggest that they did not determine the decision in either case.

For the municipalities that made a decision not to privatize, economic factors, objection to buy-back provisions, risk, difficulty in dealing with private providers, and legal and political reasons were involved. Only one respondent indicated that the reason not to privatize was based on the conclusion that privatization clearly costs more than other available options. The other respondents deciding not to privatize placed the economic considerations in a context of noneconomic factors. For instance, one reported that the privatization cost estimates were higher than expected but "the firms were generally uninformed of the privatization concept" and the city would "lose control" of the plant. A second city responded that while privatization appeared economically feasible, "unfortunately, the plant for which privatization was explored was in advanced stages of design which removed some flexibility. The city and the privatizer could not agree on the construction cost component." In other words, prior decisions reduced discretion.

Other nonprivatizing respondents mentioned such factors as "loss of control" of the WTW, political problems with the buy-back provisions, and uncertainty of the tax law. As one respondent stated, "Putting all risks aside, privatization was an economically viable alternative when compared with public [revenue bonds] financing." However, the council could not put the risks aside, especially the political risk, a finding previously confirmed in studies of service contracting (Ferris 1986:294).

The case study data support the conclusion that privatization decisions emerged from an interplay of multiple factors. Virtually all the cities had to address political and contractual problems such as buy-back provisions, loss of control over employees and wage rates, general uncertainty about privatization, and the limits of local technical expertise. It is exactly such a fluid and complex setting that maximizes opportunities for discretion and innovation. Thus, a relationship would be expected between positive privatization decisions and municipal institutional and leadership characteristics and capacity.

Six of the eight respondents who privatized indicated that the decision had been strongly shaped by a leading individual. Conversely, four of the six cities that did not privatize reported that no clear leadership was present. Supplementary case study data indicate that where an active city leader made a strong professional and personal effort to proceed with privatization, the many partial obstacles were overcome. Where leadership on behalf of privatization was less active or where other internal forces, such as the city council, actively opposed privatization, it did not proceed. This conclusion is further supported by the finding that all but one of the municipalities that privatized have a city manager or comparable type goverment compared with 50 percent of those that decided not to privatize.

It thus appears that the final decision to privatize or not to privatize was, in large part, a function of the personnel involved and the institutional processes used to make the decision. Because privatization of WTWs was a new and uncharted frontier for the local decision makers involved, uncertainty as well as complexity had to be overcome. As stated, the U.S. EPA or state agencies, according to the respondents, provided little or no assistance in the local decision-making process. Rather, local governments had to rely on internal resources and legal, financial, and industry consultants. The uncertainties of tax law reform, the uncertainty of the position of EPA, the absence of precedents or experience on which to rely, and the difficulty of making clear comparative cost analyses of options all combined to maximize both ambiguity and discretion. Specific national mandates and ambivalence about public and private sector relationships placed substantial pressures on those involved in the decisions. Thus, given these constraints on action and the absence of any national or state policy or guidelines, the decision to privatize required substantial local discretion.

Summary and Conclusions

The pre-1986 experience described above remains highly relevant to the position of cities in the post-1986 tax environment. While tax incentives have been reduced, the data strongly suggest that the role of cost savings was less prominent in privatization decisions than might be assumed. The post-1986 environment remains similar in many ways to features of the 1982–86 period. Many municipalities need to build or expand treatment capacity (Watson and Vocino 1990:430). A shortage of financing exists. And national policy in this area continues to be in flux, with the transition now under way to state revolving loan funds under the Water Quality Act of 1987. The implementation of tighter nonpoint pollution and drinking water standards seems likely to increase attention to, and pressures to use, efficient opportunities in this area of infrastructure policy.

Privatization was a risky innovation that potentially provided maximum economic and compliance benefits to local authorities caught in the squeeze between reduced funding and compliance deadlines. However, no policy at any level of government existed to provide a framework for the development and implementation of privatization. Privatization of WTWs involves a complex contractual structure and relatively high transaction costs. The transaction costs include the time and money municipal officials and privatizing firms invest in working out their respective rights and obligations and in reducing these to contractual agreements. In addition, a number of legal constraints on privatization exist, including bid laws and prohibition of long-term contracts.

The experience of the first cities to consider privatization bears upon the theory-sketch. In particular, it suggests the nature of the linking mechanisms that may come into play in the early stages of negotiating a partnership agreement, absent a formal framework of national policy. The evidence shows that these mechanisms are typically both informal and personal. The nature of these mechanisms is further illuminated by the following specific conclusions, which are based on the surveys of local authorities that made a privatization decision in the 1981–86 period.

Specific Findings

1. In the early cases, information about privatization was obtained from industry publications and informational events such as seminars. As some deals were completed, professional peers of city officials became an important source of information.
2. Interest in and adoption of privatization tended to occur in certain categories of municipalities. Most of the authorities had less than 100,000 population, had growing populations, and had above-average mean family income levels. Also, the cities that considered privatization tended to need treatment capacity in order to accommodate growth rather than to respond to compliance mandates. Clearly the mandates played a role for the growth-oriented cities, because the NPDES required them to build capacity before they could expand. The interest in accommodating new residents and industry typically brought the mandates into play.
3. The early cases involved many barriers that were specific to this option rather than being simply inherent in the normal decision-making process.
   a. Cities had to overcome legal barriers (such as limitations in state law on their power to contract for periods of several years), competitive bidding requirements, and limitations on the use of tax-exempt bonds. These issues are addressed in Chapters 4 and 5. They are important because if cities do not address them adequately prior to signing contracts, they cause problems later during project operation. Chapter 10 provides a case in point: one municipal buy-back (deprivatization) of a privatized plant was motivated, in part, by the failure of the authority to secure state legislation exempting the privatizer from the property tax.
   b. Because each deal raised so many new issues, large transaction costs occurred in terms of time and money spent working out issues and paying fees of attorneys and financial advisors. Chapter 3 addresses transaction costs for the privatization project in Auburn, Alabama.
   c. Cities had to address conflicting values and perspectives concerning the role of the private sector in owning and operating

facilities that provided a service traditionally located in the public sector.

d. The unclear role of federal and state regulatory agencies in privatization deals complicated the decision-making process. A simple example here is the inability of cities to determine whether an authority could use privatization to expand an existing grant-funded facility without having to repay the original grant.

e. Privatization faced a complex burden of persuasion because of its complexity, novelty, and uncertainty.

f. For many municipalities repurchase provisions complicated the decision to privatize. The tax benefits typically depended on an agreement that the authority buy the facility back at market value after twenty-five years. That value could not be predetermined. Officials also objected to the notion of having to pay twice for the same facility.

g. The context of changing policy at the national level created conditions that favored not only the development of privatization but also the exercise of local discretion in deciding how to meet clean water policy mandates. Privatization required the local exercise of political and administrative discretion, a difficult political process.

4. The common factor that led to a decision to privatize in this setting, marked by discretion, consisted of forces (individuals and groups) in the organizational structure of local authorities who were willing to innovate and address the many barriers that privatization faced. In individual cases many of the barriers were mentioned as reasons for a decision not to privatize. The emergence of a strong leader for privatization consistently made a difference within the complex interplay of the many issues that arose. Where this leadership did not emerge, or where active opposition occurred, privatization was not selected.

5. In addition to leadership, certain local perceptions of privatization were important elements in decisions to privatize. These factors were: a perception that privatization offered more advantages than any other option; the ability to compare privatization with the other options; and confidence (lack of uncertainty) about how privatization would function. Surprisingly, perceived time and cost savings and the complexity of implementation were not strongly related to the privatization decision.

Privatization succeeded in those cases where a new structure was developed between the public and the private sectors—a structure that provided for the achievement of common goals within a framework of public accountability. Privatization efforts failed where the two criteria of common goals and a framework for accountability could not be achieved. The following chapters detail and analyze the role of these two elements. Chapter 3 illustrates how privatization developed in a specific case that meets both of the required objectives.

3

City of Auburn and the Clean Water Act
The Struggle for Compliance

The city of Auburn, Alabama, was among the first cities in the United States to privatize its wastewater treatment works (WTWs).[21] Without precedents, a model, or a context of national or state policy, the city was left to its own resources and those provided by the private sector to develop and implement a public-private partnership in the form of privatized WTWs. The development required innovative thinking, revisions of state law, and strong administrative leadership in order to execute a highly complex and risky deal. The Auburn case study provides an extensive description and analysis of how the initial WTW privatization projects took place.

Auburn has a population of 32,000, which includes some 13,000 of the 20,000 students of Auburn University. At the time of the beginning of this study, 1984, the city had an eight-member council, a council president elected at-large, a mayor elected at-large, and a professional city manager. The mayor had limited formal duties and powers and did not serve on the council. Members of the council and the mayor were elected for staggered terms of four years.

The city manager, Douglas J. Watson, was appointed by the council and was the administrative head of the government. He was employed under contract and was responsible for the administration of a government of 260 employees and a budget of $6,794,203. In 1984, Watson was serving in his second full year in Auburn, having served eleven years as manager or assistant manager in other states and cities before coming to Auburn.

In summary, Auburn is a classic example of a small-town, growing, university community. It has a highly mobile and educated professional and white-collar population. Its prevailing values emphasize the amenities of life, including sensitivity to the quality of the environment. In the 1970s and early 1980s the city faced increasingly serious environmental and economic issues in connection with its wastewater treatment facilities.

The Environmental Issue

In 1984 Auburn's wastewater treatment system consisted of two wastewater treatment works and two main pumping stations, all built before 1958. To overcome the city's hilly terrain, the sewer system was built on opposite sides of a ridge that runs through the city. The Northside Plant, an 0.8-million-gallons-per-day (mgd) plant, treated wastewater from the railroad to the northern city limits and discharged treated waste into a creek. The Southside Plant, a 3.2-mgd plant, located on the southwestern side of the university campus, treated wastewater in the southern portion of the city with the aid of two main pumping stations as well as several smaller pumping stations. The Southside Plant also discharged its treated wastewater into a nearby creek.

Problems began almost immediately following the construction of the two WTWs in 1958 and continued for more than two decades. City officials attempted to alleviate some of the problems in the early 1960s, but their efforts were ineffectual. Following the passage of the 1972 Clean Water Act (CWA), the city began to review more carefully its wastewater treatment problems. The renewed interest was mostly attributable to the deteriorating condition of the ten pump stations that transmitted wastewater to the Southside Plant. All needed repair or replacement. However, other factors, including the CWA, played a part in placing the wastewater treatment issue on the public agenda. The Southside Plant was not meeting its effluent limits and at times was violating its National Pollutant Discharge Elimination System permit; raw sewage backed up into homes and overflowed into local streams and creeks. The Northside Plant was not in compliance with EPA standards and was overloaded due to increased residential development. In addition, twelve major breaks along one of the discharge creeks allowed flooded creek water to enter the sewer system.

Beyond the general deterioration of the system, two specific factors played important roles in placing the issue of wastewater treatment on the city's policy agenda in the 1970s. One was local public opinion. In the early 1970s, Dr. H. C. Morgan, a member of the university faculty and subsequently (1976–80) a member of the city council, began a public relations campaign to educate city officials, community leaders, and the general public on the wastewater problem. He walked every creek and stream in the city and took hundreds of pictures that showed the extent of the pollution problem in the immediate community. He conducted slide presentations at civic clubs, showing polluted streams and in-operative pump stations. Through these presentations and newspaper stories about the sewage problem, the general public developed for the first time an awareness of the wastewater problem.

The Economic Issue

In addition to the perceived environmental local need for new WTWs, national water policy became a factor in local decision making during the 1970s. The CWA set in place a substantial federal program to clean up the nation's polluted water. Shortly after its passage, Auburn became involved in the U.S. EPA's construction grant program. The city received more than $1 million to finance initial planning steps conducted by professional engineering consultants. For ten years the city actively worked to solve its sewer problems through participation in the EPA construction grant program. In 1979 the city completed a "201 Facilities Plan," which consisted of the development and review of four basic plans and various treatment options. The plan also called for the elim-ination of most pump stations and the construction of two new WTWs at sites that would allow for a natural gravity flow of wastewater.

However, grant funding under the CWA was not a reliable option for financing the WTW construction the city needed. The CWA amend-ments of 1981 reduced EPA funding from 75 to 55 percent and reduced grant-eligible costs. In particular, grant funding for increased treatment capacity was eliminated. While Auburn needed to achieve compliance, it also needed expanded treatment capacity. The net result of these changes was that if the city was able to get on the state priority list and receive any funding at all, the support it could receive would cover only 33 percent of project costs for only the Southside Plant. And, overall, the city was placed low on the state priority list because of major sewer problems elsewhere within the state. Auburn officials were told that at least they had two secondary treatment plants, even if they did not work well or were overloaded. Auburn thus faced a problem shared by many cities. An established source of construction funds had been decreased while pressures to build or expand treatment works had increased.

The Management Problem

In 1982, the city council made finding a solution to the wastewater problem a high priority. This decision was driven in part by the concern that a state-enforced moratorium on adding customers to the WTW systems would hinder economic development of the southside and would prohibit the university from constructing new buildings. This concern was complicated by the fact that the university had the option of building its own treatment facilities, an option the city opposed. Any limit on construction meant limiting business and industrial growth and job opportunities. In addition, the Southside Plant was constantly malfunctioning and polluting the local streams. The Northside Plant was operating at full capacity, a condition that would lead to a moratorium being placed on new housing units. These factors, coupled with EPA compliance requirements and the community desire to have a clean water environment, generated sufficient interest to place improvement and expansion of wastewater facilities on the active agenda of the city. The obvious questions were: How to proceed? What was needed? And, how to pay for the project?

When Watson came to Auburn to serve as city manager in August 1982, he brought both experience and professional training to the office. He emphasized goal setting, planning, and the establishment of budget priorities reflective of goal priorities. Shortly after assuming office he met with the president of the council to review council priorities and the budget process that was already under way. Although the council had identified two high-priority projects—street repair and wastewater treatment—the budget under review reflected neither priority. Out of a total budget of some $7 million, only $50,000 was designated for street improvements and nothing was designated to address the wastewater problem. However, as a result of the general realization that the WTW issue had to be faced, the council had increased sewer fees by 20 percent in 1981 and in 1982. Neither increase was sufficient to finance the needed projects. Watson informed the council that he would work on the funding problem and report back.

At this point the council knew of the wastewater problem primarily as an environmental and citizen complaint problem motivated, in part, by the work of Dr. Morgan. Watson saw the problem primarily in terms of inadequate WTW capacity for future residential and industrial growth, particularly if the state regulatory agency were to place a moratorium on development in the city. His first effort to address the problem was to determine if the existing WTWs could be upgraded. Upon finding that this solution was not practical at either plant, he turned to the second option—new WTWs. In the fall of 1982 he and the city engineer went to the state EPA agency to discuss construction funding for the Southside Plant and planning funding for the Northside Plant. They were informed that it would be five years or more before any funding might be available for the Southside WTW and even longer for the Northside Plant.

In early 1983 Watson continued to search for funding sources for WTW construction. As a result of these efforts, he was approached in the spring of 1983 by an engineering company executive in the region who was a former administrator in the U.S. EPA. Since the 1981–82 tax revisions, the company had been exploring the possibility of applying privatization (design, construct, finance, own, and operate) to the WTW area. He introduced the privatization concept to Watson. Independently of these events, a local resident and former university engineering faculty member, then with a design and engineering firm within the state, was also exploring the possibility of WTW privatization. After meeting with the city manager to discuss privatization, he presented a proposal whereby his company would develop a group to do the whole WTW project—design, construct, finance, own, and operate. However, the financing was the key element of the proposal for both parties.

By the summer of 1983, Watson had identified and tentatively evaluated four alternatives: (1) finance the construction of new sewage treatment facilities utilizing a grant from the EPA; (2) self-finance new facilities (the city sells bonds and builds facilities on its own); (3) upgrade and extend the life of the existing Southside and Northside plants; or (4) privatize the WTWs.

Decision Options

Option 1. EPA Grant. As indicated, by 1982 the city had received more than $1 million to finance Steps I and II of the EPA construction grant process. These steps included survey and engineering work. Step III funding had been applied for and, if granted, would be used for Southside WTW construction. However, with the 1981 changes in EPA funding, the city's chances for any funding were small and the potential grant percentage for just Southside construction was reduced to around 33 percent of eligible costs, equivalent to $3.1 million of the $20 million needed for the complete project. In addition, if granted, EPA funding would not be available until 1987 at the earliest.

Option 2. Self-financing. The state constitution exempted debt incurred for sewer improvements from the constitutional debt limitations placed on general municipal bonds. Thus, self-financing of the WTWs would not encumber the city's debt capacity. The city could finance 100 percent of construction costs through the issuance of bonds or through a combination of EPA construction grants and bonds. Two major factors were involved in the analysis of this option. One: the EPA construction grant, if approved for the Southside Plant, would not be available until 1987. Two: the interest rates on municipal bonds were high (10 percent or more) and would require a substantial increase in sewer user fees. Advantages of 100 percent self-financing were that the project could proceed quickly and with minimal state regulatory involvement.

Option 3. Upgrade and Extend the Life of the Southside and the Northside Plants. The third option essentially meant maintaining the status quo and hoping for future national or state policy or funding changes that might alter, for the better, options for addressing the WTW problem. The risks involved included continuing noncompliance with state and EPA standards with resultant fines or moratoria on additional service as well as the increasing political problems associated with local demands to provide a clean water environment for the community.

Option 4. Privatization. The fourth option provided a nontraditional alternative for addressing the WTW problem through private sector finance, construction, ownership, and operation of the WTWs. Public-private partnerships in the form of municipal contracts with private sector companies to provide a particular service, such as garbage collection, had been successfully implemented in communities across the United States for years. However, in 1983 no municipality had engaged in comprehensive privatization, and thus no one knew its applicability to the WTW area. The option faced multiple legal, political, and contractual hurdles.

A preliminary economic analysis of all of these options except privatization was conducted in 1983 (see table 3.1). Because the 1981 amendments to the CWA eliminated 75 percent EPA funding, this option was not possible and was thus eliminated. City financing of just the

Table 3.1 Service Fees Required to Finance WTW Options

Description	Rate per 1,000 gallons	Monthly Minimum	Average Family/ Month
Current rate	$ .96	$ 2.88	$ 6.72
New north and south plants (75% EPA grant)	$ 1.45	$ 4.35	$10.15
New south plant (100% city financing) Existing north plant	$ 1.90	$ 5.70	$13.30
New south plant (55% EPA grant)* Existing north plant	$ 1.55	$ 4.65	$10.85
New north and south plants (100% city financing)	$ 3.73	$11.19	$22.38
New north and south plants (privatization)	?	?	?

*A 55 percent grant is equivalent to 33 percent of construction costs. Projections were based on construction costs at current dollars and not at the time the grant would have been received.

Southside Plant was not cost competitive, requiring a fee of $1.90. Even mixed grant and self-financing of the Southside Plant would require $1.55, and city financing of both plants would cost $3.73. The cost of privatizing one or both plants was unknown. However, the initial discussions of privatization had suggested that it would cost from 20 to 40 percent less than the self-financing option.

By late summer of 1983, Watson began preparing recommendations for his upcoming 1984 budget message. With respect to the WTWs, he eliminated the self-financing option and recommended that a study be made of the privatization option. Several factors supported this recommendation. Substantial benefits were available to the privatizer under 1981 and 1982 tax code provisions and could be passed on to the city. Also, potential cost savings were associated with fast-track construction, noncompetitive bidding, increased on-site construction flexibility, and greatly reduced regulatory involvement and requirements.

Two additional factors supported privatization. First, the privatizer would operate the WTWs and assume responsibility for compliance with national and state water quality standards. Second, construction and operation of the new WTWs could proceed immediately. The plants would be on-line within a year as compared with the projected five to ten years required to construct and place in operation a WTW built with EPA funds. Thus, fast-track construction not only would save money but would bring the city into compliance before the 1988 deadline, avert a moratorium on development, and solve the problem of local stream pollution.

The privatization option still faced serious and substantial hurdles. First, no precedent existed to serve as a guide. In 1983 only two cities in the United States besides Auburn (Chandler, Arizona, and Norco, California) were considering privatization. No one had yet executed a WTW privatization deal. Second, state law prohibited a municipality from entering into a long-term contract for this purpose. Third, state law required competitive bidding on all municipal contracts over $2,000. And fourth, the transaction costs and requirements to execute a privatization project were enormous.

In addition to these barriers, the unanswered questions were numerous. What happens to the currently employed sewage plant personnel? What if the privatizer goes out of business? What happens at the end of the twenty-five-year contract? Will tax laws in effect require the city to buy back the plant after they had paid to build it? Is this double payment? Will the council be held accountable by the citizens for WTW problems even though it has no responsibility for ownership and operation? What happens if the city in the future wants to add a government-financed unit to the existing privatized plant? Could the city mix private and government-owned facilities? Should the city sell a private company a traditional public service in order for that company to make a profit? Could the city explain to the citizens how a private company can own and operate a WTW for profit more cost-effectively than the city could do so without a profit? Could the city explain a substantial increase in sewer fees, particularly to transfer the service to a profit-making, private firm?

Decision and Results

Watson decided on a course of action as he prepared his 1984 budget message. He concluded, at least tentatively, that privatization could work and would be the least expensive and quickest way to resolve the WTW problem. However, he appreciated the fact that privatization was a new and untested concept in the area of WTWs. He also knew that for the concept to have a chance it would have to be perceived widely, on the council and in the community, as both a politically and an economically sound option. First, however, it had to be given a fair hearing to even get off the ground.

In October 1983 he recommended to the council that he be authorized to issue a request for proposals (RFP) for the privatization of the Southside WTW and to establish a committee to evaluate the privatization option and the responses to the RFP. Watson believed that if he made a privatization recommendation alone, it might flounder. In addition, he wanted to keep the options open until a validated consensus was formed. In essence, his recommendation to the council was a proposal for how to arrive at a recommendation.

The council approved the recommendation and authorized him to develop and issue an RFP and to recommend to the council nominees for a Sewer Privatization Review Committee. For the next two to three months Watson met with a number of people to learn about privatization in order to prepare the RFP, identify committee nominees, and prepare for the initial committee meeting. In February 1984 the council approved the manager's nominees to the Sewer Privatization Review Committee and added to the committee the president of the council, who felt that if the mayor was to be on the committee he should also be a member. Included on the committee were: a university professor of civil engineering; the city finance director; the mayor; the university comptroller; the chairman of the city Industrial Development Board; the city engineer; a local attorney and former city attorney and mayor; the city auditor; Dr. H. C. Morgan, the university faculty member who had led the public education effort of the WTW problem; a member of council who was also a member of the university engineering faculty; the city attorney; the president of the council; and the city manager. The committee met in late February and the manager briefed the members on the WTW problem and the current status of the options. The committee was given a tour of the WTW facilities and was asked to select a chair and set a schedule for the completion of its work. Dr. Morgan was selected as chair, a recommendation Watson had made privately to some members of the committee. The committee organized itself into three subcommittees—legal, engineering, and financial—and prepared to review RFP responses due by March 5, 1984.

Watson made extensive preparations for the work of the committee prior to its first meeting. Given the preliminary work done by him and the charge to the committee, the committee was, as its name states, a privatization review committee. The other options for the construction of WTWs would be considered only if privatization proved to be not feasible or not acceptable. By early 1984 the city manager, the mayor, and the Sewer Privatization Review Committee were all, in essence, working toward the adoption of the privatization option. Initial financial analyses supported privatization. Contacts with potential privatizers, financial consulting firms, legal counsel, national and state EPA officials, and related parties all resulted in the feeling, if not the conclusion, that privatization was feasible. An informal decision seemed to have been reached to proceed with privatization, if all the hurdles could be overcome, if the initial financial analyses were correct, and if an acceptable contract could be executed.

During this period, the mayor, Jan Dempsey, was an active and informed participant in the process. She met with potential privatizers, state and federal EPA personnel, and financial and engineering consultants. In these meetings she established a set of relationships that led to the development of confidence in the city's commitment and ability to address and manage the wastewater issue. In addition, and very importantly, the mayor, the manager, and the committee were all instrumental in establishing the financial and managerial soundness of the city—an essential requirement for the financing required in privatization.

Watson and the committee were fully aware that they were addressing an innovative solution to the WTW problem. Thus, while the hurdles were substantial and the risks significant, the decision-making process was enhanced by proceeding in a challenging, even exciting, context of creative and professional thinking involving New York and Boston lawyers and bankers, national and international industrial executives, and local university and community professionals.

Of immediate concern were legal barriers to privatization. In this regard the city was fortunate that the legislature was in session during the period the privatization review was proceeding. By March 1984 the city manager had given to the local legislative delegation a proposed draft of legislation that would authorize privatization if the city decided to proceed in that direction. To implement WTW privatization, the bill enabled a privatizer to use industrial development bonds (IDBs), allowed the city to contract for more than three years, and enabled the city to create a Governmental Utility Services Corporation (GUSC) exempt from the property tax and the state bid law. Letters explaining the bill were sent to the mayors of all the cities on the state EPA grant construction funding list and to all members of the legislature. The bill was written specifically for Auburn and therefore required unanimous support from the local legislative delegation. However, it was a bill of general application and was subsequently supported by the Alabama League of Municipalities. The bill was amended in the legislature to include other utilities and was passed and signed by the governor in May 1984. The remarkably fast passage of this legislation resulted from a combination of fortunate timing, expert legal counsel in drafting the bill, and excellent relationships between city officials and legislators. Substantively, the bill was successful because it provided for a potential solution to a major problem at no cost to the state.

The process at this point was highly competitive. In late March the review committee heard general proposals from eight potential privatizers. Included in this group were the regional and the state engineering firms that had first introduced the privatization concept to the city manager. The state company was represented by a local resident and longtime personal friend of the mayor and of other members of the committee. However, in spite of these ties, the committee concluded that it was essential that the private partner be a large national company with an established record of WTW design, construction, and operation. The proposers were reduced to four, and the review committee listened to oral proposals from these four companies to finance, construct, own, and operate the WTWs. Following the presentations, the firms were required to respond in writing to a set of questions designed to result in comparable responses from the four proposers. Given the innovative character of the transaction, each proposer had a somewhat different structure and approach to addressing WTW privatization. Thus, these subsequent sessions with the proposers were long, complex, and intense for the proposers and for the committee. As one of the participants later observed, "the apples and oranges problem at this point was horrendous. We just could not get these companies on the same page."

In April the firms were reduced to two and each was given an additional set of questions. Both were large national firms with extensive experience in the design, construction, and operation of WTWs. In addition, each was large enough to finance the project with AAA bonds marketable at low interest rates. Upon completion of the review process a firm was selected and given three weeks to submit a draft contract. However, after seven weeks had gone by no contract had been successfully negotiated. At this point, Watson reconvened the committee and recommended that negotiations proceed concurrently with both of the

Figure 3.1 City of Auburn Debt Service Comparison of WTW Options

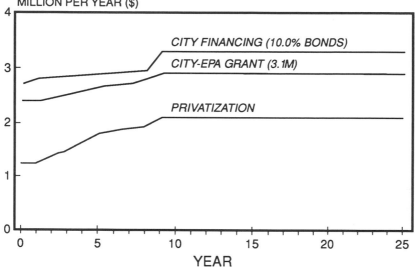

Source: Goldman and Watson 1985.

finalists. After some initial objections from the private companies, concurrent negotiations were conducted. They resulted in the acceptance of a draft contract with the second proposer, Metcalf & Eddy, Inc. (M&E). During the course of the negotiations, the firm initially selected changed its key personnel directly involved in the contract negotiations. Thus, the change in privatizers at this point appears to have been a product of the quality of the personal working relationships between the committee and the top executive personnel of the companies.

The M&E proposal was for the privatization of both the Northside and Southside plants and would require a doubling of the sewer fee. However, the fee would only increase to $1.92 per thousand gallons as compared with $3.73 (table 3.1) if the city financed the construction of both plants. And the debt service costs were substantially lower for privatization than for the other options (see figure 3.1). Essentially, the lower costs were the results of the privatizer sharing with the city, in the form of equity in the project, the tax savings generated by the 1981 Economic Recovery Tax Act. In addition, cost savings were projected due to the integrated design-construct-operate structure of privatization.

In early July, upon Watson's recommendation, the council approved the formation of the Governmental Utility Services Corporation (GUSC) of Auburn and appointed three board members, all members of the privatization review committee, including its chair, Dr. H. C. Morgan. With the adoption of this action the city moved closer to a final decision on how it was going to address the wastewater problem.

In late July, the city manager presented to the council an oral and written report that included a description of the four options the city had to address the wastewater problem, a financial analysis of each option, letters from the state environmental agency and the EPA requiring compliance action, and a draft contract between the city and M&E to privatize both the Southside and the Northside WTWs. The council adopted a resolution that authorized the signing of an interim agreement with M&E. Following this action, the city manager and Dr. Morgan made privatization presentations to the Auburn Realtors Association, the League of Women Voters, and all of the local civic clubs. The presentations were designed to make two points. They convinced the general public and the community leadership element that the WTWs were needed and that privatization was the least costly way to address the need. Dr. Morgan's slide presentation documented and established the need for new WTWs. Watson provided data on the various options, including comparative costs. Interestingly, questions of accountability, the transfer of a traditionally public service function to the private sector, personnel issues, and related matters that could have been problems were not raised.

Between August and December the council held public hearings to get community response to the privatization proposal. No major issues developed in the course of the public hearings. Of immediate concern was the necessity to double sewer fees if the privatization option was adopted. However, after the need for the WTWs had been established, the fact that any of the other viable options would cost even more essentially neutralized the cost issue. The city manager had adequately addressed any personnel issues by arranging for personnel transfers within the city or for employment with M&E. The legal issues were resolved by state legislation. Potentially related environmental regulatory issues were resolved by not addressing them. That is, the state environmental regulatory agency treated the privatization of the WTWs as a type of independent self-financed project and thus not subject to extensive agency review or action. The state agency involvement at this point was limited to the establishment of discharge limits and issuance of permits. The potential political issues of accountability and responsibility never materialized, in part because it appeared that these issues

Figure 3.2 Responsibilities of Privatizer and City of Auburn in the
Privatization of Wastewater Treatment Plants

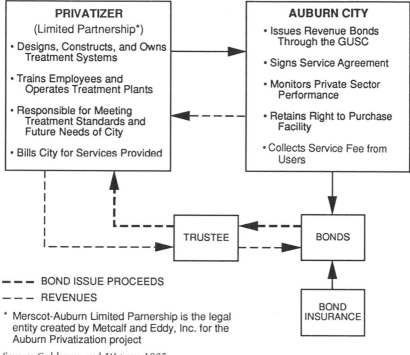

PRIVATIZER
(Limited Partnership*)
• Designs, Constructs, and Owns Treatment Systems
• Trains Employees and Operates Treatment Plants
• Responsible for Meeting Treatment Standards and Future Needs of City
• Bills City for Services Provided

AUBURN CITY
• Issues Revenue Bonds Through the GUSC
• Signs Service Agreement
• Monitors Private Sector Performance
• Retains Right to Purchase Facility
• Collects Service Fee from Users

TRUSTEE

BONDS

BOND INSURANCE

— — — BOND ISSUE PROCEEDS
— — — REVENUES

* Merscot-Auburn Limited Parnership is the legal
entity created by Metcalf and Eddy, Inc. for the
Auburn Privatization project

Source: Goldman and Watson 1985.

were addressed adequately in the service contract. In fact, the privatizer
in several presentations stated that the contract provisions provided
more accountability than had existed when the service was provided by
the city.

In December 1984 the city signed a contract with M&E to finance,
construct, own, and operate the city's WTW facilities. Actually, the
contract between the city and M&E consisted of 106 separate documents, the major one being the service contract. The privatization deal
was a highly complex, and thus costly, arrangement to execute (see
figures 3.2 and 3.3). Numerous parties were involved and the central
issue, assignment of risk, required a complex set of financial and legal
arrangements.

The service agreement (SA) was the major document that established
responsibilities and risk assumption. The SA included provisions for a
twenty-five-year contract for the construction, ownership, and operation

Figure 3.3 Structure of Auburn Privatization Agreement

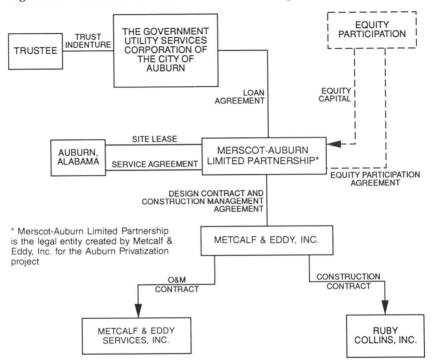

Source: Goldman and Watson 1985.

of both of the city's WTWs. Because of the tax incentives and Internal Revenue Service requirements, the SA had to stipulate that at the end of the contract period the city could buy back the WTWs at fair market value. On this point, the city officials' position was that they had no intention of ever buying back the WTWs. M&E's position was that at the end of twenty-five years the WTWs would have little or no market value anyway. In either case, the buy-back issue was avoided. Additional provisions in the contract included numerous contingency provisions for default or failure to perform and corresponding sanctions. A rate stabilization fund was established to maintain a constant fee structure over the life of the contract. Under the terms of the SA, M&E was to assume full responsibility for meeting EPA compliance requirements, including being the official holder of the state EPA permits. Auburn would continue to collect wastewater treatment fees and would pay a regular operations and maintenance service fee to M&E.

In December 1984, $36,230,000 in tax-free bonds were issued to finance the project, which included new connector lines as well as the two new WTWs. The proceeds were then loaned to a limited partnership created by M&E and the city to handle the project. The bonds received high ratings of AAA and AAA/A-1+ from Moody's and Standard and Poor, major national bond rating companies. The "Dr. H. C. Morgan Pollution Control Facility" (Southside Plant) began operations in December 1985, six months ahead of schedule and one year after its construction began. The Northside Plant began operating in July 1986. The projections show that the city will save $25 million in capital costs and debt service over the life of the twenty-five-year contract with M&E. However, final conclusions as to the ultimate effectiveness of the privatization of the WTWs remain to be developed. In fact, some questions cannot be answered until the end of the contract period when the buy-back provisions become operative. In the meantime, the city had won its struggle for compliance with the CWA and had resolved its wastewater problems.

Conclusions

The Auburn case study concentrates on the events and activities leading to the decision to privatize. Although these events preceded the stages of project design, construction, and operation, they are of interest for two related reasons. First, they illuminate the organizational and management steps and strategies that produced agreement between the public authority and the private firm to proceed with the project. Second, in doing so, they shed light on the theory-sketch developed in Chapter 1. In particular, they illustrate some of the different kinds of interorganizational configurations and other mechanisms that can assist the linking of the two sectors in privatization.

The case study confirms a point that is important but so obvious that it might be taken for granted. In privatization the roles of the public and private sector players are changed. The public authority—Auburn—gave up ownership of an operational responsibility for a service activity that by common practice and also by its nature is in the public domain. The policy history shows clearly that in recent decades the treatment of wastewater has generally been assumed to be a public responsibility. The equally basic fact that the city was raising rates for this service points to the essentially public nature of wastewater treatment. In the terms proposed by Moe (1987), the requirement of a fee payment brings into play the uniquely legitimate coercive power of the state. Changes occurred in the role of the private sector firm as well. It assumed not only ownership of the "public" facility but also the responsibility to meet the permit limits. In this regard the comment of a state regulatory official was revealing: "It's okay with us if a private firm holds the discharge permit, because politically it's a lot easier for us to fine a private company than a unit of local government." In addition, the private firm agreed to oversight mechanisms that allow public sector access to and review of market costs data that are normally kept confidential.

No national or state policies existed to provide a framework of expectations and routines for proceeding with this partnership. Responsibility for developing the framework fell to an individual, the city manager. The elements of the resulting framework consisted, in part, of the strategies the manager used to anticipate or respond to barriers to agreement. These strategies can be interpreted as mechanisms that helped to link the two sectors. The details of the case study make clear that these mechanisms include "interorganizational configurations" as invoked by Charles Wise (1990). And these configurations vary in terms of their formality and also the kinds of organizations they link. That is, we might expect that the "linking mechanisms" in public-private partnerships would all link the public and the private sector to each other directly. Indeed, some mechanisms do link public and private actors, but others link two or more public actors, and still others link two or more private actors.

For example, a formal public-public mechanism in the Auburn case is the state law passed to make privatization in Auburn and other localities possible. This arrangement is formal in that it is expressed through positive law. It is interorganizational in at least two ways. First, the city, the legislature, and interest groups reached agreement through intermediaries, including financial and legal counsel. Second, the law shifts formal power over an area of activity from one level of public organization (the state) to another (the local corporation). Examples of informal public-public mechanisms include the frequent and sometimes lengthy meetings and discussions involving the mayor and city manager, the city council, the privatization review committee, and representatives of state and federal environmental regulatory agencies.

Private-private linking mechanisms also played a conspicuous role in the Auburn case. One example of a formal private-private interorganizational configuration is the vertical reorganization that M&E undertook to better coordinate its design and operations function. This formal

Table 3.2.   Linking Mechanisms in the Auburn Case

	Type of Mechanism	
Type of Linkage	**Formal**	**Informal**
Public-public	Change in state law; blue-ribbon committee is formed	Meetings of city officials among themselves and with regulatory officials
Private-private	Vertical reorganization of firm to link design and operating units	Fast-track relationship of designers, builders, and suppliers
Public-private	Personnel agreement	Industry seminars for officials; donation of park

reorganization of functional units facilitated the use of an informal configuration, which was the fast-track method. Here the privatizer worked informally with the contractor, subcontractors, and suppliers to get the job done far faster than usual. (The importance and extent of private sector vertical reorganization is analyzed in Chapter 4 and Chapter 9).

In addition to these public-public and private-private mechanisms, public-private arrangements developed as well. The personnel agreement was a formal arrangement of this type. It guaranteed existing public employees an opportunity to relocate within the public sector or to remain with the wastewater treatment facility as it moved into the private domain. Many examples of relatively informal public-private configurations can be seen in and between the lines of the Auburn case study as well. For instance, industry-sponsored seminars sprouted to educate public officials about privatization at the time the Auburn negotiations were drawing to a close. An especially interesting mechanism, however, appears in the case of a public park that the privatizer gave to the city. Metcalf & Eddy, Inc., took one of the properties that had been part of the old treatment works, redesigned and refurbished it, at its own expense, and donated it to the city for a public park. This interaction was informal in the sense that no contractual provision required or even mentioned it. It was interorganizational in that a transfer took place between the two sectors. The linkages this arrangement put in place were affective. The private sector undertook an eleemosynary deed, and the citizens have a recreational facility to enjoy.

Thus, in the details of the Auburn case study we see not only that interorganizational configurations emerged to facilitate the privatization deal but also that they were richly varied. Some were much more formal than others. And, in addition to the public-private linkages we would expect to find, public-public and private-private mechanisms also played an integral role in the deal (see table 3.2; two distinctions are used to make up the typology of linking mechanisms: type of mechanism—formal or informal—and type of linkage—public-public, private-private, or public-private).

In summary, the Auburn case study provides a description and an analysis of a successful execution of one of the initial WTW privatization projects. The development of the project was complex and was dependent, in large part, on a number of formal and informal relationships on both organizational and personal levels. It provides a model form of comprehensive privatization.

4

System and Process

Local officials considering privatization in the mid-1980s typically tried to assess what would happen economically, politically, administratively, and personally under this option.[22] Sometimes the assessment was fast and informal, consisting of back-of-the-envelope calculations that pointed to a clear result. Other reviews were comprehensive, as in the case of Auburn. Three vignettes illustrate how a quick analysis on just one dimension, economic benefit, could clarify what would happen under privatization.

> The manager of one prosperous suburban town in the Pacific Northwest reported that, after talking with industry representatives and attending a privatization seminar, he spent about an hour in front of his microcomputer "costing out" the available alternatives. A couple of dozen Lotus runs indicated the town could do at least as well with grants and self-financing as it could with privatization. Thus, there was no reason to consider privatization further.
>
> About the same time, a politically influential bond lawyer for a city in another part of the country reportedly performed a different kind of analysis. His fee for handling bond issues was typically a certain percentage of the amount of the issue. If the city issued bonds to complement an EPA grant, he would do the transaction and receive the fee. Under privatization, on the other hand, there would be no such fee: the privatizing firm would handle the financing transactions itself. Even though city officials were interested in this option and had started talks with a well-

established firm, privatization in this case never got off—or into—the ground.

Not all the easy decisions based on economics were negative: the mayor of one privatizing city stated that the costs under this approach were so much lower than under any other scenario that the city "had no choice" but to proceed.

Thus in some cases an economic analysis led to a quick and unambiguous assessment of what would happen under privatization.

Specific political and managerial issues could be dispositive as well. One not uncommon report came from a city manager in Texas: "City officials here just feel like wastewater treatment is a basic public service and they shouldn't give it up." And more than one city backed out of a deal because, as one official put it: "We thought we had a firm agreement, but when we sat down at the contract table, the privatizer had a new representative who went back on some of the verbal commitments his predecessor had made."

For policymakers in many cities, however, the question of "what happens in privatization" was far less easily resolved. Advocates pointed to tax benefits as long as they were available. But more fundamentally, they argued that privatization was inherently more efficient than grant funding (frequently the most attractive alternative) in terms of plant design, construction, and operation. The advocates also urged that accountability could be protected through well-drawn contracts.

Critics, on the other hand, pointed out that little if any systematic information was at hand to show whether privatization would work in fact as the theory suggested. Now, some years after the first debates took place, some results are available. They address the questions of the implications of privatization for the design, construction, and operation of wastewater treatment works.

Design and Construction: A Comparative Case Study

This chapter addresses the implications of privatization through a comparison of system and process in the design and construction of treatment works under privatization and under EPA grant funding. Design and construction are important because they set the stage for plant operation and because they represent a large investment. Even small relative efficiencies in these phases can yield large absolute dollar savings. And with the elimination of most of the tax incentives in 1986, the question of inherent efficiency in design and construction has gained prominence.

The Case Study Approach

The analysis consists of a qualitative case study comparison of the two kinds of plants, supplemented by quantitative data summarizing size, cost, and time of construction.[23] The qualitative case study compares the city of Auburn privatized case and the grant-funded case of Blake. Blake is a pseudonym used to preserve confidentiality. The qualitative case study analyses are supplemented with quantitative data from seven privatized and seven nonprivatized cases. In addition, national EPA data on grant-funded facilities were examined to assess the external validity of the case study data. Data were collected on the privatized and comparison plants through mail surveys and on-site visits conducted between the summer of 1986 and the spring of 1988.[24] The site visits included in-depth interviews with officials of engineering firms, local government units, and state regulatory agencies as well as collection of documentation ranging from offering statements and service contracts to local ordinances, rate structures, National Pollutant Discharge Elimination System (NPDES) permit limits, records of plant operations, and relevant state agency records.[25]

Rather than trying to detail the separate experiences of seven privatized plants and a similar number of comparison cases, this chapter describes the experience of a representative privatized plant and its publicly owned and operated comparison case. The privatized plant is in Auburn, Alabama. The comparison grant-funded plant, Blake, is also in the Southeast and was selected because of its similarity to the Auburn plant. Both were built in the mid-1980s by the same contractor, cost roughly the same, and process similar amounts of wastewater. Differences exist as well. The Blake plant is in an enclosed concrete structure for aesthetic reasons, processes more industrial waste than the Auburn plant, must meet stricter effluent limits, and has a more advanced technology. These points notwithstanding, engineering and construction specialists recommended the Blake plant for use as the comparison facility.

Table 4.1 summarizes information about the two plants, the wastewater they process, and the time and cost of construction. Table 4.2

Table 4.1 Auburn and Blake Wastewater Treatment Works

	Auburn	**Blake**
Capacity[a]	5.4 mgd	8.2 mgd
Type of wastewater processed by plant	Domestic	Domestic and industrial
Effluent limit (BOD5)[b]	30 mg/l	7 mg/l
Planning starts[c]	August 1984	April 1975
Construction starts[c]	November 1984	April 1984
Plant goes on-line[c]	December 1985	July 1986
Construction complete[c]	June 1986	October 1986
Plant cost[d]	$9,250,000	$15,497,000
Cost/gallon[d]	$1.71/gallon	$2.15/gallon

[a] A plant's capacity is the amount of water it is designed to treat routinely, expressed in millions of gallons per day (mgd).

[b] BOD5 is "five-day biological oxygen demand," one commonly used index of pollution. It measures oxygen needed to remove organic pollutants in the wastewater and is expressed in milligrams per liter (mg/l). The lower the number, the more stringent the standard the plant must satisfy. The limit is set for each plant by the state regulatory agency based on the general requirements of the Clean Water Act and the specific conditions of the stream into which the plant discharges wastewater.

[c] Events are dated by the month in which they took place. A plant "goes on-line" when it begins processing wastewater; it usually (but not always) does so some months before construction work is complete.

[d] Plant costs refer to the costs incurred in designing and constructing the processing plant, not including collector lines and pumping stations. Cost/gallon is the design-plus-construction cost divided by the plant capacity in gallons. These data were obtained from the municipalities, the state agencies, and the privatizers as appropriate. Given the unique circumstances that affect the cost of any treatment plant, the results must be used with caution.

presents similar information in the form of averages for the two sets of plants: privatized and grant-funded.

A brief review of tables 4.1 and 4.2 sets the stage for an in-depth comparison of grant funding and privatization. On the privatized projects, both design and construction went far more quickly than in the grant-funded cases. The Auburn plant began processing wastewater just thirteen months after construction began, a brief period by any standard. The aggregate data in table 4.2 provide similar results for the two sets of plants.

Cost calculations are far less conclusive. Tentative comparisons can be made on the basis of cost per gallon of processing capacity. It is the quotient of the design and construction costs for a given facility divided

Table 4.2 Time and Cost for Design and Construction of Privatized and Grant-Funded Wastewater Treatment Works

	Privatized Plants	Grant-Funded Plants
Number of cases	7	7
Mean months for design and construction	22.7	59.7
Mean months for construction	15.9	27.3
Cost/gallon		
Range	$1.00 to $4.20	$1.20 to $4.00
Median	$2.00	$3.00
Mean	$2.24	$2.60

Note: The terms used in this table are explained in the notes for table 4.1. The caveats about cost comparisons offered there apply here also. The cost/gallon of plant design and construction is shown in terms of range for the plants in each group, median, and mean values for each group. The general tendency is toward slightly higher "average" costs for the grant-funded group. The differences are not statistically significant; a matched-cases t-test applied to the seven pairs of cases yields a value of $p < .34$. The highest individual value is for a privatized plant. The values at the high end of the range for each group reflect cases with expensive technology and expensive architectural features. Thus, privatized plants can be expensive even if built quickly and efficiently.

by the processing capacity of the facility. This measure is clearly less than ideal; however, it is the best available. For many reasons, costs are very difficult to compare for specific plants.[26] Cost per gallon figures, however, do permit some carefully qualified conclusions. In the present case, cost per gallon is moderately—but not persuasively—lower for the Auburn plant than for the Blake plant ($1.71 versus $2.15). Both these figures are lower than the mean costs per gallon for either group of plants as shown in table 4.2 ($2.24 and $2.60). This difference is not statistically significant. The difficulty of reaching firm conclusions about cost is reinforced by findings presented in Chapter 6. The national data reported there indicate that privatized plants can be at least as expensive as a national sample of comparable plants.

In general, table 4.2 provides patterns that are similar to the individual plant results shown in table 4.1 The case study of Auburn and Blake presented in the following explores the elements that contribute to the patterns appearing in tables 4.1 and 4.2. Where the experience of the additional plants differs from that of Auburn and Blake, the analysis so indicates.

System and Process in Design and Construction

WTW design and construction include multiple parties, phases, and activities. These may be analyzed in terms of system and process during plant design and construction. The term *system* refers to the set of players directly involved in developing and implementing the project; *process* refers to the interactions of the players in the system.[27]

In broad terms, WTW construction system and process include the following steps. The decision to build a new plant or add to an existing one may be driven by local interest in expansion or by administrative order from the state or federal environmental regulatory agency. The municipality typically engages a planner, often a staff person in city hall, to review alternatives and make recommendations in the form of a plan. The next step is authorization for a design (detailed engineering drawings and specifications based on the plan). If an engineering firm develops the plan, the same firm often prepares the design. The municipality and (usually) the relevant regulatory agency approve the design. Bonds are issued to pay for at least part of the costs of construction, which then proceeds. Upon completion, the owner (municipality or privatizer) provides an agent to carry out operations and maintenance (O&M). During the ongoing O&M phase the owner is responsible for meeting effluent standards under the NPDES permit.

The Grant-Funded Case: Fragmentation of System and Process

In the grant-funded case, the activities just described are centrally regulated but highly fragmented.[28] The fragmentation occurs both during planning and design in the review process and during construction. The fragmentation results from differences in system and process and typically leads to major delays.

The Review Process

The appropriate state or federal regulatory agency reviews or inspects plans, detailed designs, and project construction. In the mid-1970s, Blake's treatment plant was incapable of meeting NPDES requirements. The city applied to EPA for grant assistance. During the initial planning phase, Blake employed an engineer to develop a general project plan for submission to the state regulatory agency. He prepared the plan according to EPA guidelines. It described the project setting and wastewater characteristics and presented a benefit-cost analysis of different technologies that could be used to achieve required treatment levels. The plan also addressed the social and environmental impacts of the proposed project. The state agency reviewed the plan and returned it after some months with comments and requests for changes. The review process at this point can be lengthy. One state agency official said that his office might return up to forty pages of comments on plans for a large plant.

For the municipal and engineering personnel involved in planning the Blake plant, the review process and delays flowing from it posed two problems. First, interacting with state and federal regulatory personnel and meeting their review requirements took a lot of time and effort. Most, though not all, city officials said the negotiations were tedious, unnecessary, and frustrating. Timely compliance often required skill in procedure and willingness to accept bureaucratic requirements. State agency personnel were not unaware of municipal concerns in this regard. Their reply typically was that they were working within regulatory frameworks that they could not change and that did provide the city access to substantial grant funding.

A second problem, cited by engineers in the Blake case and in the comparison cases, had to do with municipal concern over the length of the planning phase. As one senior engineering firm official put it, "the mayor wants to see pipe in the ground." The municipal officials who became frustrated with delays in the planning stage were the same persons who later had to approve changes and work further with the engineers during construction. Thus, the same engineering official continued, the review process contributes to long-term tension between the municipality and the engineer.

Once the plan was complete, reviewed, and accepted, the process in Blake moved to the design phase. For reasons including delays incurred in the original planning phase, Blake city officials decided to employ a new engineering firm to translate the project plan into detailed designs. Knowledgeable observers not involved with the Blake project suggested the original planning engineer may have been a victim of his own frustration over dealing with bureaucratic requirements and procedures.

The completed designs were subject to time-consuming regulatory reviews. The technology involved in the Blake design was advanced and required special review by EPA in Washington. This review alone took a year to complete. With the design finally approved, the city manager issued a solicitation for bids, evaluated the bids submitted for responsiveness, and negotiated with the low bidder to reach a contract. At that point construction began. During construction, substantial delays arose from the need to negotiate change orders.

Change Orders

In a change order the parties agree that construction will deviate from the original design. On every project, construction problems arise that must be solved in this way. In the grant-funded case, change orders typically lead to delays. They must at some point be approved by the regulatory agency before the builder can be reimbursed. Thus, builders are willing to proceed with small changes but are understandably cautious about proceeding with large changes before the agency has approved them. In some cases, approval can take months. During this time construction activities proceed, but eventually critical paths are delayed pending approval.

Also, all change orders must have the municipality's approval. Obtaining it takes time and can create tension. The builder typically tells the engineer a change is needed; the engineer in turn informs the city. The parties follow this channel of communication because the engineer is retained as the city's design expert. If, as is usual, the redesign increases project costs, the city may question the designer's competence or integrity. In any case, before the contractor can proceed with the changes, formal city approval is needed. In Blake, as in many cases, approval comes from the city council, which may not meet for weeks.

The net result for Blake, and for virtually all the grant-funded comparison cases, was a long time spent in project design and construction. The system of relations in these cases encouraged neither a rational commitment to efficiency nor an affective commitment to cooperation. Indeed, delays arose precisely because the parties acted rationally to defend their own interests by doing their jobs as prescribed by law or common standards of public accountability. The central roles of the regulatory agency and municipal management as reviewers effectively put a brake on innovation on the job. One engineer stated that although EPA regulations provide for a sharing of costs savings achieved through innovative means, the procedure required to demonstrate the savings is so lengthy and arduous that few contractors bother to apply.

In the Blake case the system involved multiple actors, each operating within a relatively isolated context of objectives and incentives. This structure of relationships produced a fragmented process that resulted in lengthy design and construction phases and associated costs. Accountability was diffused among the multiple parties while ultimate responsibility remained with the municipality. Thus, the system and process were compatible with existing norms, if not with expectations of efficiency. These findings are supported by other detailed analyses of WTW implementation (O'Toole 1988a).

The Privatized Case: Integration of System and Process

Privatization alters the structure of the system of players, the process of negotiation, and the incentives for efficient choice. It integrates the players, their perceived interests, and their interactions with one another. These outcomes are reflected in the Auburn case, which is representative of the system and process under privatization. Many striking differences (numbered below from 1 to 31) appeared in the experiences of Auburn and Blake during design and construction. The account of these differences carries forward into the stage of implementation the story of privatization in Auburn.

(1) The designer-owner did not have to complete all designs and specifications before construction began in Auburn. This situation came about in part because (2) the state agency did not require a review of these materials; it saw its role as one of enforcing permit limits. If the privatizer produced a plant that was inadequate, the agency would require whatever improvements were needed to achieve compliance. It should be noted that this approach was not uniform across state agencies. For example, the South Carolina regulatory agency required the same reviews of the privatized plant in Greenville that it did of all grant-funded plants. (3) A related but distinct point is that EPA regional and national offices were not involved in the review of designs. The effect was to remove a series of negotiating points, and potential veto points, from the planning process.

(4) The community took the view that the privatizer was an established engineering firm in the wastewater field, that the municipal engineer had reviewed the general plans and found them appropriate, and that the contract with the privatizer provided adequate safeguards should the design or construction work prove faulty. In one sense, this is

not much different from the typical experience of grant-funded cases: no authority felt its principal contractor would fail to perform satisfactorily. The difference, though, is that the privatizing communities maintained this confidence knowing that the traditionally supportive framework of state agency reviews was reduced or even largely absent.

(5) The privatizer was free under these conditions to shape the process in ways not possible on grant-funded projects. This difference played out in several ways. For instance, (6) the design called for relatively little redundant or back-up equipment. In case of breakdowns during operations, the privatizer's O&M unit, which had (7) participated in the "value engineering" of the design, knew it would be able to bring in needed equipment much more quickly than a city operating a single facility would be able to do. Thus, redundant systems could be omitted and related costs cut. In Auburn and in other privatized plants the designer could point to places where additional equipment would have been required under grant financing. On the plant site at Pelham, Alabama, an area the size of a small house is empty; under grant financing it would hold a filtering unit costing more than $200,000.

By contrast, (8) the privatizer is free to incorporate into its design items that EPA might not allow as an eligible cost under its grant policies. For instance, the Auburn facility includes a lime tower that will be used to clarify effluent, if needed, under difficult processing conditions. This tower in all probability would not have been approved as an eligible cost under EPA grant financing. Of course, an authority with grant funding could elect to include such a tower in its design and simply absorb the cost through its own part of the project financing. What is different in this case is that the privatizer could elect to include the equipment it deemed necessary without having to take time to pursue the issue of eligibility with EPA.

Another distinctive result of system and process in privatization is that (9) the designer can specify the brand of equipment desired. On grant-funded projects, equipment purchases must be let for bids, and the builder must accept less expensive equipment "of comparable quality" to the desired brand. Designers and builders consistently said, however, that they knew from experience which brands of equipment worked best in the long run and they could save O&M costs by being able to specify them by name.

Under privatization, then, the absence of bid-law requirements tends to reduce total costs but (10) has the added effect of reducing competition. The privatizer can choose the product it wants outside of any short-term framework of competitive bidding for the individual subcontract. In fact, (11) in some cases the privatizer can elect to incur extra costs. For instance, if specially designed equipment is needed, or a piece of equipment needs to be obtained quickly, the supplier can be paid extra fees and bonuses to produce what is needed on the desired schedule.

Another kind of difference that is frequently mentioned is the (12) absence of the requirements of the Davis-Bacon Act (see Report 1988:11 and Savas 1987:149) in privatized projects. That act specifies that wage rates on federally funded projects must reflect norms in the geographic region. The effect is often to raise wages above the local market level. Because Davis-Bacon requirements do not apply to privatized projects, labor costs are cut. Here too is an added consequence: (13) project resources are redistributed away from labor.

(14) Privatizers also said they had the option to omit some "luxury items" that cities would normally build into grant-funded plants for appearance and comfort. As one engineer put it, city officials who are spending mostly grant money rather than their own money have little reason to omit features they want. On the other hand, one privatizing city chose expensive design features, for aesthetic reasons, that would not have been eligible for grant funding.

(15) A very important difference is that the privatizer is free to take advantage of the "design/build fast-track" process. In this arrangement, design elements are completed and fed to the builder as required, and schedules, personnel, and purchases are coordinated on site. This coordination enables the privatizer to reduce substantially the time needed for design and construction. In the Auburn case, construction began a month before the service contract was signed.

Several additional differences emerge in this context. For instance, (16) the city's review role was relatively limited after the service contract was signed. The privatizer and construction subcontractor met with the city engineer on a weekly or monthly basis to report on status, but these meetings were largely voluntary and informational on the part of the privatizer. A related but distinct point is that (17) the city did not play a prominent role in reviewing change orders. If the privatizer wanted significant changes, the change orders were provided for information to the municipality rather than being submitted to it for possibly weeks or even months of review.

The construction price had already been bargained with the privatizer, who (18) assumed the burden of cost overruns. The state regulatory agency was (19) only minimally involved in the review process leading to the issuing of permits, and (20) neither it nor EPA reviewed change orders. Thus the builder and the privatizer were free to proceed quickly, and (21) they had a shared interest in doing so. As in the grant-funded case, the builder had the advantage of reduced overhead if work was completed quickly and equipment and crews moved to other sites. However, the builder also (22) could receive bonuses for rapid project completion. The privatizer wanted the plant to go on-line (begin processing wastewater) quickly so that it could begin receiving service fees and also reduce the costs of having its own experts on site to monitor construction. In the Auburn case the privatizer also wanted the plant to go on-line before the end of 1985 in order to retain certain tax benefits. The plant went on-line on December 28, 1985.

In virtually all cases where changes were advisable, the privatizer and builder were able to (23) reach agreement quickly on site rather than submitting formal change orders to the municipality and the state regulatory agency for review and approval. All parties agreed that changes were handled quickly and effectively on this project. In-depth field interviews with resident engineers, construction workers, and supervisors suggested that (24) an important affective (conscious and subjective) component to cooperation occurred on the job site between the privatizer-designer and the builder. The people who worked on this project seemed (25) genuinely excited about it.[29] The builder and designer appeared willing to share their expertise in order to complete construction more quickly and to do a better job. While this aspect of the process is difficult to quantify, it nevertheless was clearly present. No plant of this size could have been built in a year without the closest cooperation among the participants.

In general, design and construction in the privatized cases uniformly proceeded quickly and relatively cleanly. By contrast, in the matched set of grant-funded locales, considerable variation was experienced in the implementation process. One factor that seems to have made a difference in these cases is (26) the presence of a "facilitator" or "fixer" in the grant-funded setting. In one sense, the role of facilitator was common in the system and process of privatization—that was in effect the project manager's job. Both kinds of projects routinely involved individuals who were positioned to coordinate separate organizational units. But the difference in grant funding was that these individuals rarely capitalized on this opportunity. In only two grant-funded cases did such a person energetically engage this role. In one of these cases, the key figure was the chief of public works. He was effectively able to make the grant process function. He worked closely with regulatory personnel and the designer and contractor to facilitate timely decisions and construction schedules. He also effectively used local legislators to get timely responses from state regulators. In the operations stage he was able to cut both labor and energy costs. In essence, he was able to orchestrate through management ability essentially the same result that comes from institutionally integrated design, construction, and operations. (For a presentation of this case, see O'Toole 1988a).

While design and construction thus moved forward quickly and smoothly in all of the privatized cases and in a few of the grant-funded cases, it is important to note that the fact of private ownership created several expectations of future processes that would not routinely arise in the grant-funded setting. Again, the Auburn case is representative. The tax benefits that helped accelerate construction also forced the community to accept some financial risk. The municipality agreed, as required by tax law provisions, (27) to pay fair market value if it opted to repurchase the facility at the end of twenty-five years. While this provision may seem to be a legal requirement rather than a part of the "process," it does define a risk-laden option that by definition could not arise in the grant-funded setting.

Private ownership contained the seeds of additional activities that would not routinely arise in the grant-funded context. For instance, the municipality retained both (28) the right to contract with an O&M firm other than the privatizer's affiliate and the right of first refusal if the privatizer exercised its (29) option to sell the facility.

(30) The sheer bulk of the legal work needed to frame the privatization arrangements among the parties was exceptional. The contractual relationships in the Auburn deal were both numerous (106 separate documents) and complex. More generally, (31) the transaction costs involved in developing the deal were correspondingly high. One indicator here is that of the $35 million in the bond issue that financed the Auburn project, $23 million went to meet design and construction costs; the remainder went to pay for interim financing, insurance and other credit enhancements, and the fees of counsel and financial advisors.

In light of the many differences that appeared in system and process between privatized and grant-funded plants, an obvious question concerns success in implementation: did the plants work as they were supposed to? This question is hardly idle. Engineers interviewed in the case studies frequently referred to plants that had never functioned as designed. Indeed, one of the grant-funded plants used as a matched comparison case had difficulty achieving compliance from the first day it began operations. This result, which is not unique among grant-funded plants, occurred notwithstanding the extensive routine regulatory agency reviews and inspections of design and construction.

Because the plants in question had been in operation for only very short periods, or in one case had not yet gone on-line, information about success in operations is at best fragmentary. However, both the case studies and the aggregate data collected from the EPA Region IV provide some answers concerning success of implementation. In general, most newly built plants of all types work well. In the matched set of cities, only one grant-funded plant and no privatized facilities experienced any significant difficulties.

Conclusions

The case study comparisons provide direct evidence on some parts of the theory-sketch set forth in Chapter 1. The evidence supports some of the hypotheses strongly, is ambiguous on others, and appears to disconfirm others. Here we consider some of the main points; the detailing of conclusions is reserved for Chapter 11.

Efficiency and Competition

Plant design and construction are hypothesized to be more efficient in terms of time and cost under privatization than under grant financing, due to differences in the dynamics of the two sectors. The privatizer's efficiency derives from the inherent dynamics of the competitive market plus the organizational ability to coordinate broad ranges of activity relatively free from bureaucratic intrusions designed to maintain accountability. Thus competition, time, and cost factors all seem closely related in theory. The case study results, however, suggest a far more complex picture.

The Issue of Time. The data clearly support a finding that in terms of time needed to complete design and construction, system and process yield greater efficiency under privatization than under grant financing. The Auburn plant was one of several privatized plants that required a little over a year from the beginning of construction until the plant went on-line. The average length of design and construction was 22.7 months for the privatized plants and 59.7 months for the comparison cases. This finding compares to periods of two to three years and seven to eight years, respectively, reported by Hanke (1985).

Multiple factors aided rapid project completion in the privatized cases. The system changed in that the number of key players shrank. Process changed in the direction of greater coordination of activities among, and changed roles for, the key players. And, to use Holden's (1964:643–45) conclusion concerning municipal governance: *"The . . . partners were able to predict each other's behavior within an atmosphere of trust"* (emphasis in the orginal).

Two other conclusions Holden reached apply here. He found first that *"the main politically relevant values of the participating units must be compatible"* (emphasis in the original). In privatization the common motivating value is efficiency. In the grant-funded case, by contrast, the agency introduces the at least partially competing values of the regulatory process. Indeed, some interviewees pointed out that it is rational for the agency to approve a design that offers multiple back-up systems to forestall any plausible possibility of failure. Other interviewees went somewhat further and suggested it may be in the agency's interest to approve an expensive design in order to "compensate" the city and the engineer for transaction costs incurred through regulation.

Holden's other conclusion is that *"Participating units must have the capability of responsive practical action"* (emphasis in the original). The case studies suggest that this capability can be substantially reduced by design reviews and change order negotiations in the grant-funded case. Contrary evidence was offered by interviewees in two of the comparison cities. They indicated that frustration, delay, and friction could be greatly reduced on grant-funded projects through careful attention to relations with the other players in the system. Even in these cases, however, the time needed to complete design and construction was over a year more than the time needed for any of the privatized cases.

The Issue of Cost. Because each WTW project presents some unique or unusual conditions, it is extremely difficult to compare project design and construction costs. It is thus not surprising that the evidence on cost is ambiguous. The case studies clearly suggest that system and process in privatization tend to reduce construction costs. However, the complexity of plant comparisons makes it difficult to draw firm conclusions from the modest (and statistically nonsignificant) difference in mean costs per gallon for the two groups ($2.24 per gallon for the privatized plants versus $2.60 per gallon for the comparison plants; Hanke 1985 reports cost efficiencies of 20 to 50 percent). The absence of a clear pattern in cost data is confirmed by aggregate data analysis presented in Chapter 6: the privatized plants on average appear more expensive than a national sample of comparable plants. The difference disappears, however, if one takes into account that in some privatized cases local officials did not capitalize on the opportunities for economic efficiency that are inherent in the integrated system and process of privatization. Or they elected to build into their plant very expensive features that had more to do with appearances than with the function of wastewater treatment. It should be noted, though, that similar decisions were made in the case of some grant-funded plants.

The Issue of Competition. As discussed in Chapter 1, market competition is widely regarded as a principal source of efficiency under privatization. It is clear that privatizing cities can draw on market competition if they wish to do so. Auburn and several other privatizing cities solicited and received multiple proposals and evaluated them through procedures including direct "head-to-head" presentations by the privatizers to city officials. Not every city took advantage of this option: in Mount Vernon, Illinois, officials opted to negotiate with only one firm. Chapter 8 tells this story in detail.

Once the contract is signed, however, competition is altered in more than one way. As indicated, the privatizer is free from bid-law requirements, so that the selection of equipment is not subject to the same kind of competition as in the grant setting. In this case, an incentive for efficiency remains: the privatizer is committed to build the plant and operate it at a fixed price. Thus savings through efficiency will result in profit. Less clear is the market impact for privatized O&M contract operations. Typically, the city signs a twenty- to twenty-five year O&M contract, which may be renewable at specified intervals. However, if the city is dissatisfied with the privatizer's O&M performance or cost, the contract and not the market provides the remedy and, as Holcombe (1988b, 1988c) concludes, the privatization setting often does not involve a pure market structure. Rather, the structure is a partnership in which both parties agree to ignore or limit certain competitive opportunities. The prospects for a competitive market in this field over the longer term are uncertain. This situation in turn raises an issue of accountability.

Accountability and Redistribution

In the grant-funded case frequent reviews with the municipality and the regulatory agency provide an ongoing framework for accountability. This framework is changed in privatization. The mechanisms of accountability shift to the formal contract and the sense of shared interests on the part of the privatizer and the city. While the evidence in this regard is more qualitative than the evidence on time, or cost, or even on competition, it nevertheless presents a clear picture. The mechanisms of accountability under privatization differ fundamentally from those of regulation. The interviews pointed strongly to informal processes and shared trust anchored in confidence in the contract. Whether the changes represent a strengthening or weakening of accountability is in part a matter of perspective. City officials we interviewed focused on concerns over reduced control: privatization reduces political accountability. Privatizers, on the other hand, said they felt there was increased accountability. Because they are responsible for coordinating all project activities and for meeting contract commitments, they alone are responsible if problems arise or if costs exceed estimates. The privatizers consistently stressed that the value of their long-term reputation and competitive market position provided an economic rather than a political mechanism for accountability.

Regardless of the perspective one adopts, accountability questions do arise during design and construction. They range from who handles complaints (privatizers and local officials both tended to be involved) to what happens if the plant does not conform to design or the privatizer goes bankrupt (no such cases exist). Longer-term issues also arise. For instance, even if the contract provides for a change of O&M agent, a city government whose officials are unhappy with the privatizer's O&M agent may lack the technical staff to run the plant itself. And there is no guarantee the city can find another O&M contractor able to operate, at an acceptable price, a plant that was designed for someone else to run. This situation reflects one way in which the mechanisms of efficiency, as discussed above, may affect accountability. The same problem arises if the privatizer wants to sell the facility. The added accountability issue in case of sale is that unless the city is able and willing to buy the plant back, the new owners may be investors with little concern for the city or the plant other than as sources of revenue. In this case, risk allocation and assumption, which are critical elements in the privatization contract, become even more difficult and tenuous.

Privatization had distributional consequences too. For instance, federal Davis-Bacon wage requirements do not apply during construction. As noted earlier, while this situation reduces construction costs, it also redistributes resources by reducing the wages of the people who are performing the different construction tasks. This result is addressed further in the following section on compatibility.

In sum, the city can secure mechanisms of accountability through contract. The more risk-averse it is, the more accountability it will want and the higher the price it is likely to pay. The signed contract, though, represents a long-term commitment by the city to whatever accountability arrangements it specifies. Several municipal officials felt that it was in some way inappropriate to give up control of accountability options in this manner. Their concerns point to the issue of compatibility.

Compatibility

Compatibility has to do with the broad array of political and administrative costs to the state, its subdivisions, and its citizens of transferring responsibility for a function such as wastewater treatment from the public to the private sector. Moe's (1987) discussion indicates that compatibility may be an issue in the case of wastewater treatment: where water quality and supply are involved, the coercive power of the state is routinely called into play in the administrative process. The data needed to make a full assessment concerning compatibility will gradually become available as existing plants mature. However, qualitative data already available on the design and construction phases show that the issue arises in a couple of ways.

First, the system and process of the privatization deal itself can generate compatibility issues. For instance, the reduced involvement of city personnel in the design and construction of the plant, not to mention its ongoing operation, means that the privatizing city is investing in a basic infrastructure service arrangement about which its staff is likely to have little detailed knowledge. If serious problems arise with the privatizer, no reservoir of expertise may exist within city government concerning the intricacies of the design, issues that may have arisen in construction, the details of how problems were resolved, or the many subtleties of keeping the plant running efficiently under a range of operating conditions. Certainly this situation can arise in grant-funded cases if after some period of plant operation the city personnel who were involved in design and construction have moved elsewhere. The point, though, is that the same system and processes that make privatization efficient may tend to reduce civic competence (to paraphrase Sundquist 1984).

A different and more subtle set of compatibility issues arises, not from the privatization deal itself but from the broader context of public policy in which clean water is "one, but only one" among multiple objectives (see O'Toole 1988b). For instance, several national policies attempt to create or preserve equality of opportunity in employment conditions. One such policy that is of special interest during construction is the Davis-Bacon Act. Its consequences in terms of efficiency and redistribution have already been indicated. From the perspective of compatibility, the result of the lowered construction wages appears to be to "lower the status" (Palumbo and Maupin 1987:9) of labor on public infrastructure projects by lowering the price it can command. This outcome may appear to raise only a small distributional issue when viewed in the relatively narrow frame of implementing national clean water objectives. But the assessment of any implementation strategy in terms of its compatibility with the nature of the state will rest in part on its cumulative effects on a broad range of policy goals or constitutional principles, many of which will not be obviously related to the production of clean water.

To summarize: privatization yields efficiencies of time and cost by altering the system and process in design and construction. Under privatization, system and process interact to reduce competition during design and construction. Analysis of the case studies strongly suggests that they also raise issues of compatibility, have redistributive consequences, change accountability mechanisms, and may trade off accountability for efficiency, depending on the context and details of the particular case. These details are defined in the legal, economic, and political contexts in which privatization takes place. Chapters 5–7 address these contexts.

5
Law and Policy

The investigation now shifts focus from privatization itself, and how it works, to the broader legal, economic, and political context within which it works. As these systems vary, so too do many, if not all, of the factors and relationships identified in the theory-sketch in Chapter 1. This chapter examines how national and state law interact with issues highlighted in Chapter 1, such as time, relative economy, competition, coordination, goal negotiation, and accountability.

Privatization is shaped dramatically by both national and state law. Without adequate foundations in state law, it cannot take place. And at the national level its accessibility as an option for infrastructure policy implementation depends especially heavily, and in complex ways, on both the general direction and the details of tax law.

National Law

The federal tax code contributed to the privatization movement in the wastewater treatment field in multiple ways during the mid-1980s. First, tax laws passed in 1981 and 1982 offered the private sector significant incentives to invest in infrastructure projects. Second, the EPA project grants program provided the standard financing arrangement against which municipalities evaluated the privatization option. As the EPA pursued its national municipal policy and as revisions of the Clean Water Act reduced the level of grant funding available for wastewater treatment project financing, the tax benefits of 1981 and 1982 made privatization potentially appealing to many municipalities.

The Deficit Reduction Act of 1984 placed some limitations on tax-exempt leasing and the use of tax-exempt industrial development bonds. However, significant incentives to privatize, in terms of tax law, remained in place for two more years. In 1986 and 1987 the context of national law changed dramatically. The Tax Reform Act of 1986 substantially reduced the tax incentives for private sector investment in infrastructure projects. And the Water Quality Act of 1987 provided for a transition from a national project grants program to a system of state revolving loan funds.

The examination of these tax laws benefits from historical context. In brief, tax policy with respect to municipal bonds has been a political and judicial issue for much of the twentieth century. This story emerges clearly in the report of the Anthony Commission on Public Finance (1989:6–12). The use of municipal bonds to support infrastructure development is traceable to the 1820s. In the case of *Pollock v. Farmers' Loan and Trust Co.*, the United States Supreme Court held unconstitutional a federal tax on state and local government bonds. The *Pollock* decision, handed down in 1895, was overturned in the 1988 case of *South Carolina v. Baker*, which permits Congress to restrict the issuance of tax-exempt bonds.

The *South Carolina* decision followed many decades of debate. An early version of the federal tax code exempted state and local bonds from taxation, but "Andrew J. Mellon, Secretary of the Treasury under Presidents Harding and Coolidge" recommended "elimination of the exemption" (Anthony Commission 1989:6). From 1950 to 1980 the use of municipal bonds grew dramatically. In addition to general obligation bonds, backed by the issuing government's "full faith and credit," cities also increasingly used revenue bonds secured by much narrower pledges of credit. In the words of the Anthony report (1989:7): "In the 1950s, revenue bonds were being issued for highways, turnpikes, airports and public utilities. By the 1970s and 1980s, they were also financing housing, non-profit hospitals, pollution control equipment for private industry, sports stadiums, convention centers and public power projects."

As the volume of municipal bond activity grew, so too did pressures on Congress to tax interest earnings. "*The Revenue and Expenditure Control Act of 1968* . . . contained the first restrictions on the use of tax exempt debt by issuers and was the first of a long list of legislative provisions reflecting Congressional reaction to the expanding use of municipal bonds" (Anthony Commission 1989:7). The contraction of opportunities for bond use was followed, however, by a period of expansion. During the 1970s Congress eased somewhat the restrictions it had put in place in 1968. And in the early 1980s, President Ronald Reagan's philosophy supported the use of tax incentives for private investment in capital-intensive projects. These incentives supported the development of the privatization option.

Privatization on the Wave of Tax Incentives

The Economic Recovery Tax Act of 1981 and the Tax Equity and Fiscal Responsibility Act of 1982 provided for investment tax credits and accelerated depreciation schedules. Additional advantages included options to use tax-exempt industrial development bonds and benefits from arbitrage, meaning temporary reinvestment of bond proceeds. The investment tax credit (ITC) was equal to 10 percent of the property costs for the treatment facility. Not all elements of the facility qualified, but estimates indicate that at least 80 percent of the facility costs would be covered by the 10 percent ITC (Goldman and Mokuvos 1984:128). In the usual case, the credit could all be claimed during the first year of operation, thus providing a near-term incentive to the privatizer.

The accelerated cost recovery system (ACRS) also provided near-term incentives to the privatizer. The ACRS provided for depreciation of some of the facility property on a five-year schedule and other parts on an eighteen-year schedule. Clearly, questions can be raised about the reasonableness of allowing depreciation over five years of parts of a facility designed to last for twenty years. These questions notwithstanding, the ACRS provided substantial potential incentives for private investment in wastewater treatment works.

Drawing on the benefits of these incentives, the privatizer could contribute up to 25 percent of the total project cost in the form of equity capital. The remainder of the costs could (but did not have to) be financed with tax-exempt industrial development bonds (IDBs). The use of IDBs represented a new practice in the case of treatment work financing. Typically cities issued general obligation (GO) bonds backed by their full faith and credit. The advantage in this arrangement is that the full faith and credit provisions secure an attractive interest rate for the bond issue; the disadvantage is that the bond issue is counted against the city's outstanding debt. Where cities have debt ceilings, the GO bond issue draws against it. IDBs, however, are not GO bonds. They are issued by an authority empowered by state law to do so. They are secured by a range of mechanisms that can draw attractive interest rates. These include reserve funds, required minimum payment levels (as in take-or-pay agreements), and credit enhancements such as bond insurance and letters of credit.

The industry literature contains various estimates of the costs that the privatizer can recover through combinations of the tax incentives just summarized. Goldman and Mokuvos (1984:128) mention a range of 20 to 35 percent of project costs recoverable through the ACRS and ITC. The exact size of the benefits is difficult to estimate for the general case. The case studies of privatized and comparison cases reported in Chapter 4 made clear that it is extremely difficult to trace through and pin down the exact cost components, including profit, of any project. In any event, the overall impact of the provisions was clear. To use the phrasing of Goldman and Mokuvos (1984:128), transactions that were "attractive" suddenly became "very attractive."

Tax Incentives in the Wake of Deficit Reduction

It was not long before federal legislation reduced the incentives: the pendulum swung in the other direction. The Deficit Reduction Act of 1984 placed a cap on the issuance of tax-exempt IDBs in individual states in a given year. It also restricted the availability of the tax benefits for projects involving municipal leasing.[30] Despite the limitations that arose, capital-intensive privatization continued to be an attractive alternative for project financing.

The 1986 Tax Reform Act, however, removed many of the remaining incentives for privatization (Sullivan 1986; Scully Capital Services 1987:34–35). Where regular GO bonds or revenue bonds are used, the tax exemption continues unless more than 10 percent of the bond proceeds are for private use. Industrial use on the same basis as the general public would not be a private use. Where tax-exempt "facility bonds" are used, the facilities must be privately owned but dedicated to public use. "Depreciation of privatized sewage disposal facilities is allowed over a period of 15 years without tax exempt financing and 24 years with tax exempt financing. Municipal sewers have a depreciation period of 20 years without tax exempt financing, and 50 years with tax exempt financing" (Sullivan 1986:2). There is a cap on the issuance of tax-exempt private activity bonds by states. A 20 percent minimum tax must be satisfied by the coporate taxpayer. Arbitrage allowances are limited to at most $100,000 plus some interest on reserve funds. And the 1986 act eliminated investment tax credits.

The general effect of the 1986 law on privatization of wastewater

treatment works was to reduce "the incentive for private equity formation" and to lower "the expected equity contribution from 20% to 6%."
Further, the tax law changes "shifted the plant performance risk back to
the municipality" and "placed restrictions on refunding, reserve funds,
and bank bond holder interest deductions, which increased the cost to
municipalities for traditional financing options." An important point,
however, is that not all types of infrastructure project fared as poorly in
the 1986 tax reform as treatment works did. This point is addressed in
the conclusions to this chapter. (All quoted material in this paragraph is
from Scully Capital Services 1987:33–34).

In sum, municipal bonds have long been used to finance infrastructure projects of many kinds. The extent to which interest on these bonds
is taxed or otherwise limited has a direct effect on the cost of infrastructure development. Federal policy in this area has been something of a
roller coaster in the past two decades. Tax reform in 1986 reduced or
eliminated incentives that had made privatization very attractive. Of
course, these incentives could be restored, and some observers urge that
they should be (see, for example, the Anthony Commission on Public
Finance 1989). One very broad implication of these shifts in national
policy is that the privatization option, while drawing its energy from
private sector initiatives and the dynamic of the private market, is heavily
dependent on fundamentally political decisions in the public sector. Tax
policy represents one important set of such decisions. It expresses,
through national law, a vector of policy forces. National law thus shapes
and is an instrument for shaping the functioning of privatization. A
similar picture emerges even more clearly at the level of state law.

State Law

The capacity of cities and other political subdivisions to enter into
privatization depends fundamentally on state law. Generally, a local
government can only do what state laws authorize. Absent appropriate
state legislation, municipalities routinely would be unable to privatize a
treatment work. State law must provide them with the authority to issue
bonds, make long-term contracts, compel use of facilities, and avoid
competitive bidding. Several states have passed legislation that in varying
degrees and ways makes privatization possible for local authorities. This
section provides an overview of some different approaches states have

taken. The point is that state law provides not only specific options for drafting the details of privatization contracts but also a general context that can influence the overall position of the parties in some important ways. Put differently, state law provides the field on which the elements of privatization play out. The objective here is to suggest the many different directions in which state law can tilt the playing field.

The *Compendium of State Privatization Legislation* (Privatization Council 1987) catalogs state laws relevant to privatization on the books as of late 1986. The preface to the *Compendium* notes that in the early 1980s "many states . . . found themselves with existing laws which would not permit the type of transaction contemplated by privatization." In the mid-1980s, many states enacted or considered legislation designed to address actual or potential legal barriers. In some cases at least, the privatization industry, meaning financial and engineering firms interested in privatization, assisted in the development of these laws. The instances in which this happened represent one way in which the privatization option affected its own legal setting: the relationship was interactive.

State legislation concerning privatization at the time of tax reform in 1986 showed great variation and was in a state of flux. About half the states were considering or had enacted privatization statutes concerned directly with water or wastewater treatment. Some of these statutes were sketchy; others presented fairly comprehensive packages of issues. An additional set of legislative enactments or proposals had to do with leasing or financing. Appendix A gives an overview of state law as of 1990. State privatization laws are reminiscent of state primary laws: so much variety occurs in them that mastering their intricacies requires specific legal expertise and creates substantial information costs and, in turn, high transaction costs for privatization deals.

Among the more comprehensive laws, there is variation in the issues emphasized and the interests reflected. No one law covers all the issues raised by a typical privatization transaction. Taken together, they suggest the range of issues susceptible to state law and the relevant political processes. It is important to note that the approaches states take in privatization laws are not exclusive of one another. Individual state laws reflect special attention to certain legal issues and thus to certain social interests. A review of state laws reveals five distinct models, each emphasizing a different interest. These include finance, public interest, procurement, referendum, and joint funding.[31]

Alabama Finance Model

The finance model empowers WTW authorities to issue bonds to finance privatized projects. An example appears in the law of Alabama (*Alabama Code*, sections 11-97-1 to 11-97-27, 1984). Alabama's statute authorizes the formation of public corporations having many general and specific powers. For instance, it empowers authorities to acquire, construct, or expand facilities. It further authorizes localities to borrow money and issue and sell bonds that do not expose the full faith and credit of the state, county, or city. The statute also exempts corporations established under it from all taxes and from state laws that require competitive bidding and that limit the duration of contracts.

In general, the tone of the Alabama act suggests that its organizing objective is to allow a public corporation to participate in a privatization deal and retain tax benefits in doing so. This is not surprising, as the act was written by parties involved in the privatized project in Auburn, Alabama, during the period of contract negotiations. The intent was clearly to make the privatization deal feasible from a financing standpoint.

California Public Interest Model

State law also can focus on protection of the public interest and preservation of local government powers and jurisdiction. California privatization legislation provides an example (*California Government Code*, sections 54250–56, 1986). This fairly brief law gives the local agency authority over a great many aspects of program management, including selection of a privatizer through competitive bidding not based solely on price, holding of a public hearing, and provision for a local referendum. In order to find that the privatization project is not a public utility and may therefore be exempt from its regulation, the state regulatory commission must determine that "the local agency retains sufficient jurisdiction to protect the public interest" and that the agreement "adequately addresses all aspects of the provision of service which would otherwise be subject to commission regulation."

In sum, the California legislation may be read in part as an effort to ensure public control over the privatization project and the development and operation of the facility. Part of that effort involves prescribing a procedure for public hearing and notification.

New Jersey Procurement Model

The emphasis on public notice and procurement procedures takes on a more central role in the legislation of other states, such as New Jersey (*New Jersey Statutes Annotated*, sections 58:27—1 to 58:27—18, 1986). The New Jersey legislation sets forth a detailed process for negotiating, reviewing, and awarding contracts. The focus here is on the administrative issue of procurement procedure rather than substance. The list of contract requirements mandates only that these issues be addressed, not that they be addressed in any particular way.

Utah Referendum Model

In other states, the political act of referendum is at the heart of the privatization law. Utah provides an example (*Utah Code Annotated*, sections 73-10d-1 to 73-10d-7, 1986). In 1984, the Utah legislature passed "the first comprehensive state privatization statute" (Saltiel and Avruch 1986:41). It is of particular interest because it provides for accountability through public referendum. "The governing authority of any political subdivision considering entering into a privatization project agreement shall issue a notice of intention setting forth a brief summary of the agreement provisions and the time within which and the place at which petitions may be filed requesting the calling of an election in the political subdivision to determine whether the agreement should be approved. The notice of intention shall specify the form of the petitions. If, within 30 days after the publication of the notice of intention, petitions are filed with the clerk, recorder, or similar officer of the subdivision, signed by at least 5% of the qualified electors of the political subdivision (as certified by the county clerks . . .) requesting an election be held to authorize the agreement, then the governing authority shall proceed to call and hold an election."

Washington Joint Funding Model

A different emphasis, having to do with public-private funding, appears in the legislation of Washington (70.150 *Revised Code of Washington*, 1986). In 1986, the Washington legislature passed the Water Quality Joint Development Act, which permitted privatization. The act is of interest because of its innovative linking of state financing to the privatization process. The act states that where a facility is wholly or partly owned by a service provider, the public body "shall be eligible for grants or loans to the extent permitted by law or regulation as if the entire portion of the facility dedicated to service to such public body were publicly owned. The grants or loans shall be made and shall inure to the benefit of the public body and not the service provider. Such grants or loans shall be used by the public body for all or part of its ownership interest in the facility, and/or to defray a part of the payments it makes to the service provider under a service agreement if such uses are permitted under the grant or loan program." The effect of this language is to permit state loan or grant funds to be used to support a privatization project. The emphasis on benefit to the public rather than to the service provider reflects concern that the state support be directed explicitly toward municipal welfare rather than private sector profit.

Additional legislation (Substitute House Bill 523) enacted in Washington in 1987 provided for a state bond issue of up to $50 million to provide support for privatized sewage projects and also solid-waste facilities. This follow-on legislation provided that "Disbursement of funds with respect to a facility owned or operated by a service provider shall be equivalent in value to disbursements that would otherwise be made if that facility were owned or operated by a public body. Payments under this chapter for waste disposal and management facilities made to public bodies entering into service agreements . . . shall not exceed payments made to public bodies not entering into service agreements." In sum, Washington law not only permits privatization but offers support for it in the form of permission to use state grant or loan funds that shall be equivalent to what would have been provided to nonprivatized projects.

Within state laws dealing fairly directly and comprehensively with privatization, several issues are emphasized. The Alabama law pays considerable attention to the conditions needed to ensure that the public corporation can issue bonds. The California statute emphasizes the public interest and the jurisdiction of the local unit of government. The New Jersey legislation is oriented toward substantive and procedural public interests during procurement. Utah provides an additional procedure for public control of the privatization process: referendum. Finally, the Washington state legislation lays a groundwork for supporting privatized projects through grants or loans.

The condition of state law with respect to privatization is still in flux and appears to be related to the role that a particular state's environmental regulatory agency plays. The different pieces of legislation reviewed here represent different approaches to engaging the complex public and private interests that the privatization deal combines. This is not to suggest that any one of the statutes reviewed serves only one set of interests or one institutional perspective. However, different interests and institutional arrangements receive differential treatment across state laws.

The volatile history of national law suggests several conclusions. First, and most obviously, it confirms the extent to which privatization is dependent on national policy. When attractive tax incentives were in place, innovative deal making began and a whole privatization industry developed. At a time of growing tension between needs for infrastructure development on the one hand and needs to cut federal expenditures on the other, privatization appeared to present a plausible response to both kinds of need. When the tax benefits went away, utilization of this strategy declined, even though the needs remained and the concept is viable.

A second conclusion is that in this set of circumstances several political factors were at work. As Chapter 2 illustrates, the policy changes that affected privatization so strongly were not intended primarily to deal with wastewater treatment or even infrastructure needs generally. Rather, they were designed to adjust the flow of money into and out of the U.S. Treasury. (An analysis of the cost of privatization to the Treasury is included in Chapter 6.) The reduction of tax benefits in 1986 for wastewater treatment plants reflected both political and economic judgments. As one interviewee at the Office of Management and Budget (OMB) put it, the political judgment was that local users of wastewater treatment facilities—not the federal government—should be paying for the service they were getting.

The reduction in tax incentives also reflected the economic judgment that those incentives had produced a net loss of revenue to the Treasury. The tone of the interviews at OMB implied that these two judgments were sequentially interdependent. OMB's driving interest was and still is in budget reduction. If it could be assumed that privatization took money out of the Treasury, the political argument could easily be advanced as an ideological justification for what was essentially a move to cut costs. Thus the issue of the cost to Treasury of the original tax benefits emerges as a key element in the story of privatization.

One noteworthy aspect of the political judgment (that the federal government should not pay for these projects) is that it was not consistently applied across different types of infrastructure projects. Several industry interviewees commented that solid-waste projects emerged from the 1986 tax law changes with significantly more benefits intact than remained for wastewater treatment facilities. The explanation commonly offered was that the solid-waste industry had lobbied more effectively than the wastewater industry to keep benefits.

These points indicate that the relationship of privatization to national law is much more complex than simple dependence on tax benefits. Important as they are, these benefits turn out to reflect a pattern of political and economic judgments—and interests—rather than a policy on water pollution. This theme continues at the level of state law. The foundation it provides for privatization is necessary but not neutral: it can tilt in any of several directions. Thus, the legal context of privatization is varied enough to provide some initial details for the theory-sketch developed in Chapter 1.

The theory-sketch in Chapter 1 addresses issues at two levels. At the microlevel of the privatized project, it considers matters such as time, efficiency, accountability, and competition. The discussion section at the end of Chapter 4 explores some of these issues in light of the case studies. The review of the legal context leads to some preliminary findings at the macrolevel of issues in the theory-sketch. These issues have to do with how privatization changes the roles of the public and private sectors and with the mechanisms through which it harnesses and meshes their distinctive dynamics.

The story of national tax law provides some insight to these questions. One major consequence of the tax benefits that drove the early deals was the shifting of some responsibility for project finance from the public to the private sector. Much more is involved here than simply the privatizer's equity contribution. At the national, regional, and state levels, the entire grants mechanism was disengaged along with its sometimes cumbersome procedures for ensuring accountability. These economic and political functions did not disappear into thin air: they moved elsewhere and to different locations in each case. The financing role of national government shifted from the highly regulated grants mechanism to the far less restrictive mechanism of the tax expenditure. Indeed, interviewees both in industry and in the OMB in Washington, D.C., talked about the tax benefits as "unregulated grants from the IRS."

The accountability mechanism, on the other hand, shifted to the framework of state law and regulation and to the management skills and contractual expertise available to the individual local authority. Also, by virtue of its comprehensive role in project development, often including ownership, the privatizer inevitably tended to take on some of the burden of accountability as well. When asked what mechanisms placed this burden on them, however, the privatizers consistently pointed to just one, and it was economic in nature. If they performed poorly, they said, they stood to lose in terms of both reputation and business. This mechanism, while plausible, is hardly fine-tuned to the individual case. It operates through the invisible hand of Adam Smith at the aggregate level of the market where the individual case is by definition of no consequence. As the recurring debate over amending the Bill of Rights makes clear, however, accountability in a democratic system must function in part at the level of the individual. In privatization, then, the mechanisms that emerge to link the two sectors take on special importance because they can be designed to carry the burden of accountability at the level of the individual case.

The review of state law reveals more than a dozen such strategies. These are mostly mandates that certain conditions be satisfied or procedures incorporated into the contract or negotiations leading to it. Some of the mechanisms they establish operate prior to the closing of the deal and the signing of the contract with the privatizer. Others operate on a continuing basis after the deal has been closed. A few of the mechanisms that operate mainly prior to the closing include: (1) mandating competition, (2) mandating public hearings, (3) requiring proof of personnel qualifications, and (4) referendum.

Mechanisms that tend to operate beyond the closing of the deal and into the life of the project include: (5) setting public utility regulation as the default condition, (6) requiring that effluent remain public property, (7) mandating review of the contract to show that it allows acceptably high levels of public jurisdiction over the facility, (8) assigning the authority exclusive power to set rates, (9) requiring provision for adequate maintenance, (10) requiring provision for monitoring, (11) requiring provision for amendment of agreement or for periodic contract renegotiation, (12) requiring that the contract address the allocation of specific risks, and (13) requiring that the privatizer agree to report regularly to the authority on its operations, income, and expenditures.

The importance of these linking mechanisms is illustrated by a brief examination of two examples. Both deal with disclosure of information as a means of linking the two sectors and engaging the dynamic of each.

The New Jersey statute contains two provisions that have to do with sharing of information. One is intended to preserve competition prior to the closing of the deal: the New Jersey statute takes a step to level the playing field by requiring that the contents of one vendor's proposal cannot be disclosed to other vendors. This provision reflects the dynamic of the market, as discussed in Chapter 1: that is, it preserves the secrecy of information that is a condition of the competitive market. The mandate or mechanism in this case operates to support the dynamic of the market within the political process by which the local authority selects an implementation option and an agent to execute it.

The New Jersey statute also requires that in the contract the privatizer agree to make periodic disclosure to the authority in the form of an operating performance report and audited balance sheet of the wastewater treatment system. As also discussed in Chapter 1, this requirement speaks to the dynamic of the public sector: information is openly shared to maintain accountability. What the reporting requirement does, then, is to support the dynamic of the public sector within the private sector operation of the facility long after the deal is closed and the project has started running as a "business." Thus, both these statutory provisions operate to invest the operation of each sector with an attribute of the other sector. It is far from accidental that the thrust of the mandate is precisely the opposite in one of these mandates from what it is in the other: the public sector is mandated to preserve secrecy, in the manner of the private sector; the private sector is mandated to share information, in the manner of the public sector. Through these mechanisms, the dynamics of both sectors are preserved and linked in privatization.

6
Economics

This chapter examines two important economic questions concerning privatization.[32] First, what are the relative costs for design and construction of privatized and nonprivatized facilities? That is, does privatization result in lower costs for the design and construction of facilities relative to other options such as grant-funded or self-financed projects? Second, what are the costs of privatization to the U.S. Treasury under different tax scenarios and, again, relative to other options? Chapter 7 translates these costs into relative costs to the communities under varying contractual arrangements between the community and the privatizer.

Two conflicting cost arguments permeated the development and discussion of privatization during the 1980s. The first argument, supportive of privatization and discussed generally in preceding chapters, particularly Chapter 4, is that the private sector can design and construct capital-intensive facilities more cost-effectively than can the public sector. This chapter provides a statistical analysis and test of that proposition with the conclusion that the proposition is supported with some caveats.

The second argument, while not necessarily in opposition to privatization, inhibited its development in the late 1980s. Specifically, the argument is that the 1981 and 1982 national tax code revisions that provided tax incentives to the private sector to invest in public works resulted in a net cost to the U.S. Treasury and thus needed to be and were eliminated, in large part, in the 1986 tax code revisions. The 1986 revisions did, in fact, slow, at least temporarily, the pace of privatization developments in the late 1980s. This chapter provides an analysis and test of the net cost to the Treasury proposition. Importantly, the data do not support the proposition. The implications of this conclusion are substantial and multiple. In summary, it means that while the New Federalism of President Reagan was promoting greater private sector involvement in the public sector arena, the tax code revisions of 1986 removed major incentives for that involvement. Further, the 1986 revisions were based on incorrect assumptions and conclusions about the impact of the tax incentives on the U.S. Treasury. The result is a proverbial and classic case of the left hand not knowing what the right one is doing—that is, time absence of any coherent or coordinated policy on privatization.

A Comparison of Construction Costs

To test for the efficiency of construction costs under varying public and public-private arrangements, two statistical analyses were conducted, one using data on 25 nonprivatized wastewater treatment works (WTWs) in the Southeast and the other using a national sample of 112 nonprivatized WTWs. In both analyses the construction costs of the facilities were compared with the costs of 7 privatized facilities. All of the facilities are recent, the oldest having been completed in 1982. While the ages of the facilities are close to each other, the privatized facilities are newer, on average, and this factor was taken into account in the statistical analysis. Because the privatized facilities are located in various places around the country, while one nonprivatized population set used for analysis is located in the Southeast, locational effect was taken into account in the statistical analysis. The analysis of the Southeast data was completed first and, inasmuch as the national data are in most respects the same as those of the Southeast analysis, the following discussion focuses on the Southeast data. Linear regression analyses were used to measure the effect of privatization on construction costs, given that the facilities vary in their construction times, construction dates, capacities, and locations.

Privatized Construction Costs

The data analyses reveal that privatization of WTW construction can be, but is not necessarily, more cost-efficient than nonprivatized WTW construction. The data in table 6.1 are the results in the Southeast analysis of three regressions that use as the dependent variable the cost of the facility, in millions of dollars.[33] Independent variables include privatized (PRIV), construction start date (STDATE), construction time

Table 6.1 Regression Analysis of WTW Construction Costs in the Southeast with Six Independent Variables

CONSTRUCTION COSTS REGRESSION

Independent Variables	1	2	3
Privatized (PRIV)	4.24*	4.50*	
	(2.95)	(2.05)	
Construction start date (STDATE)		-1.65*	-1.05
		(2.62)	(1.78)
Construction Time (CON MOS)		-0.23*	-0.17*
		(2.79)	(2.08)
Average treatment flow (FLOW MGD)		0.69ᴬ	0.67ᴬ
		(2.39)	(2.17)
Effluent quality (BOD5)		-0.02	-0.04
		(0.32)	(0.70)
Location (SOUTH)		-2.91	-5.58*
		(1.24)	(2.71)
Intercept	5.23	148.86	100.86
R-squared (t-statistics in parentheses)	.23	.50	.42

*Significant at .05 level.

(CON MOS), average treatment flow (FLOW MGD), effluent quality (BOD5), and location (SOUTH).

The coefficient of 4.24 indicates that privatized facilities are about $4.24 million more expensive than municipally owned and operated facilities in the Southeast. This finding by itself seemingly contradicts the expected results based on the privatization theory-sketch and the case studies. Further analysis, however, reveals that this finding is more apparent than real. Because WTWs vary by size, construction time, and other variables, these variables must be taken into account. The regression reported in column 2 includes these other variables.

STDATE is the date that construction was started on the facility. CON MOS is the number of months the plant was under construction before it started operation. FLOW MGD is the design flow of the facility in million gallons per day. BOD5 is a measure of the quality of the waste-water after treatment that shows the five-day biological oxygen demand of the treated water: lower values indicate cleaner water. A lower BOD5 requirement would be expected to raise the cost of the facility. The final independent variable, SOUTH, is a locational variable to control for regional differences. The results again indicate that, even after control-ling for these factors, privatization still is associated with higher con-struction costs than nonprivatized WTW construction in the Southeast.

Column 3 in table 6.1 contains the results of a regression that included all of the variables except PRIV in order to identify the privatized facilities that cost more than expected considering the other characteris-tics in the analysis. Cost analyses comparing privatized plants with the national sample of 112 grant-funded plants were also conducted. These analyses also suggest higher costs for privatized plants.

However, in the national analysis the independent variables explained only 30 percent of the variation in plant costs. Thus it may be assumed that many factors, some unique to each individual facility, affect costs and make it very difficult to produce statistically based generalizations concerning the factors that make up the cost of a particular WTW. The small number of privatized cases also contributes to the enhancement of idiosyncratic factors. And, as is developed in the following, when these factors are taken into account the data show that the costs of privatized WTWs can be less than nonprivatized ones. That is, given its inherent dynamic, privatization can be relatively cost-effective, but it is not neces-sarily so.

Actual and Predicted Privatized WTW Costs

The data in table 6.2 include the actual cost of seven privatized facilities, the predicted costs, and the difference between the actual and predicted costs. The analysis is based on the Southeast comparison data; the analysis of national data yielded highly similar results. This analysis begins to reveal why and how privatized WTWs may vary greatly in total costs while at the same time it supports the proposition that, overall, privatized WTW construction costs can be less than nonprivatized con-struction costs. In this regard, several of the individual cases warrant additional discussion.

The privatized WTW at Mount Vernon cost $5.5 million although the predicted cost was $10.0 million. The Mount Vernon facility represents a

Table 6.2 Predicted and Actual Construction Costs of Seven Privatized WTWs (Estimates in Millions of Dollars)

Plant Name	Actual	Predicted	Residual
Mount Vernon, Ill.	5.5	10.0	-4.5
Gilder Creek, S.C.	10.8	3.1	7.7
Auburn, Ala.	9.3	7.3	1.9
Pelham, Ala.	2.0	2.7	-0.7
Gilbert, Ariz.	14.9	11.2	3.7
Chandler, Ariz.	21.1	12.3	8.7
East Aurora, N.Y.	5.3	8.6	-3.3

case in which there was an existing municipal facility that the privatizer refurbished, providing one explanation about why the actual cost was less than predicted. In addition, as the Mount Vernon case study shows (see Chapter 8), the model system and process of privatization was used and resulted in lower costs. That is, the case study data indicate that the actual privatization structure used in the Mount Vernon project resulted, overall, in lower cost than was projected for other proposals, including other privatization proposals. The head of the privatizing company for the Mount Vernon project stated that some private sector WTW companies use the same system and process for privatized projects that they have historically used in grant-funded WTW construction and thus do not take full advantage of the inherent efficiencies of the privatized structure. That is, cost efficiencies in privatized WTW projects may be specific to the industry or local authority involved.

The Gilbert and Chandler facilities were each built by the same firm, and both cost more than the regression would have predicted. Both of those contracts allowed significant cost pass-throughs from the private firm to the municipality that may have increased total costs. In addition, the Chandler facility was designed for future capacity expansion and to have a more expensive and aesthetic exterior because of its location, a factor that explains at least part of the reason why the cost of this facility is greater than would be predicted.

The Gilder Creek facility was much more expensive than predicted. The facility cost $10.8 million for a 4.0-mgd facility that has a relatively high BOD5 permit level. Looking just at the statistics, it is unclear why this facility costs this much when comparable facilities tended to cost half as much. The case study analysis (see Chapter 10) revealed that site location, a political problem, and a set of system and process decisions that deviated from the privatization model accounted for at least some of the additional costs. The high cost of the Gilder Creek facility thus is a contributing factor in the statistical finding that privatized facilities appeared to cost more overall than nonprivatized facilities.

The Auburn facility also cost more than predicted, by almost $2 million. However, in Auburn treatment takes place at two separate plants and the data are for two separate WTWs constructed at the same time in the same privatization contract. If the costs could be broken down in the Auburn case into two WTWs, the overall costs would be lower for privatization, as supported in the Auburn case study (Chapter 3). The Pelham and East Aurora facilities were less expensive than predicted and each project fit the privatized system and process model.

Thus, the statistical analyses identify the relatively high-cost privatized WTWs. The case study data identify the factors that contributed to the high costs of these facilities. With only seven privatized facilities in the comparison, one high-cost facility, for whatever the reason, could produce the statistical result that privatized facilities tend to be more costly. In fact, when the regression reported in column 2 of table 6.1 is run without one of these facilities, that change alone is enough to make the coefficient of the privatization variable statistically significant in the opposite direction, indicating lower costs for privatized WTWs.

Cost Savings? Yes and No

The primary purpose of this section of Chapter 6 has been to provide a statistical analysis of the relationship between construction cost and the privatization of wastewater treatment facilities. Seven privatized facilities were compared with 25 municipally owned and operated facilities in the Southeast and with a sample of 112 facilities nationwide. After taking into account the differences in plant capacities, treatment levels, construction time, and starting date, construction costs of the privatized facilities appear to be, on average, higher than those of nonprivatized WTWs. However, further analysis indicates that these statistical results are not supported when additional factors are included. The factors that determine the costs of privatized projects are far more complex than the summary statistical analyses suggest. At best, the statistical data indicate a range of construction cost levels among privatized WTWs. An examination of the residuals of the regression equations revealed that some privatized facilities were less expensive than the average municipal facility, leading to the conclusion, consistent with the case studies, that privatized facilities can be constructed at costs comparable to or lower than municipally owned and operated facilities. The question of interest is whether the more efficiently built WTWs are the result of idiosyncratic factors or differences in generalizable characteristics of privatization.

Clearly in the privatized cases there are some facilities that had higher than projected construction costs for a variety of reasons not intrinsic to privatization. The costs of these facilities tend to mask the range of construction costs. That is, some privatized facilities were clearly less expensive to build than the average costs of nonprivatized WTWs. The case study data indicate that lower costs are associated with the system and process structure of privatization. Higher costs are associated with violation of this structure, even in privatized cases, and with cost factors not related to the dynamic of privatization, including contract provisions. The latter factor is reviewed extensively in Chapter 7. In summary, construction costs of privatized WTWs appear to be a function of a set of complex factors. Privatized WTWs can be more or less costly to construct than municipally constructed WTWs. Thus the decision to privatize the construction of a WTW may be less dependent on cost efficiencies of privatization than on factors of demand, time, political acceptability, available options, and general privatizer and contract specific characteristics.

Tax Incentives and Privatization

Changes in tax incentives made privatization projects more appealing to both the public and the private sectors during the early 1980s and less so in the late 1980s. The impact of tax incentives on privatization and on the U.S. Treasury was an important factor in the development of WTW privatization. This section analyzes that impact. Because tax law is very complex, only selected provisions that directly relate to privatization are addressed. A second caveat is that the tax issues addressed apply only to the privatization of WTWs that is capital intensive. The tax incentives discussed in this section would not apply to labor-intensive privatization. That is, a municipality that completely privatizes its wastewater treatment plant would be affected by these tax issues, whereas one that contracted out for the private operation of a municipally owned plant may not.

A review of the major impacts of the tax code revisions of the 1980s on privatization provides an important dimension to the understanding of capital-intensive privatization. As previously discussed, several tax incentives made available in 1981 and 1982 were altered in 1984 and 1986. These revisions included: (1) the change in depreciation schedules, (2) the elimination of the investment tax credit, (3) the revision of the treatment of capital gains, and (4) the change in the availability of financing through tax-exempt municipal bonds. While other changes were made in the tax law in the 1980s, these four changes were the most significant with respect to WTW privatization.

Three-Model Analysis

To analyze the effects of the revisions in the tax code, a general economic model was used to compare the impact on WTW privatization of three general ownership structures. The first is a municipally owned and operated plant that pays no taxes but can take advantage of tax-exempt municipal bond financing. The second is a privatization firm early in the 1980s that owns and operates a facility under a service contract to a municipality. The tax law under which such a firm would operate changed continuously over the decade. The 1981 tax reform provided a host of advantages, the most notable of which were the accelerated cost recovery schedule (ACRS) depreciation and the investment tax credit (ITC). However, even ACRS was phased in so that the schedule varied from year to year. Tax reform in 1984 removed some tax advantages, and the 1986 tax reform eliminated even more but lowered marginal tax rates. The early 1980s firm in the model was assumed to be able to take advantage of the most favorable tax treatment ever available in an effort to assess the maximum tax advantage that could have been available for privatization. The third case for comparison is a late 1980s privatized facility that operates under the tax law passed in 1986 but after all transition periods are over. This firm operates in the least favorable tax environment possible in the decade.

The specific differences in each case and a description of the model used for analysis are provided in Appendix B. In summary form, the model considers a hypothetical WTW that costs $100,000 and will operate for twenty-five years. An assumption of equal cost of privatized and nonprivatized facilities was made in order to focus on tax differences. The factors included in the model that differed in the three cases were depreciation, investment tax credit, capital gains, and tax-exempt

Table 6.3 Simulation Results of the Tax Incentives for Privatization with Varying Assumptions

Simulation number	1	2	3	4
Assumptions				
Discount rate (percent)	10.00	0.00	10,00	10.00
Market interest rate (percent)	10.00	10.00	10.00	9.21
Municipal bond rate (percent)	7.50	7.50	7.50	9.21
Inflation rate (percent)	5.00	5.00	0.00	5.00
Salvage value percent	10.00	10.00	10.00	10.00
Markct valuc pcrccnt	15.00	15.00	15.00	15.00
Profit rate (percent)	7.40	7.40	7.40	10.00
Results				
Municipal	$ 15,689.43	$ 35,234.86	$ 22,692.60	$ 0.00
Early 1980s privatized	13,426.63	− 11,184.41	25,592.39	− 2,262.80
Late 1980s privatized	− 16,903.84	− 51,387.93	− 13,541.65	− 16,903.84

bond financing. These factors were analyzed under varying assumptions, including the discount rate, inflation rate, salvage value percent, market value percent, and profit rate.

Four simulations were run to include the varying assumptions in each of the three cases. The data in table 6.3 show the assumed values and the present values of the tax advantages in each case. The discount rate, market interest rate, municipal bond rate, and inflation rate are all in percents. The salvage value percent is the percent of the $100,000 initial cost of the project that is used as salvage value for depreciation purposes. For example, a salvage value percent of 10 indicates a salvage value of $10,000. The market value percent is measured the same way but for the percent market value remaining after twenty-five years. An important distinction is that salvage value is in nominal terms whereas market value is in real terms, so inflation affects the real salvage value but not the real market value. Finally, the profit rate is the percent of the original $100,000 that is assumed to be earned by the privatizer as taxable income every year. For example, a profit rate of 10 indicates that $10,000 in taxable income is earned every year.

Simulation 1 in the table shows the base case set of assumptions. The discount rate is 10 percent, standard in government analysis. The actual levels of market and municipal interest rates make no difference in-asmuch as the tax advantage is generated by the difference between the two. In examining different sets of assumptions these interest rates have relatively little effect on the overall results of the model, but rates of 10 percent for the market rate and 7.5 percent for the municipal rate are used in the base case.

The inflation rate of 5 percent is a guess rather than an estimate because the factors causing inflation for two decades into the future are primarily the results of future policy variables chosen by the government. A salvage value of 10 percent is used, meaning that for depreciation purposes 90 percent of the nominal value of the project will be depreciated in the base case. The market value percent means that at the end of the contract the facility will retain 15 percent of its real value.

According to federal tax law a facility cannot be considered to be privately owned and operated if the service contract between the firm and the owner specifies that profits due to increased efficiency of operation are shared with the municipality. In essence, a privatized facility exchanges a service for a contracted fee, and the private firm takes either profits or losses from the operation. The profit rate, therefore, is an estimate because it cannot be specified in the contract. A study by Peat Marwick Mitchell and Co. (1985) estimates that a private firm would require a 20 percent return on investment after taxes to engage in such an activity. Peat Marwick Mitchell further estimates that the up-front investment on which this return would be earned equals 20 percent of the total cost of building the facility, implying an annual taxable income equal to 7.4 percent of the facility. Following the Peat Marwick Mitchell study, the base case in table 6.3 uses 7.4 percent as the profit rate.

The results of the first simulation in table 6.3 show the present value of the tax advantages of each scenario. The net tax advantage to municipal ownership is $15,689.43, which is the present value of using municipal bonds rather than taxable bonds to finance the project. This is the only tax advantage in the municipal scenario. The tax advantage to early 1980s privatization is $13,426.63; so while the two are close, under the base case assumptions there would be a net gain to the Treasury from privatization that has a present value of slightly more than 2 percent of the value of the project. In this simulation the Treasury did provide a subsidy to privatization under the early 1980s tax law, but the subsidy for municipal ownership and operation was greater.

In the late 1980s case, the tax laws impose a positive tax burden on privatization with a present value of $16,903.84. Thus, a comparison of the municipal alternative and the privatization alternative in the late 1980s shows a difference of more than $30,000, or 30 percent of the assumed initial cost of the project, that must be paid in taxes. That is, under the late 1980s tax law a clear and significant tax penalty exists for privatization efforts.

Simulation 2 uses the same assumptions as simulation 1, except that the discount rate is reduced to zero to show the dollar flow of benefits independent of their timing. This change increases the net tax benefit of municipal ownership but reduces the net benefit in both privatization scenarios. This is the case because the municipal tax advantage of tax-exempt financing is spread evenly throughout the years whereas the private benefits of depreciation and the recapture of capital gains are timed so that in both cases some taxes are shifted back in time. In addition, the cost of the capital gains tax, which is discounted twenty-five years in the base case, is not discounted in the second simulation. A comparison of simulations 1 and 2 shows that the tax benefits from early 1980s privatization were a result of shifting the net benefits up in time and the net costs back. If the dollar flows are not discounted, the early 1980s privatized project makes a net payment to the Treasury.

Simulation 3 returns to the initial scenario but reduces the inflation rate to zero. Without inflation, the tax advantages to all scenarios increase, but the tax advantage to late 1980s privatization remains negative. Inflation raises the real interest payments that must be made but also reduces the real value of depreciation and causes a phantom capital gain that must be paid at the end of the project. On net, inflation raises the tax liability of the privatized projects, although it affects the early 1980s scenario more. But while inflation is costly to the privatized projects, it benefits the municipal project because it lowers the real interest cost.

To see how much of the difference results solely from the tax-exempt financing of these simulations, simulation 4 assumes that no tax advantage exists in municipal financing. The results show that the municipality then has no tax advantage, and the net tax advantage to the late 1980s scenario remains unchanged. The early 1980s privatization case becomes more costly. Using the particular numbers in this simulation, about half of the advantage to the early 1980s scenario is due to tax-exempt financing, and without tax-exempt financing the present value of taxes paid in the early 1980s case is positive.

Any number of different cases could be examined, but these four cases illustrate the general conclusion that even in the early 1980s privatization had no tax advantage when compared against the municipal ownership and operation alternative. In order to test this conclusion against an extreme case, it was assumed that for the early 1980s case the entire facility was able to be depreciated as ACRS five-year property, less the salvage value. This assumption gives an unrealistically large advantage to the privatized firm, but the case was tested to see if privatization might ever have tax advantages beyond the municipal ownership scenario. All other assumptions were left as in simulation 1 in table 6.3.

The results show a net tax advantage for early 1980s privatization of $22,508.10, which is considerably more than the $15,689.43 tax advantage to municipal ownership and operation. In this simulation, the federal treasury would be subsidizing the privatized effort more than if the facility were municipally owned and operated. Thus, the municipal ownership and operation scenarios are close enough that if very large tax advantages are given to the privatized firm, it could produce a tax advantage for privatization over and above the advantage to municipal ownership. This is not the case with late 1980s privatization. Under the late 1980s tax structure a clear tax penalty exists that must be paid by a municipality that wishes to undertake a privatization effort.

Even during the early 1980s when a number of tax incentives existed for privatization, the tax incentives were not overwhelming enough that municipalities should have been willing to undertake privatization for the tax advantages alone. In the base case simulation, the tax advantage was for municipal ownership, not privatization, even in the early 1980s. However, the changes in the tax law from 1984 to 1986 have greatly reduced the tax incentives to privatization, meaning that municipalities and firms that privatize, in essence, pay the federal treasury a substantial amount in order to do so.

Varying the Assumptions

Discount Rates. What happens when the assumptions are changed? For example, what are the results with varying discount rates? The simulations in table 6.3 used discount rates of 0 and 10 percent and found that the lower discount rate increased the tax advantage of municipal ownership and decreased the benefit of privatization in the early 1980s and the late 1980s scenarios. The increased advantage to municipal ownership results from the fact that the future benefits are not reduced through discounting. The difference between the early 1980s privatization scenario and the late 1980s scenario results from the fact that the early 1980s tax laws allowed tax benefits to be shifted forward in time, primarily through accelerated depreciation.

Subsequent analyses used the same basic assumptions but with discount rates of 5, 15, 20, and 25 percent. This range of discount rates allows a clear illustration of the effect that varying the discount rate has. As expected, increasing discount rates lower the tax advantage of municipal finance and raise the value of both private options. Beyond some point, the tax advantages of the early 1980s scenario in the early years outweigh the costs in the later years. A high discount rate in the early 1980s scenario generates positive tax advantages that are greater than the municipal ownership advantages. For the assumptions in this model a 15 percent discount rate is sufficient for the early 1980s scenario to be more advantageous from a tax standpoint than municipal ownership. More than being just an exercise in exploring extreme assumptions, these simulations show that if a model places sufficient tax advantages in the early years of a privatization option, the tax advantages can weigh in favor of privatization.

Interest Rate. The difference between private and municipal interest rates comes from the tax deductibility of municipal rates, and in the model the tax advantage is set equal to the difference in the rates. Simulation 4 in table 6.3 assumed no difference and found results roughly in line with what would have been expected. Without this tax advantage, both the municipal and early 1980s privatized scenarios were less favorable, but the ordering in which tax advantages were greatest to municipal ownership and least to privatization in the late 1980s scenario was unchanged. Using market interest rates from July 1987, the difference in most simulations was assumed to be 1.36 percent. The first simulation used this difference in interest rates, and the remaining simulations used some larger interest rate differences of 4, 6, and 8 percent, with the expected results. The late 1980s scenario has no tax benefit because tax-exempt financing is not used, and benefits make both other scenarios more attractive but without changing the result that municipal ownership has marginally greater tax advantages than privatization.

Inflation Rate. One big variable in any long-term project is the inflation rate. The analyses examined inflation rates from 10 to 25 percent. In table 6.3 most simulations assumed 5 percent inflation, although simulation 3 assumed 0 inflation. As can be seen, inflation reduces the tax advantages to privatization because depreciation, salvage value, and interest rates are typically figured in nominal terms, so tax advantages disappear as inflation lowers their real value. However, income and the market value of the facility at the end of the project will be in real terms so will adjust with inflation. Because the items on which taxes must be paid adjust with inflation but the tax benefits erode with inflation, it is not surprising that inflation reduces the tax benefits in all scenarios. But once again, the ranking of the alternatives does not change and the maximum tax advantage still accrues to municipal ownership.

Salvage Value. Realistically, salvage value likely could not vary much in the real world. But in order to measure its effects, four salvage values of 0, 25, 50, and 100 percent were analyzed. Changes in the salvage value have a much more pronounced effect on the early 1980s scenario than the late 1980s scenario because the effect of the salvage value is on the benefits of depreciation, and the early 1980s tax law contained much greater depreciation benefits than the late 1980s tax law. With no salvage value in simulation 1, the entire project can be depreciated, and the tax benefits to privatization in the early 1980s scenario are very close to the tax benefits of municipal ownership. By eliminating depreciation, the difference is over $20,000, which is more than 20 percent of the initial value of the project. Clearly, ACRS depreciation had a major effect on the tax benefits from privatization.

Market Value. Unlike the salvage value, one could imagine that the market value of the property after twenty-five years could vary considerably. And, as expected, an increase in the market value of the property causes more taxes to be paid in the privatization scenarios. In this case the firms are better off even though they pay more taxes because their tax increase represents only a fraction of the increased value at the end of the project. Using real market values of the property at the end of the project as 25, 50, and 100 percent of the initial value, the present value of the tax payments increases in each case but not by much because this tax payment on the capital gain comes after twenty-five years. If the discount rate is reduced to 0 to show the total amount of tax benefits regardless of their timing, the total tax benefits to municipal ownership rise, because they are not discounted, while the total tax payments in the private scenarios rise, also because they are not discounted. This analysis illustrates the importance of timing of benefits when future benefits are discounted.

Profit. The final variable considered was the profit rate of the privatized facility. This is the variable that makes the most significant

Table 6.4 Simulation Results of the Tax Incentives for Privatization Varying Profitability of the Private Firm

Simulation number	1	2	3	4
Assumptions				
Discount rate (percent)	10.00	10.00	10,00	10.00
Market interest rate (percent)	10.00	10.00	10.00	10.00
Municipal bond rate (percent)	7.50	7.50	7.50	7.50
Inflation rate (percent)	5.00	5.00	5.00	5.00
Salvage value percent	10.00	10.00	10.00	10.00
Market value percent	15.00	15.00	15.00	15.00
Profit rate (percent)	0.00	5.00	10.00	15.00
Results				
Municipal	$ 15,689.43	$ 15,689.43	$ 15,689.43	$ 15,689.43
Early 1980s privatized	44,324.87	23,447.68	2,570.49	− 18,306.70
Late 1980s privatized	5,934.00	− 9,496.97	− 24,927.94	− 40,358.91

difference when varied over a plausible range. The profit rate of 7.4 percent, which means that the firm receives taxable income equal to 7.4 percent of the price of the facility, is a value that makes the early 1980s privatized and municipal ownership scenarios close in their tax advantages. Smaller profit rates increase the tax advantage to privatization because there is less taxable income but the deductions remain unchanged, while larger profit levels reduce the tax benefits. (See table 6.1.) But while the early 1980s scenario and the municipal ownership scenario are close and the amount of taxable income is a crucial variable, the late 1980s scenario never provides a tax advantage to privatization unless the profit rate is at or close to zero. Under the late 1980s tax laws, a significant tax penalty always exists that must be paid for choosing the privatization option.

In the first simulation in table 6.4 it is assumed that no taxable income is generated by the privatizing firm. A capital gain is generated at the end of the project, as before, by assuming that the market value of the facility is 15 percent of the initial purchase price. Under these conditions early 1980s privatization generates a tax benefit larger than municipal ownership but without producing any profits for the private firm. In the late 1980s scenario municipal ownership is still better than privatization from a tax standpoint, even if no taxable income is generated from the project.

Even a profit rate of 5 percent, which may not be unreasonable, leaves the privatized facility in the early 1980s with tax advantages over the municipal facility, but a 10 percent profit rate returns the tax advantage to municipal ownership and operation. Given the structure of the tax laws, the key variable in determining whether tax advantages to privatization in fact occurred early in the decade is the amount of taxable income generated by the privatized facility.

In this section a number of scenarios were examined with a wide range of assumptions in order to examine the relationships between tax provisions and privatization. Overall, it appears that a key variable in this relationship is the amount of taxable income generated by a privatized facility. If the taxable income is high enough, the tax paid on the income offsets the tax advantages such as the investment tax credit and accelerated depreciation. Lower taxable income results in a net tax advantage to privatization in the early 1980s tax climate but not in the late 1980s. The break-even area seems to be an annual taxable income in the range slightly below the 7.4 percent of the cost of the facility used in the base case, but this area could vary depending upon the other assumptions.

The amount of taxable income actually generated by the private owner of the facility is uncertain and by law cannot appear as a part of the service contract between the municipality and the private operator of the facility. In order to qualify for tax purposes as a privately owned and operated facility, the service contract between the municipality and the facility's owner cannot reduce the payment to the operator if the plant generates more profit because it is operated more efficiently. It is, therefore, not possible to know ahead of time the amount of taxable income that will be generated.

The question of tax advantages under the early 1980s tax laws could be debated, depending upon the profitability of the privatized facility. The amount of profit, unlike the interest rate, will not typically be established at the outset; efficient operation will make the facility more profitable, and inefficient operation could result in losses. But while there is room for debate about the tax advantages of privatization in the early 1980s, it seems clear that in the late 1980s a significant cost will always exist for choosing the privatization option, even if the privatizing firm makes no taxable income at all. Regarding current tax policy, then, it is unambiguously clear that the 1986 tax law provides a tax penalty for privatization.

The results of these analyses are based on simulations that necessarily fall short of reality because the tax situation of every privatization effort will be different. Facilities will have different mixes of depreciable assets, firms will be in differing situations with regard to their ability to take advantage of provisions in the tax code, and in the relatively simple model used only part of the tax code was modeled. The tax advantages to privatization will vary depending upon individual cases, thus limiting the ability to draw general conclusions applicable to all privatization efforts. To try to take account of this variability, cases were examined that gave especially unrealistic tax advantages to privatized firms, and those cases give some reason for drawing general conclusions.

One main conclusion is that the key variable that determines whether there is a tax advantage from the federal treasury to privatized facilities is the amount of profit generated by the private firm. At low levels of taxable income, the tax laws in the early 1980s could generate substantial tax benefits to privatization. At higher profit rates, the tax advantages disappeared. The simulations suggest that even when tax laws were the most favorable, no substantial subsidy for privatization occurred and there may not have been any subsidy for privatizing rather than municipally owning and operating a facility. Again, the real world results would vary from case to case, but the early 1980s tax laws appeared to put privatization on a par from the tax standpoint with municipal ownership and operation.

The tax changes from 1984 to 1986 have changed the picture considerably, and it is now especially disadvantageous to privatize. The conclusion is that municipal ownership and privatization appeared to be close in their tax advantages early in the 1980s, allowing a choice between these ownership structures based on other considerations, but the tax system in the late 1980s imposes a clear disincentive against privatization.

The Economics of Privatization

The economic issues analyzed in this chapter offer some surprises in terms of either the theory-sketch of privatization or widely held assumptions that were consistent with the sketch. The main points concern the costs of privatized projects relative to other projects and the tax costs of privatization to the U.S. Treasury.

The theory-sketch generates an apparently straightforward hypothesis about project cost: other things being equal, privatized projects cost less than similar grant-funded projects. The status of tax benefits is irrelevant to this hypothesis. While the concept of project costs seems simple enough, in practice it is very difficult to operationalize. This problem has many sources: the complexity and individuality of each plant; the complexity of sorting through the details of project costs; lack of neat and simple measures on which to base comparisons; and the impossibility of locating matching cases that allowed control of all variables except the use of privatization.

Given these factors, conclusions must be qualified. The analyses offer evidence that privatized facilities can be less costly than grant- or self-financed facilities if, all other factors being equal, an integrated (design, construct, and operate) system and process are used. Cost is not the same as efficiency, however, although the two can be related. The case study evidence in Chapter 4 strongly suggests that the inherent dynamic of privatization favors relative efficiency. Thus some tension exists in the statistical and case study findings on efficiency and cost. Two factors help resolve the contradictions. The first is that local authorities have the option of building plants with expensive design features very efficiently. The second is that even though the privatization dynamic offers efficiency, it does not guarantee it. As the privatizer in Case Study 2 in Chapter 8 suggested, it is possible to design and build a privatized plant no more efficiently than a typical grant-funded plant.

At issue in the second section of this chapter is the cost to Treasury of privatization projects. It seems plausible to assume that the tax benefits that assisted privatization deals prior to tax reform in 1986 resulted in a net loss of revenue to the national Treasury (Watson and Vocino 1990:428). This assumption is explicit in the references interviewees made to "unregulated grants from the IRS." This assumption also surfaced fairly clearly in interviews with officials at the Office of Management and Budget. The effect of the 1986 tax reform was interpreted as leveling the playing field so that local users would pay the costs of their own sewage treatment rather than having federal taxpayers foot the bill.

Economic analysis of several scenarios, however, suggests a different result. Rather than leveling the field, the tax reform of 1986 tilted it strongly against privatization by imposing severe net tax penalties on privatizers. Perhaps even more interesting is the finding that pre-1986 privatization offered relative tax advantages only if the privatizer's profit was relatively low—precisely the situation in which the privatizer would be unlikely to make the investment in the first place. Indeed, as the privatizer's profit rises, the net tax flow becomes positive to the Treasury in relation to other scenarios. This would appear to be a "win-win" situation. The effect of these findings is to call into serious question the assumption that privatization, assisted by pre-1986 tax benefits, results in a net loss of revenue to the Treasury. Rather, the evidence suggests that even with those benefits, privatization is revenue-neutral and that the pre-1986 benefits functioned to place privatization on an even footing with other options.

7
Contracts
Costs and Risks

The formal contract between a local authority and a privatizer is the document that allocates risk and establishes accountability in a privatized project. The way that risk is shared in a privatized project is directly related to the incentive structure of the contract and the ultimate total costs. If one party to the agreement bears the risk in the event of some occurrence, then that party has an incentive to minimize the cost associated with that occurrence. For example, the party that must pay the cost of any major repairs to a facility has an incentive to see that major repairs over the lifetime of the project cost as little as possible, and the party that is responsible for the operation and maintenance expenses of the facility has an incentive to see that operation and maintenance cost as little as possible over the life of the facility.

If all costs were known ahead of time, the contract would simply specify which party would be responsible for which costs. But some costs will be uncertain, perhaps dependent upon unforeseen contingencies, and some costs will depend upon the behavior of the parties to the contract. In allocating the responsibility for the costs, it would be efficient for the operator of the facility to be responsible for the costs directly under the operator's control and for the municipality to be responsible for other costs. Under this distribution of responsibility, the municipality would be exposed to less risk than if the facility were municipally owned and operated, inasmuch as the operating costs would be the responsibility of the private firm, and the private firm would be at risk only for those costs over which it has direct control. In practice, the typical privatization contract assigns to the municipality additional responsibilities and risks over which it has little control. Thus, privatizing firms do not have as much of an incentive to be efficient as would be possible in these areas, and as a result, the municipality must engage in more oversight of the firm to ensure that it keeps its costs as low as possible. This finding focuses particular attention on the need for ongoing monitoring arrangements, as provided for in the Kettl model. The discussion at the end of this chapter explores this point more fully.

This chapter briefly examines six privatization contracts that were written in the 1980s. The contracts represent one of the first (Auburn) as well as one of the most recent (Mount Vernon) privatized WTWs. In addition, the contracts represent five different privatizers and three different types of privatized projects. Auburn, Gilder Creek, Gilbert, and Mount Vernon are comprehensive WTW privatization projects while Culpeper is an industrial park project and Pine Bluff is a pumping station project. The specific motivations, contexts, and terms of the contracts vary in each case, so there are six very different contracts to examine rather than variations on a standard contract. The common ground among the contracts is that in each case a municipality (in one case, a regional authority) desired additional wastewater treatment facilities and decided that the best way to produce the facilities was to contract with a private firm to design, construct, own, and operate them rather than rely on the traditional municipal construction, ownership, and operation or municipal ownership and contract operations. In one privatized case, Mount Vernon, ownership is not a part of the privatization structure and will be discussed separately.

The following provides a brief overview of each case. Subsequently, how risks and responsibilities are allocated or shared between the private firm and the municipality is compared and analyzed.

Case Summaries

Auburn, Alabama. The private firm provides the entire city's wastewater treatment services. Two new facilities were built by and are owned and operated by a private sector firm. The city owns the sewer system that delivers wastewater to the firm. There is a twenty-five-year contract, after which the city has the option to buy the WTW at fair market value. O&M fees are set in the contract, but the fees are renegotiable every five years. The renegotiation clause of the contract is vague and provides only limited guidelines.

Gilbert, Arizona. Gilbert is adjacent to Chandler, which also has a privatized wastewater facility, and the same firm constructed WTWs for both municipalities. Gilbert needed additional capacity for development, and developers agreed to pay for the facility through a connection agreement that specified how much of the cost is to be borne by each party. The city is responsible for a base fee and an operating fee. The city is also responsible for maintaining a $1 million replacement fund out of which extraordinary expenses are paid. This fund is to cover most major repairs and replacements, even if they are anticipated. The city has some oversight over the use of this fund and retains ownership of the money but is ultimately responsible for these expenditures.

Gilder Creek, South Carolina. The Western Carolina Regional Sewer Authority (WCRSA) oversees this facility along with a number of others. The facility was needed because of a consent order with the state to provide cleaner water. (There was a twenty-year contract with the privatizer, renewable after that. However, after this analysis was completed, the WCRSA bought the Gilder Creek WTW from the privatizer. The privatizer will continue to provide O&M services on a contract basis. The public purchase of a privatized WTW is a new event and is discussed in Chapter 10.) A service charge formula put the WCRSA at risk for most costs but gave it the option to buy the WTW at five-year intervals. Changes in the tax laws that affect the tax liability of the firm are one of the factors for which the WCRSA was responsible, but the contract stated that if the fees were altered for this reason, the authority had the option to buy the facility at that time, in addition to the option to buy back every fifth year.

Mount Vernon, Illinois. The WTW facility existed before the privatization agreement, and the firm upgraded the facility and provides all O&M in exchange for a fee, adjustable for inflation and for influent level. The contract was executed after the 1986 tax code revisions and the city retains ownership of the facility. The upgrade was necessary because of a consent decree with the state of Illinois.

Culpeper County, Virginia. This facility serves only an industrial park and provides water as well as wastewater treatment. The facility is on municipal land and is granted a ninety-nine-year lease, after which the facility goes to the municipality at no cost. The firm sets its own rates, but the agreement specifies that they be no more than 1.5 times the rate charged by the town of Culpeper.

Pine Bluff, Arkansas. The firm in this agreement does not treat wastewater but pumps wastewater from city facilities to a city treatment plant. There is a twenty-year contract, renewable, with a minimum charge fixed in nominal terms and a volume charge that adjusts with the consumer price index.

Contract Analysis

The brief presentation of the six contracts shows that considerable variation occurs not only in what the privatizing firms do but also in the terms of the contracts. As stated previously, the Pine Bluff facility does not treat wastewater but only transports it. The Culpeper facility serves an airport industrial park but not the municipality. The Mount Vernon facility is owned by the municipality rather than the privatizer, although the privatizer is solely responsible for operation and maintenance. In the remaining three cases considerable variation occurs in the contract provisions.

The facilities at Gilder Creek and Mount Vernon were motivated by court orders to improve water quality, while the Culpeper and Gilbert facilities were the two most clearly motivated by future local development. The Auburn project was motivated by a combination of compliance and growth needs and community desires for a clean water environment. In short, significant differences exist in the motivation for building new facilities and in the types of services that the facilities provide. An analysis of contract provisions in more detail identifies the cost-related incentives in the contracts and the way that risks are allocated or shared between the municipalities and the private firms.

Culpeper and Gilder Creek Contracts

Two different approaches to providing incentives for efficiency are embodied in the Culpeper and Gilder Creek contracts, and a contrast of the approaches provides a productive starting place for looking at contract terms. The Culpeper case provides the simplest incentives for efficiency while Gilder Creek uses a more indirect approach.

Culpeper is an unusual case among the contracts examined because the Culpeper facilities are intended to serve only an industrial park, so residential rates and service are not influenced by the privatization project. For a two-year period, the county agreed to subsidize the project until construction was complete, but after that the private firm was on its own. The county is responsible for the quality of wastewater inflow into the plant and for requiring connection to the facility for those in the service area. The firm owns and operates the facility, determines fees, and bills customers. A limit is put on the fees because the contract specifies that rates cannot exceed 1.5 times the rates charged by the town of Culpeper.

The facilities themselves are on land owned by the county and leased to the firm for ninety-nine years. The service agreement specifies that at the end of the lease the facility becomes the property of the county with no compensation paid. The county also has the right to purchase the facility at its appraised value any time after twenty years.

This contract gives the firm an incentive for efficient operation because all costs of owning and operating the facility are the responsibility of the firm. Thus, the firm has an incentive to implement any method of treating the wastewater at lower cost. After the start-up period, the county has no responsibility for the cost or operation of the facility, so all risks in this contract are borne by the privatizing firm.

The Culpeper contract nevertheless raises several questions. First, does the firm have too much of an incentive to cut costs, thereby giving it an incentive not to produce the highest quality service? For example, one might normally expect that the firm would never exceed the minimum possible water quality. Second, the cost of this contract to the service recipients may be higher than necessary. Because the contract specifies that rates will not exceed 1.5 times what might be considered a fair cost of the services rendered, there may be an incentive to peg initial charges high to compensate for expected or unexpected increases in costs to the privatizer. These might legitimately arise due to, for example, more stringent water quality standards, a poorer quality influent from industrial park customers than would be expected from residential customers in Culpeper, or a subsidy in the Culpeper rates coming out of general revenues. Another reason for higher costs for the privatized firm would be the risk the firm bears that it might have to pay for unanticipated extraordinary costs. In any case, the Culpeper contract leaves the privatizing firm much more subject to the risk of loss than is typical in these contracts. The additional risk borne by the firm is likely to manifest itself in the form of higher rates.

An alternative possibility is that the rates in Culpeper are not higher but the firm is willing to bear the additional risk in exchange for the opportunity of cutting its costs and making more profit. When more costs and contingencies are covered by the municipality, the ability of the firm to alter its strategy and make more profit is reduced. Thus, it may be that the rates are comparable to what a municipal facility would charge, and the firm is compensated by the opportunity to make more profit by cutting its costs without having to pass the savings along.

One provision in the Culpeper contract that would eventually keep the firm from overcharging its customers is the provision that after twenty years the county can buy the facility from the firm at its fair market value. If for any reason the county is dissatisfied with the rate structure, the quality of service, or any other aspect of the facility, the county has the option of buying the facility and operating it itself.

This provision was even stronger in the original Gilder Creek contract. Twenty years is a long time, perhaps extending through the useful life of the facility. The Gilder Creek contract, however, specified that the authority could purchase the facility for any reason after five years and had the same option at five-year intervals after that. This provision had the potential to be an effective mechanism for ensuring satisfactory service because there was a relatively timely way for the authority to terminate the contract and assume operation of the facility.

The Gilder Creek facility was designed and originally owned and operated by the privatizing firm. The firm warranted the quality of the facility and had complete liability for the facility, including the liability for any fines resulting from the facility's operation. Cost overruns in construction were also a risk assumed by the firm because the service charge provided for a fixed amount to be assigned to cover construction costs. The privatizing firm was also responsible for routine operation and maintenance expenses because the fee for O&M cost specified in the agreement adjusts only for inflation.

The service agreement specified two major factors that were the responsibility of the authority. The cost of major repairs and replacement were passed through in the service charge and therefore were not a risk to the firm, and the cost of changes in the tax law that materially affected the firm's tax liability could also cause an adjustment of the service charge. In the event of tax law changes that would alter the service charge, however, the authority had the option to buy the facility immediately, in addition to the option to buy that arises every five years.

Some important differences between the Culpeper and Gilder Creek agreements are worth noting. First, the fee structures have significant differences in the two cases. As indicated, the maximum fee at Culpeper is set to 1.5 times the fees at the town of Culpeper, without any reference to the cost of the privatized facility. Therefore, once the fees are set, absolutely no incentive exists for the privatizing firm to goldplate or overbuild the facility. Once the contract is signed, the private firm's behavior cannot adjust the fee, so the firm has an incentive to produce the services as inexpensively as possible. Setting a fee schedule in this way, with reference to other facilities rather than the one whose fees are being considered, makes it unnecessary to examine in detail the cost structure of the facility whose fees are being set by the agreement.

At Gilder Creek, by contrast, the fees were set with reference to that particular facility. The service fee was the sum of four components. The base charge was fixed and was set to reflect the capital cost of the facility. The O&M cost was fixed in the contract according to the inflow into the facility and was adjusted for inflation. Presumably, the expected actual O&M cost was used as a basis for the initial figure, but once the facility was operating, the actual O&M costs were not a factor in determining the service fee. This arrangement gives the firm an incentive to produce services as inexpensively as possible rather than to inflate expenses in order to increase the O&M part of the fee. In contrast, the extraordinary repairs and residue disposal were passed on at their actual costs. This pass-through had two effects that differentiate the Gilder Creek contract from the Culpeper contract.

The firm had little incentive—except for the buy-back provision—to keep costs down in these areas. Importantly, because repairs could be passed on to the authority, the authority exercised more oversight during the construction of the facility to make sure that design and construction of the facility were undertaken in such a way as to minimize the amount of repairs the facility would need. Quite clearly the firm had an incentive to save money during construction and operation and to risk higher future repairs because the repair cost would be passed through in the service fee.

A second difference between the two contracts is the way that risks are shared between the two parties. As the above discussion makes clear, the Culpeper contract places virtually all risks with the privatizing firm, whereas the Gilder Creek contract shares the risks between the firm and the wastewater authority. This is not necessarily undesirable from the authority's standpoint because it may be able to negotiate a more favorable rate in exchange for assuming more risk, but it is an important difference between the two contracts.

A third important difference between the two contracts is the difference in the buy-back provision. At Culpeper, the government may buy back the facility at fair market value after twenty years. This time frame for buy-back is typical of WTW privatization contracts. At Gilder Creek, in contrast, the authority had the option of buying back the facility after five years and at five-year intervals thereafter, making it much easier for the authority to get out of the privatization agreement if it ever appeared undesirable. This kind of buy-back provision would seem to be an excellent way to make up for any other shortcomings in the contract. If for some reason things do not work out the way that those in the authority had expected, they can buy the facility and operate it themselves or even buy it and then sell it to another private firm.

Other Contracts

These two contracts provide a frame of reference for looking at the other contracts. The other privatization contracts have much in common with the Gilder Creek contract, with the important exception that none of them allows the government to purchase the facility until the end of the contract term, unless for some reason—such as default by the firm, unsatisfactory service, or force majeure—the firm is not fulfilling its part of the agreement. Although there would be no reason to end the privatization agreement unless the service was for some reason unsatisfactory, the important difference is that at Gilder Creek the authority did not have to prove anything to get out of the agreement, whereas the potential exists for a legal battle in the other cases if the authority decides that the terms of the contract are not being fulfilled.

Pine Bluff, Arkansas. The Pine Bluff contract is unique among the contracts examined because the privatizing firm at Pine Bluff provides only facilities to pump wastewater from the city's collection system to the city's treatment facilities, and the private firm does not treat wastewater. The fee structure at Pine Bluff is constructed to give an incentive for efficient production of the service because it consists of two components, neither of which can be controlled by the firm. A fixed base fee is intended to cover the construction costs of the facility, and a volume charge adjusts with the volume of wastewater processed, and it is adjusted with the consumer price index. Unlike most other contracts, no provision exists for the municipality to participate in extraordinary expenses, so the full price of the service to the municipality is guaranteed in the contract. However, a direct comparison of terms cannot be made because of the substantial difference in the services provided.

Mount Vernon, Illinois. The Mount Vernon Contract also differs from the others because the private firm contracted to upgrade an existing facility and the title to the facility remains with the municipality. These differences by themselves need not have a major impact because the contract gives the firm total responsibility for upgrading, operating, and maintaining the facility. The service fee formula used at Mount Vernon has nine terms in it but can be divided into three basic components. First is the facilities availability component, which is a fixed amount designed to cover the capital costs of the facility. Second is the operation and maintenance component, which is specified as a function of the amount of influent. The third component contains seven pass-through items, which are the cost of residue disposal, insurance costs in excess of the originally agreed-on amount, real estate taxes, any required testing costs, maintenance and repair costs of the existing facility, Illinois Interstate Commerce Commission costs, and energy use credits, which are subtracted.

The pass-through component that raises the biggest question is the maintenance and repair of the existing facility. Potential exists for confounding maintenance costs on the new and the existing facilities, thus requiring some oversight. The incentive to maintain and repair the existing facility in the lowest-cost manner is removed by making this a pass-through item. There are obvious reasons why the firm would be reluctant to agree to maintain the existing facility in exchange for a fixed price, but it is still desirable to have the operator be responsible for these costs. However, repairs to the new facility are not passed through in this service agreement, as is the case at Gilder Creek and at many of the other privatized facilities.

Another provision of the Mount Vernon contract states that if the operation and maintenance expense falls below a specified limit, the municipality gets a refund on some of the O&M fee it paid. This provision may limit the incentive of the firm to operate the facility in a manner efficient enough to have to return some of the fee to the municipality, and it increases the oversight that the municipality needs to exercise. Possibly the O&M fee specified in the contract is deliberately on the high side, and this provision is inserted in order to guarantee the firm a cushion on O&M expenditures while shifting some of the O&M risk to the municipality.

Gilbert, Arizona. The Gilbert facility was designed to produce additional capacity for development, and a group of developers agreed to pay for the facility through a connection agreement. Once completed, the municipality is responsible for a base fee and an operating fee, much like the contracts discussed previously. The municipality is responsible for any major repairs, thus taking away some incentive to operate the facility efficiently and requiring closer oversight on the part of the municipality.

The service contract specifies that it is a one-year contract, renewable annually, but has no serious provision for the municipality taking over the facility until after the twenty-fourth year, when the municipality has an option to buy. Thus, nonrenewal of the contract, while legally possible, would not be realistic unless the municipality already had another facility to take the place of the privatized one or unless it could negotiate a purchase.

Auburn, Alabama. The contract at Auburn specifies a base service charge that is fixed by the service agreement and an additional service charge that adjusts for inflation. The inflation adjustment has two components. Seventy percent of the adjustment moves with the consumer price index, and the other 30 percent is based upon the actual cost of electricity to the facility. However, if the inflation adjustment is negative, no adjustment is made for inflation and for the volume of influent. Like many other contracts, the municipality is responsible for equipment replacement, thus lessening the incentive of the firm to maintain the equipment and requiring additional oversight on the part of the municipality.

The Auburn contract is unique among those examined because despite the fact that a schedule of fees is specified in the contract for the twenty-five-year life of the agreement, there is also a provision that the service charge be renegotiated every five years. The renegotiation is supposed to take place on a fair and reasonable basis, making it appear that although the municipality and the firm have a twenty-five-year contract, the fee structure is only solidly determined for five years. A possibility thus exists that the costs of inefficient operation could be passed on to the municipality, and this possibility in turn requires greater oversight on the part of the municipality.

There is no easy way to summarize the terms of these greatly varying service agreements. The typical case, however, leaves the municipality in the position of being much more than just a purchaser of services from a private firm. The municipality typically shares a substantial amount of financial risk with the firm and therefore has the responsibility to exercise oversight over the facilities to make sure that the municipality does not pay too much. With the exception of Gilder Creek, the contracts do not allow an easy way out of the agreements should they prove unsatisfactory. An additional point of commonality is that the typical contract makes the authority a partner in the provision of services and that the privatization agreements produce a public-private partnership in the provision of wastewater services rather than a private firm selling a service to a public entity.

The facilities that most clearly fit the model of a private firm selling a service to a municipality or directly to users are the Culpeper and Pine Bluff facilities. The firm at Culpeper sells water as well as wastewater services directly to the user rather than going through an authority. It has almost complete liability for the operation, and it sets its own rates subject to an easily observable cap on the rates. Pine Bluff, the facility that only transports but does not treat wastewater, also sells services at a set fee to the municipality, leaving the city liable for nothing other than paying the fee in exchange for the service.

The Mount Vernon facility is also operated in a manner much like an exchange of service for a contracted fee, especially considering that title to the facility remains with the municipality. The municipality remains responsible for major repairs to the portion of the facility that existed before the privatization agreement, presenting a potential conflict, but the firm is responsible for repairs to the part of the facility it constructed. One question about the extent of the public-private partnership at Mount Vernon centers on the provision that a part of the O&M fee can be returned to the municipality. This arrangement places some of the responsibility for O&M expenditures with the municipality rather than with the private firm.

The facilities at Auburn, Gilbert, and Gilder Creek all have provisions for the overseeing authorities involved to pay for major expenses, the limits of which are not specified in the privatization agreements. This responsibility requires more comprehensive oversight on the part of the authorities and makes the projects more of a partnership between the authorities and the firms than a contract agreement where a firm sells a service to an authority at a specified price.

The privatization contracts examined show that both the public and the private sectors share significantly in the risks of producing the service. A substantial amount of public sector oversight is required in order to assure that the service is being provided as efficiently as possible. With so much public sector risk bearing, some of the advantages that in theory can result from privatization are sacrificed because the authority must monitor the private firm much more closely than if it were just paying a price in exchange for a service. A notable characteristic in most of the privatization contracts is how heavily the public sector is involved in bearing risks that would normally be borne by the business that provides a service in the private market.

In actuality, the share for each party of the total project cost is the result of the relationship, as defined in the contract, between allocation of risks and incentive provisions. In general, WTW privatization contracts assign substantial risks and responsibilities to the public authority. To the extent that authority risk sharing and oversight are required, some of the theoretical economic advantages of the private market are diminished. However, public accountability is retained. The result is that a new public-private structure is developed. Interestingly and importantly, this new structure calls for the private sector to submit to and participate in the rules of the game (dynamic) of the public sector much more so than is required of the public sector to participate in the private market. Thus, privatization, from this perspective, is a paradox. Rather than the public sector becoming more like the private, just the reverse occurs in privatization. In somewhat different terms, the change of roles proposed in the theory-sketch appears to take place, but it is not necessarily symmetrical in nature. Chapter 11 explores some of the implications of the ways in which both sectors change roles.

The theory-sketch proposes that in privatization the contract is, or at least can be, structured to allocate risks and costs in a way that a private market opportunity is provided while public accountability is preserved. While the analysis of privatization contracts necessarily is more qualitative than the analyses of project construction time or cost, the results are nevertheless striking in the degree to which they call into question some premises of the theory-sketch while supporting other premises.

The review of contracts makes fairly clear that the assignment of risk through contract provisions is a subtle matter. Economic risk, like political power, has a mercurial quality. Slight shifts—or omissions—in the contractual structure shift risk quickly from one location to another. Thus it is not very surprising that risk is, in fact, shared between the parties in most of the privatization contracts. Most contracts pass risk from the private sector firm to the public sector authority. The extent to which this shift happens, however, is surprising. The analysis suggests that more than one contract leaves the local authority with less than adequate accountability mechanisms in place. Some contract provisions give the privatizer an incentive to cut costs on construction and pass them through to repair costs during plant operations, costs that the authority would have to defray. Considerable variation also occurs in the ease with which an authority can get out of the agreement if it should prove unsatisfactory. In one case, the authority has to prove nothing to get out of the agreement. In other cases, the burden of persuasion or proof on the authority is considerably higher. Finally, in at least some cases a provision giving the authority first right of refusal in case the privatizer wants to sell the facility is included in the contract apparently as an afterthought. Yet, such a provision is needed to place the authority on what might be called accountability square number one: control over who ultimately provides an essential public service.

These findings bear in several ways on the theory-sketch. First, in some cases the contract alters roles: the local authority assumes risk in a manner we would more likely associate with the private firm. Second, under some provisions the importance of oversight by the authority during design and construction is increased dramatically, because the privatizer has the incentive to defer costs to the O&M stage. It might be argued that one subtle effect of this situation is to inject an element of public accountability, in the form of responsibility for fair play, into the role of the private firm. Third, the contracts illustrate accountability mechanisms that can be used to retain accountability for the authority. The relevant provisions here have to do with buy-backs and contract termination and with how user fees are determined.

8

Mount Vernon
Post-1986 Tax Reform Privatization

Mount Vernon was the first city to privatize a wastewater treatment work (WTW) following the 1986 tax reforms that removed most of the tax incentives designed to get private sector participation in public works projects.[34] The case thus represents a privatization project that relies clearly on the system and process of privatization, rather than on tax incentives, to make it a viable option for public infrastructure construction. The case also presents several other important features of infrastructure privatization, including: the politics of the process; use of foreign capital; how the WTW ownership issue was handled in a case in which federal and private funds are involved; and the active role of the Illinois Environmental Protection Agency (IEPA).

Mount Vernon is located in south-central Illinois and had a 1986 population of 20,500. The city has a combined manager-council and strong mayor form of government. In the 1980s the city was considered to have one of the highest potential growth rates in Illinois. It is served by four interstate highways and six rail lines and is near the St. Louis international airport. Economic growth was threatened by environmental problems resulting from inadequate wastewater treatment.

The Environmental Issue

In the early 1980s Mount Vernon faced a wastewater treatment crisis. The city had built a tertiary wastewater treatment plant in the 1970s. However, the facility never worked very well and had insufficient capacity to meet current demand. In 1986, after several years of attempting to

meet state and federal effluent standards, the city was placed on restricted status by the IEPA, which banned new connections until the
problems could be addressed. If the problem was not addressed quickly,
the city would lose its potential for substantial economic expansion. In
addition, the effluent from the WTW was discharged into a creek that
flowed into the city's drinking water supply.

Although the city had made efforts to be in compliance with standards
through improvements made in 1977, the improvements never worked
well. The city in 1986 was still paying for the bond issue that funded
those improvements. While the city had recently gone through an
economic recession, a major wave of industry was coming to the area in
the form of foreign auto factories, and Mount Vernon needed to get off
the state environmental regulatory agency's restricted status so it could
provide sewer connections to the new industry that could locate in
the city.

Other problems faced the city. The pre-1986 city council was kept in
the dark about the wastewater treatment problems and, although the
city first received warnings in 1983, it was not until 1986, when the city
was put on restricted status, that the council first addressed the problem.
At that time, options were limited. Unemployment was at 18 percent
because, in part, of the moratorium. User fees were as high as the
council believed they could be. The city could not finance a WTW
project out of its own budget because it was still paying for the earlier
improvements.

Because of this set of conditions the WTW problem became a political
issue resulting in changes in the city organizational and political structure that set the stage for solving the WTW problem. A strong mayor
who had served two terms eight years earlier and had secured numerous
grants during his tenure was reelected. A new city council was elected,
and nearly everyone on the council had either business or engineering
experience in their backgrounds. The citizens also adopted home rule
and the city used the home rule powers to restructure the tax base and to
appoint a professional city manager to run the city. The intent was to use
the newly adopted sales tax as a base for a pay-as-you-go structure to
fund and upgrade an expansion of the wastewater treatment facilities.
However, any effort to address the WTW problem faced a range of
regulatory, financial, and political problems.

Decision Options

Mount Vernon, as stated, had attempted to address the wastewater problem as early as 1984. Environmental Management Corporation (EMC), a St. Louis water and wastewater contract operations firm, was employed to help the city operate and maintain the existing WTW facility. While improvements were made, the plant capacity was insufficient to handle peak flows. A plant upgrade and expansion projected to cost some $9 to $14 million was required. The first option considered to meet this need was to secure federal funding. Although Mount Vernon qualified for an EPA grant, the most the city could receive was $2.3 million, which was insufficient.

The city next looked at self-financing. This option had inherent problems for several reasons. The moratorium had hurt the city financially and money was not available to pay for the WTW renovation. The only way self-financing was affordable was through a plan called pay-as-you-build, in which improvements would be made as they could be financed through the increased sales tax. This solution would have cost some $9.5 million and compliance would not have been reached until 1994. According to the mayor, Rolland Lewis, the IEPA rejected the pay-as-you-build option because of the time frame and was thus planning to file a lawsuit against the city. The self-financing time frame was also not acceptable because the city would lose the opportunity for economic expansion.

Additional problems arose for the self-financing option. The IEPA rejected a bond payment plan backed only by expected sales tax receipts. In addition, the sales tax revenues were being used to upgrade the existing WTW. Prospective financial backers were unsure about this method of payment because of a restrictive covenant on the 1975 bond that financed the 1977 improvements. Because the bond payments were almost exclusively derived from sales tax receipts instead of user fees, the city could not be insured, even though it had never missed a bond payment.

In August 1986, EMC presented a proposal to the city council to finance, design, build, own, and operate the existing and expanded facility. EMC, along with its affiliate, Paric Corporation, was formed in 1982 for the specific purpose of branching into privatization, using the design, build, and operate structure as a way to provide a cost-effective and productive service. However, it had difficulty in selling the idea to cities. According to Jerry King, president of EMC, "the most effective design, build, and operate happens when all of the workers are involved in the same structure." However, this structure can only work in a noncompetitive bidding process. This process, according to King, is threatening to public officials because it requires a higher degree of trust and is politically riskier for the politician because it leaves room for the charges of favoritism or, at worst, corruption. However, in the post-1986 tax environment, the company believed that substantial savings were possible in privatized projects because of noncompetitive bidding and integrated design, build, and operate structures.

According to King, this structure was the future of privatization because tax benefits were artificial inducements and encouraged the same kind of proposals as were seen in the grants era of competitive bidding. If noncompetitive contracts were allowed and the company could control the factors, then companies would take extra risks to present the best proposal.

This concept was, however, very difficult to sell to the city. According to Paul McKee, chairman of Paric Corporation, it took a long time (five to six years) to get the concept across for several reasons, including bureaucratic reluctance to be innovative, mistrust, and the political process. With respect to the political process barrier, McKee referred specifically to the view held by some that the solution to the WTW problem was a political one, that is, extension of the deadline dates for compliance, renewal of the grants program, and the fact that no public policy existed to guide the adoption, if not the enforcement, of privatization. Further, he noted that enforcement of compliance requirements varied greatly from state to state. The privatization option was more viable in a state in which enforcement was strong, which was the case in Illinois.

Because of the unique structure of the noncompetitive arrangement and the fiscal situation in which the city found itself, a formal feasibility study was not done. However, because of the high public visibility and interest in the WTW issue, the mayor placed the WTW decision-making process on the public agenda. The public was very involved and informed through extensive media coverage of the issue. The new city manager was invited to speak to many civic groups and he always received questions concerning the WTW situation, primarily because business leaders were concerned about the limits for expansion imposed on the city. He said that, remarkably, the WTW problem was a topic of discussion for the entire community and that he spent forty to fifty hours a week, at first, just on the WTW issue.

Other problems were encountered in addressing the WTW privatization option, including financing, IEPA approval, and the question of whether or not private and federal funds could be mixed in the upgrade and expansion of a grant-funded WTW. With respect to financing, the city mandated a solution that required no new taxes and no increase in fees. In spite of these hurdles, regulatory, political, and economic issues forced the city to address and resolve the WTW issue.

Decision Results

Costs and benefits were involved in each of the options considered. In the city manager's evaluation, while some EPA money was available, it was not enough and did not provide a timely solution. Timing was also a liability in the self-financing option, but it had the advantage that reduced debt service would have occurred in the pay-as-you-build plan. However, neither of these met IEPA requirements. With privatization, advantages existed in several areas. Public support was high, an opportunity existed to shift city responsibility and liability, and the timing was optimal. The liabilities appeared primarily in transaction costs—the contractual paperwork and the attorney fees—and in the difficulty of structuring a privatization deal in the post-1986 tax reform context. Specific issues included facility ownership, the mixing of the existing and new facilities, and restrictive covenants that remained on the existing facility.

These issues were resolved by adopting a hybrid form of privatization in which formal ownership of the WTW remains with Mount Vernon. EMC-Paric, however, acts as owner for the duration of the twenty-year contract. This arrangement was possible because of the 1986 tax code revisions. A major implication of this arrangement was that it technically allowed the city to avoid the potential legal and financial risk involved in meshing federal and private funds in the same facility. The financial structure of the deal (see figure 8.1) included a total of $6.4 million, substantially lower than the projected $9–14 million of the other options. Industrial development bonds were issued by the city and the funds ($5.025 million) were then loaned to EMC for construction of the facility. The remaining funds were used for engineering and transaction costs. EMC operates the WTW and Mount Vernon makes monthly payments to EMC in a twenty-year service agreement. The financing of the deal was made possible by a letter of credit (insurance) issued by Dai-

Figure 8.1 Financial Structure of City of Mount Vernon Wastewater Treatment Privatization Project

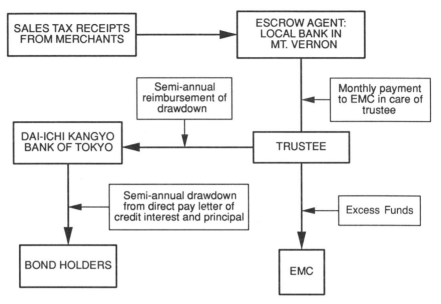

Source: Reinhardt, 1988: 9.

Ichi Kangyo Bank of Toyko. The profit for EMC-Paric comes from the 5 percent contractor's fee, the O&M fee, and any balance in the equipment reserve fund.

Analysis

The privatization solution was realistically the only option available to city officials. The pay-as-you-build solution would not have satisfied IEPA because Mount Vernon would have missed the compliance deadline by several years. A pay-as-you-build plan was, however, the only option available to the city, due to the restrictive covenant, until privatization was proposed. Privatization, even after 1986 tax reform, was chosen, according to the city manager, because it was a timely and acceptable solution. The need to comply with IEPA requirements and get out from under the moratorium for economic development purposes was very important. The fact that privatization was less costly, in some ways, was of secondary importance.

The construction time frame for the privatization option was also a critical factor. The city moved off restricted status in October 1987 because of the work EMC had already done on the WTW and because of the scheduled upgrade and expansion. Completion date for the project was scheduled for November 1988 (sixteen months) but proceeded ahead of schedule. Had the work been financed by a pay-as-you-build plan, Mount Vernon would not have had its restricted status lifted until 1991.

While EMC originally proposed private ownership, reduced tax benefits and restrictions on the existing facility made private ownership both unnecessary and unattractive. Except for ownership, however, the Mount Vernon project included all the elements of a privatization project. According to EMC, even in the absence of tax benefits, substantial cost savings were available to the city because of the integrated design-construct-operate structure that privatization made possible. The city manager, Jim Bassett, provided the following brief summation of the issues encountered during this process. In the area of legal issues, the starting point was the 1986 tax law, which changed the overall structure of the privatization deal. Because of the tax law changes and the restrictive covenants on the existing facility, it was not beneficial for EMC to own the WTW. If EMC had owned the facility, it might have been possible for the federal government to exercise a right to recapture some of the funds that had been spent on previous upgrades. Another legal issue concerned the type of bond issue and ratings the city negotiated. The city could not have gotten bond insurance because of its financial rating. With Dai-Ichi Kangyo Bank insuring the bond issue, Mount Vernon received a rating of AAA −.

In terms of economic issues, the problem arose of how to pay for the WTW. Because the council refused to raise user fees and payment was to be drawn from sales tax revenue, financial institutions were hesitant about supporting the bond issue. The city's change in its form of government to home rule added to the hesitancy. The political context of the issue added to the difficulty of finding a solution. At the same time, the change made a final resolution possible. The whole process took place in open sessions and the public was informed and eventually supportive. Mayor Lewis was given substantial credit for making the deal work, along with King and McKee. These three provided the leadership that established a trust relationship upon which a contract was executed. The major administrative problem encountered was the time involved in contract negotiations.

Two other issues encountered were the time span of the agreement and the role of the state regulatory agency. Officials at IEPA had not encountered a twenty-year agreement before and were unsure of how to deal with it. From the city manager's point of view, although the cooperation of IEPA was outstanding at the permitting and review stages, "getting there was a nightmare." While the state had provisions for privatization, it had not been attempted for WTWs before. In the final analysis, Mayor Lewis commended the IEPA for its work in making the privatization deal possible.

This case represents a post-1986 tax reform privatization project. Mount Vernon owns the WTW and holds the discharge permit, and the private company operates the facility. The city is responsible for the relationship with state regulators and is also responsible for billing the customers as well as handling public complaints about billing. EMC is responsible for quality and frequency of worker training, dealing with problems of staff morale, equipment maintenance, employee hiring, promotion and turnover, effluent quality, and public complaints concerning construction and odors.

Despite the 1986 changes in the tax code, privatization was able to work in Mount Vernon. It worked because the project incorporated the essential system and process elements of a privatized public-private partnership. In addition, the circumstances surrounding the decision to privatize contributed to its adoption. Without those particular circumstances, privatization might not have taken place. The circumstances included Mount Vernon's need to get off restricted status before the city's economic "window of opportunity" closed, the strength of the state regulatory agency, the small size and considerable eagerness of the private company, the leadership of and commitment to the project by Lewis, King, and McKee, and the willingness of all the individuals involved to seek a mutually beneficial solution.

The case of Mount Vernon lends support to some of the conclusions reached in Chapter 3. As in the Auburn case, the complexity and lack of definition of national policy created both constraints and discretion at the local level. Local political leaders took upon themselves the task of doing the work and developing the mechanisms needed to enable the local authority and the private firm to enter as partners into a privatization deal. The entrepreneurial role of the private firm also provided a major share of the energy the deal consumed. The transaction costs were very high, as the long work weeks of the city manager indicate.

Beyond these points, the Mount Vernon case suggests some important conclusions concerning the effects of the 1986 tax reforms. At the empirical level, Mount Vernon shows that privatization can work in the post-1986 tax environment, meaning that it can prove to be an attractive option to a city and agreement can be reached. At the theoretical level, interesting findings emerge concerning five elements of the theory-sketch. First, the privatization approach permits, as hypothesized, rapid project development, design, and construction. In view of the comparative case study results presented in Chapter 4, this is no surprise. Second, however, the Mount Vernon deal also worked in part because the fast-track design-build approach, combined with vendor-assisted financing involving the Dai-Ichi Kangyo Bank, contributed to a lowering of project costs relative to other options. Given the complex evidence on the relative cost issue, as set forth in Chapter 6, this finding is important. It supports the interpretation that privatization can be cost-effective relative to other options, even though it is not necessarily or consistently so.

A third theory-relevant finding is that in the Mount Vernon case the element of market competition was almost completely eliminated. Both public and private sector officials interviewed in this case study affirmed that EMC was early treated as a sole source bidder. As a result, EMC was able to save money in the early negotiating stages and to share information with Mount Vernon officials in a way that was not done, and could not have been done, in a competitively bid process. Thus, contrary to the premise set forth in traditional market theory, competition was not only reduced in this case but was practically eliminated.

From this finding flows a fourth theory-relevant conclusion. That is, in this post-1986 case, sector-based roles of the principals changed even more drastically than they did in the pre-1986 cases. The private firm was subject to none of the competitive precontract bidding that pre-1986 privatizers routinely went through. The local authority was willing to buy into this modified arrangement early in negotiations, thereby foregoing its opportunity to use precontract competitive bidding as an (economically based) accountability mechanism. The accountability burden then shifted to the state regulatory agency, which, absent national policy or guidance, was unsure about how to evaluate this innovative arrangement.

Fifth, these findings support a theory-driven assessment of the 1986 tax reforms. In removing incentives and tilting the playing field against privatization, as Chapter 6 concludes, the 1986 tax reform did more than place additional financial constraints on the parties. Rather, it contributed to and extended the changing of the roles of the two sectors within the framework of the deal.

9

Politics
Public and Private

In addition to legal, economic, and contractual issues, privatization raises a host of political and resultant administrative and organizational questions. As Henig, Hamnett, and Feigenbaum (1988:443) noted, "enthusiasts liken this policy [privatization] to a kind of world revolution. Like all revolutions, we argue, this one is best understood in political terms." Chapter 9 examines the broader public and private sector political institutional settings in which privatization takes place. While previous chapters addressed generally some aspects of the politics of privatization, this chapter focuses on the development and implementation of privatization as it has evolved in the context of national, state, and local politics and in the context of the politics of the private sector WTW industry.

Privatization, to be successful, requires changed roles and a different kind of cooperation between public and private managers who are responsible for privatized projects. This conclusion can be stated in terms of the need for vertical coordination of policy and administration among national, state, and local levels of government and horizontal coordination between the public and private sectors. The development and structure of these relationships are fundamentally products of the policy and political processes. In part, they determine who gets what, when, and how.

The chapter is organized into four sections. The first section briefly reviews the three major national political currents that shaped the privatization effort in the 1980s. These include: New Federalism and national budgetary demands, ideology, and the search for increased efficiency and productivity in the provision and delivery of public services. The second section addresses the politics of privatization at the state level, specifically focusing on a national survey of state environmental management and regulatory agencies. These agencies are central players in the implementation of national clean water policy and in establishing the context for the privatization option. Moreover, the Water Quality Act of 1987 adds weight to the state agency role as wastewater policy changes from a national grant program to a state revolving loan fund program. The third section discusses the politics of privatization at the local level where privatization decisions are made. At this level, who wins and who loses? How are the decisions made and by whom?

The last section of this chapter presents findings of case studies and of a survey of the politics, broadly defined, of the privatization industry. The driving force for privatization in wastewater treatment during the 1980s was industry initiative, not public policy. Practitioners in the wastewater treatment industry and related financial firms developed privatization conceptually and marketed the initial projects. How industry organized to address the privatization option, which the tax legislation of the early 1980s made so attractive, and how this effort relates to the public policy and political processes, particularly at the local level, are important variables in the story of WTW privatization.

Three observations are relevant to an analysis of the politics of privatization. First, most state environmental agencies exist because of national level policy initiatives, incentives, or sanctions. In the absence of incentives (positive or negative) state-level implementation of national policy is difficult. Privatization in the 1980s was not a national policy. Thus, no national-level incentives existed to support a state agency role or local-level adoption. Second, as discussed previously, privatization emerged from the private sector as a market opportunity resulting from the opportunistic consequences of changes in other national policies, specifically water and tax policies. Thus, privatization was not in the national policy channel during the 1980s, with or without incentives. And third, given these two factors, and even though privatization provided an option to meet substantial wastewater needs that existed at local levels, most authorities were very slow to consider privatization as a policy or program option. Was this reluctance to adopt the privatization solution to the wastewater problem a political or economic problem? Or both?

Privatization developed in a highly diffuse context of public policy. In large part, as the following analyses reveal, this context was detrimental to the adoption of privatization. The context was too weakly defined to support the basic processes of policy development and implementation and as such they were politically unacceptable or of little political value. As a result, ad hoc structures developed within and among industry, local governments, and regulatory agencies to address privatization. For the most part, these ad hoc structures ignored or were insensitive to the fundamental differences between the dynamics of the public and private markets. This chapter serves to identify and define these structures and their role in the development of privatization.

The National Context: New Federalism and Ideology

Chapters 1 and 2 placed the development of the privatization of WTWs in a historical context, including the national economic and political factors that motivated and shaped its development. Only a brief summary of these factors is presented here.

Three major currents converged in the 1980s to make privatization of WTWs possible. First, the election of Ronald Reagan institutionalized a change in national metapolicy from a proactive to a limited national government role. The new metapolicy was translated into New Federalism and a call for a reduction in the role of the national government and an increase in the roles of state and local governments and the private sector. National budgetary deficits and cumulative debt added political strength to the implementation of New Federalism. Two specific actions that had a direct impact on WTW privatization were the reduction and subsequent elimination of WTW construction grants and the 1981 and 1982 tax incentives for the private sector to engage public works. The result was a market opportunity for the private sector to meet public infrastructure needs (Goldman and Mokuvos 1984). The industry response is analyzed in a later section of this chapter.

The second current that merged with, or perhaps spawned, the New Federalism was the growing status of the public choice school of thought that began in the 1960s and traces its roots to Adam Smith and classical economics (Ostrom and Ostrom 1971). The school has both academic and ideological adherents, often a mix of the two, including the Adam Smith Institute, the Heritage Foundation, and similar organizations (Butler 1985a, 1985b; Heritage Foundation 1987; Moore and Butler 1987). The central thesis of the adherents of this ideology is that the private market provides, for many goods and structures, a better and more efficient and productive mechanism for making public policy decisions and for producing and delivering public goods than does the public market, the representative assembly. Adherents of this belief actively promoted the adoption of a range of public-private initiatives during the 1980s, all designed to reduce the role of government and increase the role of the private sector (Savas 1987). During this period President Reagan ordered the use of A-76 private sector contracting requirements, established an Office of Privatization in the Office of Management and Budget, and appointed a Commission on Privatization, which issued a report in 1988 that adopted completely the public choice ideology (Report 1988).

The third stream that contributed to the privatization movement in the 1980s came from some of the public providers of public services at all levels of government. Particularly with respect to WTW privatization, modern-day descendants of the turn-of-the century progressive-reform movement, primarily city managers, viewed WTW privatization as a way to meet needs efficiently and productively. In essence, at this level privatization was a good management option.

This configuration of factors provided the national context for the development of privatization at the local level and for an increased emphasis on other forms of public-private partnerships, contract services for example. What is striking and obvious in these developments at the national level is the absence of any coordinated or formal policy on privatization. In fact, during this period the U.S. EPA avoided promoting privatization because some of its components, namely tax incentives for the private sector, were in apparent conflict with OMB's attempts to reduce costs to the Treasury.

Finally, in terms of national partisan politics, contrary to the experience in Europe (Henig, Hamnett, and Feigenbaum 1988), privatization never became a partisan issue. In the 1984 and 1988 presidential elections, all of the candidates at one time or another paid homage to the concept of privatization but without much understanding of or commitment to any specifics. The term *privatization* became a general term for a host of activities, including the "privatization" of foreign policy in the Iran-Contra affair.

Within this ambiguous national context, local governments and the private sector proceeded to develop and implement privatization, specifically WTW privatization. However, with respect to WTWs, since 1972 state-level environmental agencies had played a substantial role in the construction and financing of these facilities through the U.S. EPA construction grant program. What role did state agencies play in the privatization of WTWs?

The State Regulatory Agency and Privatization

Major changes in national policy often generate major changes in the policy implementation and administration responsibilities of public agencies and officials at the state and local levels of government. As previously noted, the New Federalism of the 1980s sought to shift programs from the national government to state and local levels and to the private sector. In the mid-1980s it was at least implicitly assumed that the policy of devolution and the privatization of WTWs, while sharing a common genesis, could be implemented independently of each other. EPA's hesitancy to endorse privatization before late 1988 illustrates this point nicely. In many instances, however, the two movements were linked. The connection becomes especially obvious when a driving force for both sets of actions is national budgetary constraint. When the national government passes off financial responsibility for substantive policy to the states, opportunities and pressures develop for state agencies to accept or engage other resources, including private sector provision of services and capital. The manner in which state agencies addressed themselves to public-private partnership options influenced the development of WTW privatization.

State Environmental Agencies in Transition

The Clean Water Act of 1972 established both a national policy for the treatment of municipal wastewater and a national program for implementing that policy. The initial implementation mechanism was a program of nationally funded grants, administered by the Environmental Protection Agency through state regulatory agencies. The main state regulatory activities include issuance of permits, review of plant design and construction, grant administration, monitoring of plant effluent and stream quality, and negotiation of compliance and sanctions. As states take on added responsibilities under the Water Quality Act of 1987, their responsibilities in these areas seem far more likely to increase than to decline.

These responsibilities did not evaporate for privatized WTW cases. However, there was no established framework of expectations about how to discharge them. In grant-funded cases, national policy provided that framework of expectations. It consisted specifically of a series of regulatory reviews and approvals tied to the funding process. Under privatization that schedule no longer was applicable because there was no federal funding. Or was it? The regulatory role of the state agency remained to be exercised (or not exercised). A general policy implementation question thus concerns whether, and how, state agencies address and play this role in the increasingly common decentralized arrangements in which the private sector plays a major part. Specifically, what role did state agencies play in the development and implementation of the privatization of WTWs, given the absence of a formal national privatization policy and the ambiguous role of EPA? What was the politics of privatization at the state level?

Many of the processes and behaviors this question addresses are likely to be informal, particularly in the ambiguous context of WTW privatization. Absent formal prescriptions deriving from national policy, less formal structures of communication seem especially likely to arise at the state agency level to coordinate behavior. As Chester Barnard observed in *The Functions of the Executive*, "formal implementation activities arise out of and are necessary to informal activities; but, when formal activities are undertaken, they create and require informal activity" (quoted by Denhardt 1984:93). In terms of policy implementation theory, this view certainly accords with the "bottom-up" approach to implementation that emphasizes relatively informal behaviors and interactions at the local level. But even the core notion of the "top-down" approach seems to contain the seeds of this view. The absence of a federal mandate, including incentives or sanctions, translates into a lack of control over what people at the state level do with respect to an implementation problem (Goggin et al. 1990:11).

In the absence of national and state policy, as we shall see, agency personnel nevertheless had to develop information, perspectives, and positions that relate directly or indirectly to public-private partnership forms, including privatization. How does this development take place? For instance, what do agency personnel know, think, and tell cities about privatization? What are their preferences? Has the agency developed an informal position on privatization or reviewed its status as an option under state law? Has it promoted enactment of state legislation supportive of privatization? The answers to these questions necessarily affect privatization as one mechanism for achieving clean water objectives.

Theoretical Underpinnings

Beyond the practical need for information as a basis for policy design, state regulatory processes, as they relate to privatization, are of interest for theoretical reasons. The following discussion develops theoretical underpinnings for an examination of these processes in the area of clean water policy.

As the New Federalism proceeds and regulatory responsibility shifts correspondingly, new issues will arise (Meier 1985). Some of these issues will be empirical. For example, in the case of WTW privatization an immediate question is the extent to which state agencies engaged this option and developed information, issues, points of view, and mechanisms for proceeding. Some more theoretically informed issues arise as well. For instance, when national mandates remain in place but responsibility for accomplishing them is shifted to the states while national funding for implementation is eliminated, constraints and pressures, as well as discretion, are very likely to increase for state authorities. What kinds of responses can we expect from state agencies, and what factors will shape these responses? In the politics of federalism, many studies document the relationships between federal incentives and policy diffusion and implementation (Montjoy and O'Toole 1979; Welch and Thompson 1980).

A number of theoretical approaches exist to address these issues (McGarity 1986; Treiber 1985). One approach, a "comprehensive analytical rationality" model, emphasizes regulatory attention to all aspects of and all potential solutions for a given problem (McGarity 1986:416 and passim). This model suggests that to understand the regulatory process we need to attend to the many ways in which regulators engage possible solutions to problems, not just how they implement a particular solution.

A second approach to understanding state regulatory behavior considers informal and reflexive activities (Treiber 1985). This approach is apposite here for two reasons. First, the framework for analysis speaks to exactly the kind of fluid, transitional situation that we see as policy responsibilities devolve from federal to state agencies under the New Federalism. Second, the approach seems particularly well-suited to examining regulatory processes as they relate to implementation options (privatization) that are not clearly defined in a legislative mandate and that are not routinely the subject of extensive and clear rules or guidance from the federal agency.

A synthesis of these two approaches produces the following questions in examining the role of state agencies in the development and implementation of WTW privatization. What options are available for implementing national policy? Are some of these options more firmly grounded in positive law than others? How do the agencies engage these different options? What do they know, want to know, think, do to learn, tell others, and decide with respect to these options? How do these options interact with one another, and how do the agencies deal with the potential for interaction? With what groups do the agencies communicate on these issues, and about what do they communicate? What formal decisions and positions do agencies establish, and what kinds of informal, reflexive activities take place—or fail to take place—as implementation proceeds? These activities are fundamentally political, not economic, even if economic pressures shape them to some extent.

How Do State Agencies Engage Privatization?

To address these questions, state environmental regulatory officials were surveyed in the summer of 1988 and a number of on-site case studies were conducted. Survey data were collected after the first round of WTW privatization and just prior to the promulgation of a privatization policy by the U.S. EPA. In all, thirty-nine survey cases were completed through a mail questionnaire and follow-up telephone interviews.

The questionnaire addressed how states, as represented by their responsible regulatory officials, engaged privatization. There were four main areas of emphasis. First, were agency officials aware of privatization, and did they regard it as feasible in general? (They were and they did.) Second, did they do anything to address privatization in the terms discussed in the preceding section? (They did.) Third, was there variation in the extent to which agency officials addressed privatization? (There was.) Fourth, was there a pattern to the variation observed? (Yes, to a limited extent.)

The survey results clearly indicated that state agency officials were aware of privatization even though it was not a formal policy for which

Table 9.1 State Agency Perceived Barriers to WTW Privatization

Type of Barrier	Number (%) Who Perceive
Economic	16 (44%)
Political	13 (35%)
Legal	9 (25%)
Administrative	8 (22%)
Other	7 (21%)

they had responsibility. Thirty-four of thirty-nine states (87 percent) reported that they had read about privatization in industry journals. Some had additional knowledge. Seven respondents (18 percent) reported instances of privatization in their states, and officials in sixteen states (41 percent) indicated that cities or other authorities in their jurisdictions had seriously considered privatization. The respondents were split, however, on the overall feasibility of the privatization option in their states. Nineteen (49 percent) said it would be feasible, twelve (31 percent) said it would not, and the rest were undecided. When asked what barriers might stand in the way of privatization, they also gave mixed responses (see table 9.1). The question on political barriers was phrased in terms of the roles of the public and private sectors. The question on administrative barriers referred to accountability and responsibility of the agencies involved.

Additional information on the respondents' assessment of the private sector role in water treatment emerged from a question on factors affecting water quality. Respondents ranked six factors "in terms of the amount of positive effect they had had on improving wastewater treatment" in their state in the past five years. Ranked in order of decreasing amount of positive effect, the factors were:

MOST POSITIVE EFFECT
—Construction Grants
—Permitting Process
—Clean Water Standards
—Regulatory Sanctions
—Local Desire for Clean Water
—Private Sector Activity
LEAST POSITIVE EFFECT

Table 9.2   Experience of State Agency Personnel with WTW Privatization

Experience IN THE PAST YEAR DID YOU:	Response NUMBER (%) SAYING YES
—read about privatization in trade or industry journals?	34 (87%)
—discuss it informally in agency?	26 (67%)
—discuss it with an industry agent?	24 (62%)
—want more information about it?	19 (49%)
—discuss it with a municipal agent?	18 (46%)
—receive an inquiry about it?	17 (44%)
—attend a seminar on it?	14 (36%)
—receive EPA guidance concerning it?	11 (29%)
—assess the feasibility of privatization under state law?	11 (28%)
—want more EPA guidance?	10 (26%)
—talk about privatization with a state legislator or staff person?	10 (26%)
—attend an in-house meeting at which privatization was on the agenda?	9 (23%)
—request information about it?	6 (15%)
—adopt an agency position (formal or informal) on privatization?	5 (13%)

In summary, state agency officials who were responsible for water policy implementation were aware of privatization and had "engaged" it to the extent of having some knowledge about its occurrence in their states and some opinions concerning it. While officials were divided on the feasibility of privatization, they were nearly unanimous in their evaluation of the overall role of the private sector in contributing to water quality. That is, they placed it at the bottom of the pile.

Against this background, a second question was asked. If officials knew about privatization, and in several cases cities in their states actively considered it, had their agencies developed a policy with respect to it? In this case the answer was also unambiguous. Thirty-four of thirty-nine respondents (87 percent) reported no policy in general toward privatization. In sum, there was awareness and some evaluation of this option but very little in the way of direct engagement in the form of established policy.

This combination of findings leads to a pair of questions. Why were there so few formal determinations of policy? And, absent such formal determinations, what if anything did agency personnel do to address the privatization option? To explore these issues respondents were asked whether they had done or experienced fourteen different items during the preceding year (see table 9.2).

The majority of respondents had read about privatization in trade journals, discussed it informally in the agency, and had discussed it with an industry agent. Formal experience with or actions taken regarding WTW privatization were reported by less than a majority, including getting guidance from the U.S. EPA.

The state agency survey results support findings based on on-site state agency interviews. The strongest pattern in the data concerns the role of public agencies and private industry in the development of privatization. Clearly industry initiatives drove the privatization option. The state agency position was, at best, reflexive, not active. The two most extreme response distributions underscore this interpretation. Eighty-seven percent of respondents indicated they had read about privatization in industry journals; the same percentage indicated their agencies had taken no position on it, formally or informally.

The pattern of policy processes in the state agencies related to WTW privatization appears to have been informal, internal, and reflexive rather than formal, external, and proactive. Respondents from 67 percent of the agencies indicated in-house discussions (concomitantly, in fully one-third of state agencies privatization may not even have been discussed). The percentages were typically lower for behaviors that are more formal or outward looking: 23 percent reported having attended an in-house meeting, and only 13 percent adopted even an informal agency position. Only 28 percent had taken a step toward policy in the form of evaluating privatization under state law; and just 26 percent had discussed it with a state legislator or staff person.

The pattern of discussions concerning privatization also is revealing. The primacy of industry activity appears again: 62 percent of respondents had discussed privatization with industry representatives. The role of the municipalities as partners to the private sector is reflected in the 46 percent of respondents who had discussed privatization with municipal representatives.

Absent from the data is any sense of movement in the state agencies toward active engagement of issues concerning privatization. Although 44 percent of respondents had been asked about it, only 15 percent had

made an inquiry about it. Barely half (49 percent) wanted more information about privatization, and just a quarter (26 percent) reported
wanting more EPA guidance than they had received.

The view from the states clearly focuses on public mandates rather
than private initiatives. They see public mandates as either the more
productive force for achieving clean water policy objectives or as a more
relevant political object of their role. Indeed, it appears plausible that the
state agencies view their mandates and procedures as the motor and
transmission driving local authorities and the public toward clean water
objectives. They may view the private sector entrance into this arena
with skepticism or even concern. The notion of mandates suggests a
theory-based explanation for the lack of organized initiative at the
agency level to deal with privatization. The existence of federal incentives plays a central role in the diffusion and implementation of mechanisms for achieving national policy goals (Welch and Thompson 1980).
Where incentives are lacking, the states are less likely to address themselves to the mechanisms in question. At the time these survey data were
collected, privatization was a nonissue in terms of clean water policy
implementation. No incentives, either positive or negative, existed for
states to address it. Incentives existed at the local level—cost savings,
economic development, and compliance requirements—and the privatization activity was at that level. By contrast, the grants program
contained substantial positive (grants) and negative (fines) incentives.
Thus it is hardly surprising that relatively few states undertook positive
initiatives with respect to privatization. The municipalities that privatized
wastewater treatment facilities in the 1980s did so because of locally
driven economic or political incentives, primarily pressures for industrial
and residential development. State agencies were not confronted with
this type of incentive.

That said, there clearly was variation in the extent to which states
addressed privatization either reflexively or actively. The responses in
table 9.2 show that some steps or events were much more frequent than
others. A review of the responses on a state by state basis indicates that
the pattern of these steps or events varied across states. That is, some
states reported that none of these things had happened, some reported
that all of them had happened, and some reported a mix. The variation
in results leads to another question: what patterns, if any, can we detect
in this variation? To explore this issue, states were assigned scores
reflecting the number of events or steps that had taken place. The low

score was zero (nothing had happened), and the high score was fourteen (they had seen or done it all). In this way it was possible to identify the extent to which, overall, individual states had addressed privatization.

This ordering of cases made it possible to assess several hypotheses. For instance, did states that had more personnel dealing with water policy do more to address privatization? This hypothesis seemed plausible, inasmuch as the larger staffs would quite possibly represent more differentiated skills and interests as well as greater likelihood of slack resources to allow a staff person to deal with this new option. However, no relationship occurred between staff size and intensity of privatization-related activity.

Was the variety of methods a state used to assist in project funding related to effort to address privatization? The idea here was that if an agency had expertise in one or more ways of assisting municipalities to obtain funding (the options were state grants and state loans), it might be more disposed to examine an additional, alternative source of funding. Again no relationship occurred.

These negative findings suggest that it is not easy to determine what kinds of state agencies will actively address privatization. This pattern, or lack of pattern, can be attributed to at least three factors. The first was the absence of federal incentives, mandates, or even clearly defined policy of any kind with respect to privatization. Second, states were reacting to an unfamiliar private sector initiative or intrusion into a traditional public sector area. Third, no political incentives (pressures) existed to engage privatization. The concluding section provides comments on the broader significance of these results. However, before turning to the conclusions, one additional set of results is presented that points to the presence of an ordered and cumulative structure in what the states do when they do address privatization. Here the question shifts from "what kinds of states address privatization actively" to a more descriptive matter: "when states address privatization, how do they do it?"

To answer this question the Guttman scale technique was applied to the responses of the thirty-nine state agency officials to the fourteen items in table 9.2. (The responses on eight of the items form a scale that has a coefficient of reproducibility [CR] of 0.92. See table 9.3. See Miller 1970:93 and Babbie 1989:409, on Guttman scaling.) The scaling resulted in a vivid pattern of state agency responses to privatization.

Although it was not clear which states would proceed to address privatization, a fairly firm structure of activity characterized the manner in which states did so. The steps typically consisted of reading about privatization in trade journals, discussing it informally in-house, discussing it with an industry or business agent, discussing it with a municipal agent, discussing it with a representative of the state legislature, meeting formally about it in-house, going out and asking questions about it, and finally, reaching an agency position on it. The findings suggest that even where implementation options are not driven by federal mandates or incentives, state agencies that address those options may do so in steps that reflect a common pattern.

In this regard, it is particularly interesting to note that all of the scalable items involved a form of communication rather than an attitude or an assessment. Also, six of the eight scalable items referred to contact with a group or organization outside the regulatory agency itself. The groups in question seem to be ones that are physically near at hand, including industry, the state legislature, and municipalities. The absence of EPA from these items confirms the ambiguous role that EPA played in WTW privatization and the sense of local perspective that emerges from the broader set of responses from the state agency level.

State Agencies and Privatization

As of mid-1988, responsible officials in state agencies were aware of privatization as an option and had had the opportunity to learn about it and engage it to the extent they wished to do so. The data, however, suggest an agency orientation toward public mandates and regulatory processes as the relevant political and substantive keys to achieving clean water objectives. While privatization was a national-level movement, it was not a state-level one. This orientation had fundamental implications for WTW privatization. Specifically, the private sector and the municipalities and other local authorities were carrying the privatization option. State agencies were not ready to engage the privatization option positively or to provide positive assistance with respect to it. The absence of federal incentives for the states to address privatization contributed substantially to this result. No political or economic incentives existed for state agencies to engage the privatization option.

The prospects for privatization will depend in part on the extent to which state agencies are able—and enabled—to engage this option more directly and proactively than they have done. One step in this process would be the externalization or outward orientation and legitimation of this issue for the agencies. A mechanism to contribute to this process is already engaged: in 1988 the U.S. EPA formally acted to

Table 9.3 How State Agencies Engage Privatization

ITEM: Total +	RE* 34	IN 26	BU 24	CI 18	LE 10	MT 9	QU 6	PN 5	
State									Total +
Illinois	+	+	+	+	+	+	+	+	8
New Jersey	+	+	+	+	+	+	+	+	8
Minnesota	+	+	+	+	+	+	+	+	8
Vermont	+	+	+	+	+	+	+	0	7
Maryland	+	+	+	+	+	0	+	0	6
Delaware	+	+	+	+	+	0	0	0	5
New Mexico	+	+	+	+	+	0	0	0	5
Connecticut	+	+	+	+	+	0	0	0	5
Utah	+	+	+	+	+	0	0	0	5
Louisiana	+	+	+	+	0	+	0	0	5
New York	+	+	+	+	0	+	0	0	5
Oklahoma	+	+	+	+	0	0	+	0	5
Wisconsin	+	+	+	0	0	+	0	+	5
Missouri	+	+	+	+	0	0	0	0	4
Ohio	+	+	+	+	0	0	0	0	4
Kansas	+	+	+	+	0	0	0	0	4
Rhode Island	+	+	+	0	0	0	0	0	3
Arkansas	+	+	+	0	0	0	0	0	3
Colorado	+	+	+	0	0	0	0	0	3
Tennessee	+	+	+	0	0	0	0	0	3
Florida	+	+	+	0	0	0	0	0	3
West Virginia	+	+	0	+	0	0	0	0	3
Alaska	+	+	0	+	0	0	0	0	3
Hawaii	+	0	0	+	0	+	0	0	3
Virginia	+	0	+	0	0	+	0	0	3

organize and promulgate public-private options for partnership structures in meeting national water policy objectives. The overall impact of this initiative, particularly on state environmental agencies, is at present unclear.

Though many states did not address privatization actively, some did. To the extent they did so, they followed a fairly clear pattern of activity reflecting informal reviews and contacts with a range of groups, primarily private sector ones. This finding suggests the relevance of informal, reflexive mechanisms to the ways in which state agencies implement policy in the interstices of positive law. Absent formal policy,

Table 9.3   (Continued)

ITEM: Total +	RE* 34	IN 26	BU 24	CI 18	LE 10	MT 9	QU 6	PN 5	
Mississippi	+	0	+	0	0	0	0	0	2
Nebraska	+	0	0	0	0	0	0	+	2
Arizona	+	0	+	0	0	0	0	0	2
Montana	+	+	0	0	0	0	0	0	2
Indiana	+	+	0	0	0	0	0	0	2
North Dakota	0	+	0	0	+	0	0	0	2
Idaho	+	0	0	0	0	0	0	0	1
Oregon	+	0	0	0	0	0	0	0	1
Kentucky	+	0	0	0	0	0	0	0	1
South Dakota	+	0	0	0	0	0	0	0	1
Iowa	0	0	0	0	0	0	0	0	0
California	0	0	0	0	0	0	0	0	0
Wyoming	0	0	0	0	0	0	0	0	0
Maine	0	0	0	0	0	0	0	0	0
# ERRORS:	4	3	3	6	1	5	1	2	

$$CR = 1.0 - \text{(total errors/total responses)}$$
$$CR = 1.0 - \text{(25 errors)}/\text{(8 items} \times \text{39 responses/item)}$$
$$CR = 1.0 - (25/312) = 0.92$$

*RE—read about privatization in trade or industry journals
 IN—discussed it (privatization) informally in the agency
 BU—discussed it with an industry or business agent
 CI—discussed it with a municipal agent
 LE—talked about it with a state legislator or staff person
 MT—attended an in-house meeting at which privatization was on the agenda
 QU—requested information about it
 PN—adopted an agency position (formal or informal) on privatization

this finding can assist in the assessment of policy initatives, such as EPA's recent emphasis on "public-private partnerships."

A final brief point needs to be made with respect to the politics of the role of state regulatory and environmental agencies in the development of WTW privatization, that is, the statutory posture of privatization at the state level. As Chapter 5 analyzed in detail, during the 1980s most states enacted some form of privatization law. This legislation was necessary because many of the requirements of successful privatization, including the power to execute long-term contracts, exemption from bid laws and property taxes, and the authority to contract with private sector companies, were prohibited by state law. Presumably, each of these prohibitions had worked its way through the political processes of the state and had been enacted for good reasons. To repeal or circumvent these laws required, of course, the use of the state's fundamental political process, the state legislature.

No systematically collected data are available to document the process through which the states enacted privatization laws. However, case studies reveal a clear pattern. The enactment of state privatization laws was the result of the efforts of local governments and privatizers working with state municipal leagues. In most cases, the privatizer drafted the legislation and the local legislative delegation that represented the authority trying to execute a privatized project handled the legislation. The state legislatures passed the bills because they provided a no-cost-to-the-state solution to meet local needs. The state regulatory or environmental agency, in most states, was not involved in the enactment process. This fact further supports the conclusion that, at best, state environmental agencies played only a reflexive role in the development of privatization of WTWs during the 1980s.

Local Politics of Privatization

The section on the diffusion and adoption of privatization in Chapter 2 and the three case studies presented in Chapters 3, 8, and 10 provide many specific and general insights into the politics of privatization at the local level. This section provides a brief overview of the local politics of privatization.

Privatization, specifically the privatization of WTWs during the 1980s, was essentially a set of actions and transactions executed at the local level and between local governments and the private sector WTW construction and financial industries. As documented in this chapter, the national and state levels of government provided, at best, an ambiguous context for the development and implementation of privatization and, at worst, in some states, a set of hurdles that inhibited its development. Thus, the development of privatization was dependent on initiatives and resources of local authorities, including political initiatives and resources.

The typical process for the development and implementation of a privatized project included the following. To meet either development needs or regulatory requirements, often both, a local water authority, usually a municipality, had to upgrade, build, or expand its wastewater treatment capacity. The traditional options were to self-finance a project or to secure a federal grant. By the early and mid-1980s, neither of these options was readily available, timely, or affordable. Thus, in the context of increased needs for wastewater treatment services and reduced resources to meet the needs, the private sector offered a new and innovative option—the privatization of WTWs.

The issues raised in this option—financial, legal, and political—were multiple and substantial. Should a basic public service be provided by the private sector? What if the privatizer went bankrupt? Who will the citizens hold accountable for the service—the city or the privatizer? How can a private sector company provide the service and make a profit at a lower cost than the city can? If it can, how can private sector success be explained to the citizens without its being interpreted as an indictment of public service inefficiency and waste? How is a privatization deal executed?

All of these questions had to be addressed by local authorities, and some of them became insurmountable hurdles for some authorities. As the data presented in Chapter 2 show, a privatization deal is so complex that only those authorities with sufficient managerial resources, usually professional city managers, were able to execute a privatization contract. In the cases where privatization was attempted and failed, even in manager cities, political reasons were usually the cause for failure.

Some examples will serve to illustrate and document this point. In one small manager city in the Southeast, the privatization option was considered, was found to be financially attractive relative to other options, and was tentatively adopted by the city council. However, the council subsequently decided not to privatize because the privatization deal as proposed would eliminate the participation of the city's local bond counsel. The lawyer involved was an influential member of the community, had served as the city's bond counsel for a number of years, and perceived the privatization deal as a threat to the city's and his financial interest. In fact, in the privatized deal the counsel would not have received his usual percentage fee for handling a city-financed project. In this community the project was handled in a way that was perceived to impact negatively on the local power structure, particularly the bond market. In other privatization projects the city bond counsel was included in the project and this issue was avoided.

Other political issues, however, were not so easily avoided. In a number of cases the decision not to privatize was the result of not being able to address adequately the accountability issue. Elected members of local authorities, usually city councils, argued that privatization resulted in their being held accountable by the citizens for a public service over which they had no, or at best only indirect, control. While privatizers countered with the argument that the privatization contract provided more accountability than currently existed in most cities, for some it was a difficult argument to make.

The argument was difficult to make for several reasons. Given the absence of any national policy on privatization and the passive role that state agencies played, the privatization of WTWs was left to local authorities and to private market vendors. Thus the privatization deal depended on the ability of local officials and private vendors to develop and execute a deal. In the context of ambiguous policy, public opposition to increased fees, skepticism regarding private market profits for delivery of a public service, and the absence of any precedents, the personal roles of the actors involved in the process, both public and private, were critical to successful privatization. WTW privatization was thus in large measure the result of the relationship that developed, or failed to develop, between the city and the privatizer and between both the city and the privatizer and the community.

A key variable in this process was the ability of private sector personnel to deal with local government officials. Following the 1981 and 1982 tax revisions that provided incentives for private sector companies to invest in public projects, a number of companies entered the market who had no or limited previous experience in dealing with local political authorities. As discussed in the following section, some of these companies quickly retreated from this market because of the inability to relate to local politicians and the local political process. Those companies that had previous experience with local authorities in contract services were able to engage a variety of local political processes that enhanced their efforts to secure a privatization project. These processes ranged from frequent personal contact to participation in and sponsorship of public meetings and to the donation of land for a public park. To some extent, the successful private company was perceived as acting in the community as a part of the local government, participating in the local political processes in the interest of the community.

In summary, given that WTW privatization was entirely a local decision, local politics played a part in every WTW privatization effort made during the 1980s. Given the absence of national and state privatization policy or guidance, the development of privatization was left to local authorities and to the private sector to work out. This process obviously included the local political structure, processes, and personalities. Privatization was successfully adopted in those cases where the political issues were addressed and overcome. Specifically, privatization was adopted where it was viewed as a public-private partnership based on common goals and public accountability and endorsed as such by the community. The private sector played an important role in establishing this relationship.

The Private Market and Privatization

One aspect of the privatization movement that has received little attention is how private firms organized to engage privatization. What is the politics of the private sector in the development of privatization? While the construction and engineering industry was primarily responsible for the development and diffusion of the initial efforts to privatize WTWs, little is known about the inner workings of industry's role in this area. As noted earlier, the evolution of the role of the privatization industry and its current status are directly related to the political nature and feasibility of privatization. In this respect, three questions related to the industry are particularly relevant. One: how and why did the industry first get involved in WTW privatization? Two: what organizational structures characterize the industry, and how do they relate to local political institutions? Three: how have these structures evolved, and what is the current and future status of the privatization industry?

Public and Private Markets

The entrance of the private sector into a traditional public sector service area has implications for both sectors. Privatization brings public needs and private means together to create a market opportunity. This process usually takes place in a period of economic adversity, such as characterized the early 1980s (Worthy 1984:211–42). What happens, however, when the economic and policy context changes? And what are the implications of these changes for long-term relationships between the sectors such as those on which WTW privatization is based? What are the responsibilities, political and otherwise, for the private sector when public needs are addressed by private markets? These are fundamentally questions of politics and policy.

Several characteristics of an industry that enters a new public market help to define the entry process and determine its success. These include: building on existing expertise and technology; a reservoir of managerial skill; the development of new forms of financial resources; industry flexibility to adapt to new market situations; sensitivity to the broader implications of meeting public service needs; and the reality that the profit-making objective of the private sector will take priority over the service objective of the public sector (Worthy 1984). How accurately do these characteristics describe the WTW privatization industry?

The Privatization Industry

To answer these questions, fifteen companies that were directly involved in the 1980s in WTW privatization, or attempts to privatize a WTW, were surveyed and/or interviewed. Five of these are national parent companies of WTW companies involved in privatization, and ten are directly involved in WTW design, construction, or operations. The companies are located in all regions of the United States. Eleven of the companies were interviewed on site and by telephone and four were interviewed only by telephone. Most of the companies were interviewed at least twice, once during the 1986–87 period and again in 1988.

The companies that initially entered the WTW privatization arena vary substantially in size, structure, and major line of business. Three are major engineering and construction companies without prior direct WTW experience. Three had prior experience in drinking water operations, technology, or equipment manufacturing but not with wastewater. Three had long-term experience with WTW engineering, design, and operations. And three of the companies had prior experience with privatized solid-waste ventures or other long-term contracts with public sector organizations but not with WTWs. (For example, one company is owned by a European parent company with long-term experience in drinking water privatization.) Each of these companies thus based its entrance into the WTW privatization market on prior and related, but differing, experience. And each did so as a way to strengthen its current WTW market position or to use its related experience and resources to expand its operation into the wastewater treatment market.

All of the companies saw privatization as a market opportunity. However, different companies entered the market at different times and for varying specific reasons. Some companies wanted to expand their construction business and had little or no interest in WTW operations and maintenance. Other companies saw WTW design and construction primarily as a means to secure long-term operating contracts. Some companies, during the 1981–86 period, entered the WTW privatization arena solely to secure the tax benefits available during that period. As national tax policy changed in 1986, interest in WTW privatization varied by type of company and motivation of the company for initial entrance into the market.

The Pre-1986 Privatization Industry

The argument is often made that the public sector (policy) is constantly changing and thereby provides an unstable context and partner for the more stable private industry. However, in the case of the WTW industry, the survey revealed as much, if not more, instability in the private sector as in the public. The implications of this instability for long-term public-private partnerships for the provision of basic public services, such as wastewater treatment, are substantial.

Major changes in national policy did in fact generate the initial wave of private sector interest in WTW market opportunities. This wave of private sector activity had varying influences on the internal organizational structures of the companies involved. Two of the smaller companies without prior direct WTW experience appointed WTW privatization managers with small staffs to develop privatization projects. These staffs were responsible primarily for marketing WTW privatization in medium-size municipalities, essentially a political process. Five companies made no significant organizational changes and relied on existing staff to market WTW privatization. The changes affected emphasis and personnel assignments, not structure. Most of these companies were major engineering and construction firms that saw WTW privatization as a means to expand their construction market. However, the two companies with the longest and most direct experience in and most resources devoted to wastewater treatment moved early in 1981 to develop vertically integrated organizations based on the international company model. That is, major organizational changes were made to incorporate WTW design, engineering, construction, marketing, and operations into a single structure. In addition, one company also brought into the organization a privatization financial planning capability and integrated that capability into the overall WTW privatization effort.

Two observations are relevant about these organizational, programmatic, and personnel changes in the industry. The first has to do with

WTW privatization marketing. Given that WTW privatization was not a national policy to be implemented by state and local authorities but rather was a product developed by the private market, industry had to gain access to the market as a vendor. This effort constituted a fundamentally different role and relationship than that which existed under the WTW construction grant program. Those industries with no or limited prior experience dealing with local public authorities found the process to be a frustrating one. In fact, some of the companies, after initial attempts to develop vendor relationships with local authorities, abandoned the effort altogether. Dealing with local mayors, commissioners, and elected lay members of councils was an impossible task for some companies. Those companies that had prior experience with local authorities, either in the construction grant program or in operations and maintenance contracts, were much more able to develop a vendor relationship in the WTW privatization area.

A second observation relates to the organizational structures of the companies involved. The WTW construction grant program segmented the process into design, construction, and operations stages. Different companies could and did successfully specialize in only one of these stages. However, as discussed in Chapter 4, one of the key elements of successful privatization is the integration of these components into a single structure. Some companies recognized the advantages of a single structure early on and reorganized to secure the maximum advantages this structure offered. Other companies, however, attempted to operate in the traditional segmented structure by subcontracting for pieces of the total project. As reported in Chapter 6, privatized projects varied greatly in costs. To some degree, the organizational structure of the company and the resultant ability of the firm to integrate project stages may account for these varying costs. The companies that could and did make these changes have been the successful privatization companies. Ironically, while the privatization option led to vertical integration, or reorganization, in the private sector, the public sector during the 1980s failed to attain such integration between levels of government with respect to privatization policy.

The Post-1986 Privatization Industry

The second major policy change in the WTW privatization arena that affected industry structure came in the 1986 tax code revisions that reduced the tax benefits included in the revisions of 1981 and 1982. Again, the private sector industry reacted to these revisions with varying changes in the level of interest in the WTW privatization market and with a number of substantial changes in organizational structures. Four companies either returned to their traditional WTW roles or placed the WTW privatization emphasis on the shelf until the market and policy pictures became clear. For the most part, these were the companies that had entered the market almost solely for the tax benefits during the period in which market opportunities and profits appeared to be definable in clear financial terms. In fact, two companies involved mainly in construction exited the market prior to the 1986 tax code revisions for two reasons. First, they anticipated the revisions and the extent to which they would make closure of WTW privatization deals more difficult. Second, as mentioned earlier, these companies found dealing with local government officials cumbersome and frustrating, making continued activity in the market very difficult.

Five companies, mostly those with long-term WTW experience or privatization experience in solid waste, remain committed to WTW privatization after the 1986 tax reform. They have either revised their organizational structures to reflect a change in marketing emphasis of WTW privatization or, in three cases, substantially strengthened their organizations' capability to expand further the privatization market. In most cases, this effort involves purchase of new firms, for example O&M firms, in order to provide an integrated structure for project development and operation. Thus, while the WTW private market has changed due to shifts in national policies, specifically the tax code, companies initially involved in the WTW privatization market have either retained or further developed their organizational capability to function in the market.

It is clear that the private sector responded to public policy changes as the market provided opportunities in WTW privatization. However, it is equally clear that the private sector, at the same time, responded to changing market conditions. This factor poses additional issues for long-term public-private partnerships. The provision of an essential public service cannot be dependent on market conditions. The instability of the private market poses some troublesome issues for privatization. For example, two of the major and most successful WTW privatization companies underwent leveraged buy-outs during the 1980s. One was a friendly employee buy-out while the other was a hostile takeover. This action affected company policy, structure, and personnel, apart from issues of national policy changes. In one case, in part, the buy-out appears to have contributed to the only sale to date of a privatized plant back to public ownership (see Chapter 10). In this context, the relative instability of the privatization industry becomes an important variable in analyzing the institutional relationships between public and private sectors.

Changes in national policy and market conditions have had multiple direct and indirect influences on the WTW privatization industry. Some companies, as stated, have withdrawn from the market or discontinued additional marketing efforts. Other companies have either consolidated marketing efforts or have developed long-term WTW marketing plans. While these plans differ in structure from pre-1986 plans, they retain the basic elements of privatization: integrated design, construction, and operation. This structure in turn has implications for how a private sector company relates to the public sector. For example, a small privatization firm that is committed to the concept of integrating design, construction, and operation takes the position that the 1986 tax revisions weeded out the firms not truly interested in the system and process efficiencies of privatization in the WTW market and, thus, the market is now better off without these companies and the tax benefits.

Only three companies reported that removal of the early 1980s tax incentives directly eliminated the WTW privatization market. Other companies reported that, while tax code revisions have altered the structure of WTW privatization and have changed the market, the fact that the grant program is ending while treatment needs continue to grow assures a continuing privatization market. However, these companies reported that further revisions of the tax code, particularly with respect to depreciation schedules, buy-back requirements, arbitrage, and bond caps, need to be addressed in order for WTW privatization to meet its potential.

The national and state political and policy contexts; local government political structures, personalities, and processes; and the structure, operation, and evolution of the WTW private sector industry are all key elements in the development of WTW privatization. Their roles in privatization constitute both independent and dependent political variables. The development of WTW privatization was dependent on changes in federal policies, some of which had little to do directly with wastewater treatment. State agencies, by their reflexive roles, determine the tone and fabric of regulation within which privatized deals are executed. Local governments develop, adopt, and implement privatized projects. And the WTW industry plays an important role in shaping—or not shaping—policy and execution at each of the levels.

Multiple examples exist of industry's proactive political role in the development of WTW privatization. For instance, at the national level, as noted earlier, the wastewater treatment industry was less well organized than the solid-waste industry in terms of preserving tax benefits for privatization in 1986 (Watson and Vocino 1990:429). And several of the state privatization laws on the books were developed and actively promoted by firms in the privatization industry. At the local level, the privatization deal is nothing if not a fundamentally political shaping of accountability mechanisms to fit altered roles of both public and private sectors.

In these multiple ways, the story of national policy change, state regulatory agency role, and industry evolution is an important part of the local politics of privatization. This story bears both directly and indirectly on the theory-sketch presented in Chapter 1. Its most direct relevance is to the important issue of accountability. The principal thrust of the theory in this regard has to do with the contractual framework: if carefully crafted, it can preserve accountability. But as we have seen, this is at best an overly simple and potentially misleading rendering of a very complex reality. The review of contracts in Chapter 7 made clear that the contracts that have been written contain not only variation but also gaps in terms of how they address or fail to address important issues of accountability.

If the contract is thus suspect as a stand-alone mechanism of accountability, what other features of the implementation setting might provide—or fail to provide—support? The state regulatory agencies and the privatization industry both fit this function readily. The role of the agencies is quite direct. For example, under certain contractual conditions the need for project monitoring during construction is great because the privatizer has incentives to pass costs on to the O&M phase. If the state regulatory agency, in its exercise of discretion, elects to monitor design and construction quite closely, then it will augment or supplement the accountability framework established in the contract.

The supporting role of industry with respect to accountability is a little less direct but no less important. A key aspect of this role has to do with industry stability. The privatization deals are all designed with the long term in mind. Long-term relationships imply the ability of both partners to maintain a reasonably stable and predictable role. The contracts contain provisions on renegotiation and termination of the relationship.

Such provisions are themselves essential to maintaining accountability, in part through maintaining some vestiges of the competitive market within the long-term public-private partnership.

Local authorities made very clear that they place value on the credibility of the private firm as a long-term partner. Indeed, they construed stability as a condition of their own continuing accountability: they knew and trusted the folks with whom they would be dealing. In this context, any element of the policy setting that destabilizes the private sector's continuing interest in the relationship has an indirect but strong effect on the fabric of accountability. For instance, if the privatizer goes through a leveraged buy-out and the new owners need cash to service the debt incurred to finance the buy-out, then a sale of the privatized facility may be the result. Such disruptions in a long-term partnership damage the fabric of accountability, and privatization itself loses appeal to the public authority.

In sum, then, the politics of privatization can be read as the story of how actors in both public and private sectors and at all levels of government adjust or fail to adjust their roles, behaviors, and structures in response to the politics of privatization. Chapter 10 provides a case study that illustrates what happens when these political accommodations are not made.

10

The Western Carolina Regional Sewer Authority
Deprivatization

The Western Carolina Regional Sewer Authority (WCRSA) case documents two aspects of wastewater treatment work privatization not present in the other case studies.[35] One: the privatization took place within the structure of a regional authority rather than in a single municipality or authority. Two: after the privatization deal had been executed, the WCRSA bought the WTW from the privatizer; thus the case is the only example to date of deprivatization. In addition, the WCRSA case illustrates a privatization effort in which the state agency role posed barriers to privatization compared with the neutral role played by the state in the Auburn, Alabama, case and the positive role played by the state in the Mount Vernon, Illinois, case. Finally, the case presents a privatization deal in which the system and process used in the project violated, to some degree, the integrated design, construct, and operate structure of the model privatization project. The consequence was the eventual collapse of the privatization effort.

Greenville, South Carolina, and the area around it that together make up the Western Carolina Regional Sewer Authority had a 1986 population of 399,000. The region is an area of moderate growth (4.9 percentage increase from 1980 to 1986). The particular section located east-southeast of Greenville, however, experienced very rapid growth in the 1980s and, with the recent extension of an interstate road loop, rapid development is expected to continue. Thus, a new wastewater treatment facility was needed in this area.

Thirty WTW facilities exist in the WCRSA. Seven of them are over one million gallons per day (mgd) in size, fourteen are municipal plants, and the rest are package plants (small, self-contained units). The first public facilities were built in 1925 under the jurisdiction of the Greater Green-ville Sewer District and have had several upgrades and expansions since then. In 1974 the WCRSA was created and financing for WTWs was changed from ad valorem taxes to user fees. The purpose of the WCRSA is to provide sewer trunk line and sewage treatment plant service for the region. The authority is staffed with 135 personnel to provide operation, maintenance, laboratory, and administrative services. The WCRSA has an annual operating budget of some $10.5 million.

Environmental Issue

The treatment facility serving the growth area of the region was the Mauldin "A" Plant, which was built in the 1960s well outside the city of Mauldin. As development occurred, the plant was upgraded several times from its original lagoon system to a staged aeration configuration. Nevertheless, the 1.5-mgd capacity was exceeded at times and plant performance was marginal. Due to the marginal performance and inade-quate capacity, a moratorium was placed on new development in the Mauldin basin, and the South Carolina Department of Health and En-vironmental Control (DHEC) issued a consent order requiring a new facility. Some assistance had been given by the U.S. EPA for a previous upgrade of the Mauldin facility, but a long-term and comprehensive solution was necessary. As the need for an immediate further upgrade became more apparent, further EPA assistance was pursued through the state project priority system. However, the project was given a low priority ranking by DHEC and thus no further grant assistance was immediately available. This low ranking, combined with the mor-atorium and resultant prohibition of development, made it apparent the WCRSA would need to consider alternative financing for the upgrade of the existing WTW or the construction of a new facility.

Decision Options

By late 1984 the possibility of privatizing a new facility was being seriously considered. Charles Douglas, WCRSA director, provided the leadership for the privatization effort. He defines privatization as "an activity in which the private sector provides a service to the public through a public entity" (Douglas 1987:1). Further, he identified five reasons why privatization was applicable to the WCRSA. These features included: (1) the low and untimely prospect of U.S. EPA funding, (2) the need for expanded capacity to accommodate growth, (3) the scope of work, (4) the foreseeable limit for the WCRSA to issue general obligation bonds, and (5) the public interest in privatization.

In 1984 Douglas attended an Arthur Young, Inc., seminar to learn more about the privatization option. Subsequently, in 1985, Arthur Young did a feasibility study of the project and concluded that privatization was an economically viable option and, compared to conventional public financing, could save the authority between 7 and 18 percent in debt service charges. In addition to the economic advantages, the Arthur Young study identified other benefits. Federal and state involvement in local affairs would be minimized and local debt capacity would be preserved. The authority would be insulated from construction risks and cost overruns. The privatizer would guarantee that the construction was free from defects and failures, assume responsibility for performance and permit compliance, and assume liability for any fines and permits.

Following the study, the governing body of the WCRSA authorized further pursuit of the privatization option. A site selection committee was formed of five citizens (to represent and involve the public) as public interest grew in the project. Some public meetings were attended by 300–400 people. The major public concern was over the location of the plant, however, not privatization. Because of this issue, the facility was eventually located on the site that was most expensive, but one that raised the least opposition.

A final factor that further supported the consideration of the privatization option was a decision made by DHEC with respect to any grant assistance. While the WCRSA studies supported the construction of a new 4-mgd WTW, DHEC preferred a 1-mgd upgrade of the existing facility. While the 1-mgd upgrade would meet compliance requirements, it would not meet expanded capacity needs. DHEC thus ruled that only 1 mgd of additional capacity would be eligible for grant funding and no trunk lines would be eligible for funding. With this decision, the effort to privatize the WTW became the focus of review.

The Privatization Option

As with other WTW privatization projects, the WCRSA effort confronted a number of problems. The financing of the project was to be based on the use of tax-exempt industrial development bonds (IDBs) and privatizer equity. However, state law prohibited use of IDBs for water and wastewater projects. Subsequently, in June 1985, the South Carolina legislature revised the law to allow the use of IDBs for construction of WTWs. However, they also amended the law to require that any projects under the act that involved purchase or lease had to be submitted to the applicable local council of governments for a feasibility review and a study of the fiscal impact of the project on the taxpayers.

At this point, the privatization effort became extremely complex as issues of long-term contracts and bid law requirements were addressed. Legal, technical, bond, and procurement counsel all became involved in working out the details of the project. Through a series of long and complex reviews it was concluded that the WCRSA could contract for services on a long-term, twenty-year basis. A two-step procurement procedure was authorized that would meet the requirements of the state bid law while allowing the authority to select a privatizer using both qualification and cost criteria.

In early 1985, a four-member team was appointed to direct the privatization effort. The team included legal, financial, and engineering consultants and the manager of the Engineering and Planning Section of the WCRSA. In March 1985, requests for qualification proposals were sent to twenty-four private sector firms. The proposals received were evaluated on a number of factors ranging from WTW experience to personnel and financial requirements. The proposals were evaluated by a technical advisory team and an advisory committee made up of a corporate engineer, retired banker, home builder, environmental attorney, and two WCRSA commissioners. Eleven firms submitted proposals. After a couple of additional reviews, four firms were selected for a second-stage review. The second stage required submission of financing plans and costs, preliminary specifications for modifications of the plant design already completed, and a proposed service contract.

Three firms competed in the final review. In December 1985 the WCRSA signed a privatization contract with the agents of Metcalf & Eddy, Inc., and its parent company, Research-Cottrell. The late December signing was prompted by concern about proposed 1986 tax reforms that would eliminate tax benefits for the privatizer. In fact, the 1986 Tax Reform Act did eliminate most of the tax incentives provided in the 1981 and 1982 tax reforms. However, the WCRSA transaction was completed prior to the expiration of the tax incentives, and the privatization deal was executed.

The primary factor in support of privatization at this point was the potential cost savings relative to other options (see table 10.1). Data on

Table 10.1 Comparative Annual First-Year Operating Costs, WCRSA

	Privatization	WCRSA Self-Financing	Net Difference
Debt retirement costs	$1,350,000	2,030,000	$680,000*
O&M cost (Annual @ 1.75 mgd)	513,800	351,000	-162,800
Annual service charge	1,863,800	2,381,000	517,200**

*33.5% Savings on debt retirement costs
**21.7% Savings total (first year)
Average annual savings for twenty years: $321,000

comparative costs show a savings in debt retirement costs and higher costs for O&M but an overall net cost savings for privatization. The capital cost of the facility as submitted by the privatizer was $16,621,000. Total project cost, including financing and trunk lines, was projected to be $18,166,000.

A second important reason for privatizing was the savings in time. The construction schedule placed the operating date fifteen months from start of construction. In late December 1985, WCRSA signed a service contract with the service provider, Merscot IV, Inc., the managing general partner of Merscot-Greenville Partnership (a South Carolina general partnership), essentially Metcalf & Eddy, Inc., and parent company Research-Cottrell. Industrial revenue bonds in the amount of $19,340,000 were issued by Greenville County for loan to the Merscot-Greenville Partnership to finance the project. The bonds were limited obligation bonds, meaning that they did not require a tax or debt increase for the county. In this arrangement, the privatizer had invested some $3,817,000 of equity. Figure 10.1 shows the transaction, the flow of funds, and the relationships among the issuer of the bonds, the trustee, the service provider, and the authority. The authority is obligated to pay a service charge to the service provider pursuant to the service contract. This service charge has two components, a facility base charge (FBC) and an operations and maintenance (O&M) charge. The FBC is a set cost and does not change annually; however, the O&M charge is subject to an adjustment based on a change in wastewater flow and inflation.

The WCRSA privatization project was developed and implemented at

Figure 10.1   Privatization Structure, Western Carolina Regional Sewer
Authority Project

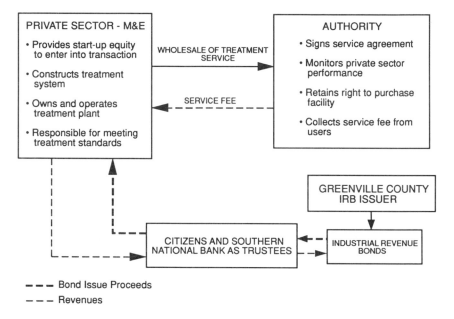

--- Bond Issue Proceeds
--- Revenues

the local level as a partnership between the WCRSA and Metcalf & Eddy,
Inc. (M&E). No national or state policy existed to provide a framework
for development of the project. However, state laws had to be revised in
order for the project to proceed and the DHEC, the state environmental
regulatory agency, played a significant role in the implementation of the
project. A four-member technical advisory team made up the basic
group that structured the project. From early in 1985, when the WCRSA
commission gave the go-ahead for the privatization feasibility study by
Arthur Young, until late 1985, this team provided direction for the
project. Evaluations of the proposals were made by a technical advisory
team and an advisory committee set up specifically to assist the WCRSA
in evaluating the participating firms. The committee made evaluations
that eventually led to a recommendation to the commission of the firm
to be the service provider.

Actions that were taken on several issues that were encountered
during the privatization decision process ultimately contributed to the
deprivatization of the deal. First, during this process, a decision was
made to proceed with completion of the WTW design before a privatizer
was selected. While initially it was thought best to leave the final design

up to the privatizer, the decision to proceed was based on saving time and to provide a better estimate of project costs that could be used to evaluate the privatization proposal. The initial design, completed before the privatizer was selected, was for an extended aeration process. The privatizer preferred a different system. In the context of the requirements and efficiencies of integrated design, construction, and operation, the changes were essential. However, the end result was increased costs of the project.

Second, several items were addressed in the legal area. It was difficult to determine final legal authority for the project. DHEC, the regional council, the authority, and others were involved at various points. In all, permits were required from ten, or more, different agencies. In addition, the issue of the use of IDBs for WTW construction had to be addressed through a revision of state law. While the revision was approved, the amendments included other provisions, such as council of government review, a fiscal impact statement, and procurement restrictions, that made the privatization effort more difficult and thus more costly.

A third issue involved the National Pollutant Discharge Elimination System (NPDES) permit. M&E applied for the NPDES permit after its selection as the service provider. Because of the level of public concern about the project, it was May 30, 1986, before DHEC issued the permit with an effective date of June 16, 1986. Most importantly, the NPDES permit that was issued contained revised, more stringent effluent and odor-control requirements. These revisions further increased the total costs of the project up to the $19.4 million level.

Because of the range of factors presented in the WCRSA case, the components of the project were not fully integrated in the manner that other case studies suggest is required for a successful privatization project. During the design phase, only the engineering firm, the WCRSA staff, and the consulting firm were highly involved. During the construction stage only the builder, an M&E subcontractor, was highly involved in the process. The WCRSA director and engineer were somewhat less involved, as was the engineering firm. In the implementation stage the WCRSA board authorized the design firm to supervise the process.

The WCRSA privatized project appeared to be an attractive public-private partnership for both the privatizer and the authority. However, from the start, the project encountered a series of factors that increased the total cost of the project and complicated the relationships among the state and local and the public and private participants. Among these factors was a generalized uncertainty about how a single privatized

WTW would function in the context of the thirty other publicly owned and operated WTWs in the WCRSA. While it is difficult to define or quantify the impact of this factor, it appears to have been one cause, from the perspective of the WCRSA, that led to the deprivatization of the WTW.

A specific problem for privatization in the authority context was that O&M costs were higher for the privatized WTW facility than for those owned and operated by the authority. This is true because the authority has in place the staff, equipment, and other resources to maintain its facilities, resources that a single community may not have. The authority already has an "economy of scale" cost advantage in O&M services.

In 1988, the facility was bought by the WCRSA from Research-Cottrell for a negotiated sum of $4.6 million, which included the estimated equity investment in the plant by Research-Cottrell. WCRSA assumed all debt on the outstanding bonds. Thus the WCRSA facility is the first WTW privatization project to be sold by the privatizer back to public ownership. In this case deprivatization occurred.

Several factors can be identified that contributed to the deprivatization of this facility, each of which addresses a core element of successful privatization. First, the sale of the WCRSA facility was initiated by the privatizer. During the course of the WCRSA project, Research-Cottrell, the privatizer's parent company, underwent a leveraged buy-out (LBO). Following the LBO, major personnel changes were made and the company needed to increase its cash position. Initially, an attempt was made by the privatizer to sell the facility to a passive financial holding company. In this case M&E would have, as a part of the deal, retained the twenty-year O&M contract. However, the WCRSA exercised its contract option to buy the facility, and subsequently a five-year renewable O&M contract was signed with M&E.

Other factors also contributed to the deprivatization of the WCRSA facility. They included a general concern about the overall acceptability of the partnership in terms of the economics, politics, and management of the deal. That is, the financial advantages of the deal for both the privatizer and the authority were never concluded to be as productive as expected and costs were higher than expected. Second, as previously noted, to some extent the WCRSA was uncomfortable with the arrangement of having a single privately owned WTW in the authority along with thirty publicly owned units. The WCRSA case is the only WTW privatization project undertaken in the 1980s by a regional authority that owned several other plants. The lessons learned in this project may indiciate some fundamental differences between a stand-alone project and a project undertaken by an authority operating additional facilities.

The state legal context of the WCRSA privatization project also contributed to the decision to deprivatize the facility. Specifically, if the state tax laws did not exempt the facility from the property tax, this additional cost would further limit the economic advantages of the deal. Problems also occurred with the procurement laws and with state agency relationships in getting a permit. And, importantly, the decision to segment the design of the facility from its construction and operation violated an important element of successful privatization. In part, the desire to close a deal before the end of 1985 may well have contributed to each of these problems.

From the perspective of some, the purchase of the facility was a good opportunity to resolve two additional and unaddressed issues in privatization. The first issue involved the question of the fair market value of the facility at the end of the contract period. The second involved the loss of public accountability and control over the unknowns in a privatized project. WCRSA ownership gives the authority control over the unknowns. Participants in this project, however, stated that privatization could have a place in some communities. It can provide a timely and quality response to meet WTW needs.

In summary, while the WCRSA project was a pre-1986 privatization deal, and thus had the opportunity to maximize tax and cost savings and system and process advantages, it nevertheless failed to do so for a number of reasons. To the extent that the project violated the requirements that make privatization work, it increased costs, lost political support, and ultimately was dissolved. This conclusion is consistent with the findings presented in the previous chapters to the effect that privatization, while initially driven by private sector tax incentives, is a product of multiple factors. Tax incentives, while helpful, are not sufficient to ensure success. Rather, the formal and informal mechanisms needed to link and sustain the sectors in their changed roles in privatization were not sufficiently present to sustain the WCRSA project.

11

Privatization
Revolution, Reform, or Regression?

Capital-intensive privatization of wastewater treatment works was promoted by the private sector in the 1980s as a means of implementing national clean water policy, meeting local clean water needs, and providing a market opportunity for the WTW industry. In terms of this study, privatization is one form of public-private partnership; it involves private sector participation in many or all aspects of infrastructure project development. These may include project finance, design, construction, ownership, operation, and maintenance. Thus, privatization differs from contracting for services in substantial ways.

This book addresses the politics and economics of privatization as one form of public-private partnership. Chapter 11 presents the general conclusions reached. The central question is one of the nature and implications of privatization in political and economic terms. Is it a passing fad, a revolution, a reform, or a regression in the relationship of the public and private sectors in the conduct of public business?

The overall conclusion is that privatization is a feasible and viable option to meet, efficiently and productively, some infrastructure needs. However, in the public-private partnership movement, privatization, at least successful privatization, is a paradox. Rather than reducing government, which it may do in some ways, more fundamentally it brings the private sector into the policy and management structures of the public sector. The private sector becomes more like the public sector than the reverse. To understand this paradox and its applied implications is to understand the requirements of successful privatization—how privatization works.

Privatization evolved as an opportunistic consequence of the changing context of national law. The larger political and economic context for the development of privatization was one of declining resources, increasing needs, a desire to reduce the role of government, and faith in the efficiency of the private market. The result was a general movement toward greater reliance on the private sector for the provision, production, or delivery of traditional public services. The first wastewater privatization deals in the 1980s reflected tax law changes in 1981 and 1982 that provided benefits to the private sector for investment in infrastructure projects. These deals included elements of private sector ownership and financing that made tax benefits available to the private sector but not to the public sector. The gross effect was to reduce project costs to the authorities involved.

In the period from 1982 through 1985, a number of municipalities and other authorities in the United States considered WTW privatization, and some adopted it. The perceived relative advantage of privatization motivated these authorities to try to deal with the numerous financial, legal, political, and administrative barriers inherent in this option. The privatization process is extremely complex, carries high transaction costs, and poses a range of implementation difficulties. More basically, the concept itself is poorly understood, is not in a policy context, and remains to be developed. Thus fewer than a dozen authorities chose to proceed. However, their example, combined with increasing infrastructure needs, continued political and ideological interest, and strong industry efforts to promote the option, continues to make privatization an option to meet some infrastructure needs despite the fact that tax reforms in 1986 removed many, but not all, of the tax benefits and changed the structure of privatization.

Several reasons exist why privatization merits attention as a national option. They include continuing national attention to and regulatory enforcement of clean water policy; continuing need for WTW project development; the growing national debt and the pressure on the national budget generated by the deficit reduction process; general awareness and expectation of increasing private sector participation in the production of a broad array of traditional public sector services; some possible salutary effects of the 1986 tax reform in this area; and continuing industry and local interest in privatization. A final reason is grounded in the political traditions and processes of the United States. The U.S. political system is a pragmatic one that encourages innovation to address specific problems. Privatization is an innovative option that has been considered in numerous jurisdictions and tried in some, with varying degrees of success. It remains available to help meet clean water objectives.

The reference to availablity raises a practical issue that has been submerged through much of the study but now surfaces: feasibility. Much of the evidence presented here bears on the feasibility of privatization in both political and economic terms. The answer to the feasibility question depends in part on the meaning assigned to the term *feasible*. A useful distinction can be made between national feasibility and local feasibility. National feasibility refers to a condition in which privatization is a well-understood and readily accessible mechanism for WTW project development that local authorities everywhere can routinely and confidently include in the menu of options to which they refer. Under this definition, national feasibility implies that privatization affords a plausible alternative mechanism for implementing national policy and meeting clean water needs on a large scale. Privatization is at present not feasible in this sense, although it has the capacity to become so.

The local feasibility question has to do with whether it is possible in practical terms for a local authority to proceed with privatization, if it wishes to do so and can reach agreement with a privatizer. Here the answer is definitely positive. Thus the question of feasibility becomes, in part, an issue of what problems have to be addressed and what steps have to be undertaken to transform the local option into a national policy and option. To answer these questions and to place privatization in the broader theoretically grounded framework of public-private partnerships and public policy, we return to the theory-sketch developed in Chapter 1.

Evaluating the Theory-Sketch of Privatization

It is useful to recall what the theory-sketch and hypotheses developed in Chapter 1 were and were not intended to do. They were intended neither to build an ideological case for privatization nor to list a set of conclusions the data would serve to confirm. Rather, they presented a reasonably coherent and testable interpretation of how privatization works and why it works as it does. The data and analyses in the intervening chapters test, to varying degrees and in varying ways, the hypotheses derived from the theory-sketch. The results of that exercise permit evaluation—and require some reformulation—of the theory-sketch.

The Politics and Economics of Privatization

Privatization is both an economic adaptation and a political strategy: It can best be understood through reference to the interaction of political and economic factors. Each of the chapters presents evidence touching directly or indirectly on this thesis, and in every case the connectedness of politics and economics is in some way apparent. Perhaps most fundamentally, during the past decade political and economic factors combined first to create, and then to uncreate, a rich soup of privatization opportunities for inclusion on the infrastructure menus of public authorities and private firms. Chapters 2 and 5 detail how the tug and pull of infrastructure needs, water policy, deficit reduction, New Federalism, and tax reforms produced a wildly fluctuating context of national policy in this regard.

In this context, expectations loosened and shifted, and outcomes were surprising in several ways. Privatization emerged in one sense as a competition between the public and private sectors for the production of a public service. The current public-private partnership movement is motivated in part by the notion that the provision of a public service can be more efficient and productive if it is done by, or in emulation of, the private sector. The cases examined in this study lend mixed support to this premise: they show variation. Buried in this variation, however, is an unexpected finding, perhaps a paradox. In the successful privatization projects, the private sector firms adopted more characteristics of, and thus became more like, the public sector rather than vice versa. Common factors in these cases included the reduction or elimination of competition (bidding) and security of market (costs) data. The cases show that sufficient availability and openness of data can exist to allow for public accountability.

Several additional surprising findings deserve mention. First, it seems plausible that decisions in the early privatization cases would have been shaped mainly by economic factors. However, these factors turn out to be secondary to issues of need, local leadership, and perceptions of the privatization option itself. Restated in slightly more general terms, political factors engaged and tended to outweigh economic factors.

Second, common sense also would seem to suggest that privatization, under the tax laws of 1981 and 1982, resulted in a net loss of revenue to the U.S. Treasury when compared with available alternatives. However, the economic analyses in Chapter 6 show that privatization, with the tax benefits of the early 1980s, is essentially revenue neutral to the Treasury when compared to municipal self-financed projects. While this issue is not a direct part of the theory, the results concerning it do bear on the theory. One of the economic hypotheses suggests that in privatization the nature of the good changes from collective to toll. That is, if the private sector takes over from the public sector, the public subsidy will stop and users can be forced to pay for the service they take. The position taken by OMB on tax incentives casts doubt on this interpretation as long as the incentives are in place. The OMB perspective is that through tax benefits, plants are financed by Treasury dollars. Thus, government (meaning the general taxpayer) is subsidizing local service, and the premise of transition from collective to toll good is illusory. The results of the economic analysis, however, support the premise as stated. If tax benefits result in no net loss to Treasury, then privatization does not provide a special subsidy for service. Rather, in the post-1986 form it represents an additional charge (tax) on the consumer.

Third, when the tax benefits were removed in 1986 it seemed possible that the entire privatization industry would lose interest in the privatization option. This turned out not to be the case. What did happen was that firms that had been active in privatization for purposes of obtaining tax benefits did drop out, but firms with long-standing organizational commitments to wastewater treatment remain active and interested based on the integrity of the framework (system and process) of privatization.

These counterintuitive results provide a cautionary backdrop for the discussion that follows: the interaction of politics and economics in privatization is complex and unpredictable enough to limit opportunities for simple comprehensive formulations. The results concerning the main elements of the theory-sketch, however, do offer some partial insights into the mix.

Economics: Time, Cost, Competition, and Efficiency

At the core of the case for privatization are premises alleging inherent efficiencies of time and cost deriving from market competition. It is clear that privatization does much more than provide possible tax benefits; it dramatically changes the system of players involved in project development, the ways in which those players relate to one another, and the processes by which projects are designed, built, and put into operation. The expected savings in time are easy to detect: privatized facilities are designed and completed in a far shorter period than grant-funded facilities or even self-financed facilities developed through more conventional methods.

Expected cost differences are less readily discernible. The statistical analyses do not support the proposition that all privatized plants were designed or built more cheaply than their grant-funded counterparts. The qualitative case studies, however, clearly show that privatized projects can be constructed at less cost. In other words, it is possible to design and build an expensive plant efficiently through privatization. And it is possible that not all privatizers take full advantage of the efficiencies inherent in the privatization system and process of integrating design, construction, and operation.

Privatization challenges the premise of competition. In the theory-sketch, market competition drives economic efficiency and arguably enforces accountability if contracts allow for periodic renegotiation of the privatization relationship. Paradoxically, however, the efficiency of privatization turns out to derive from the absence of competition during design and construction. And this is not all. When the loss of tax benefits reduced the financial attractiveness of privatization after 1986, an apparent result was to reduce the competitive aspect of privatization deals even further. In view of the central role that the premise of competition plays in the theory of public-private partnerships generally, these findings appear to carry import beyond the limits of privatization.

Politics: The Need for Accountability

Important political issues in privatization include public accountability, the relationship between privatization and political institutions, and the multiple objectives of the state, some of which can be lost (affirmative action and prevailing wage rates) in a shift of traditional public services to the private sector. Many authorities that considered privatization, including some that proceeded with it, were deeply concerned about loss of public accountability and control over the public facility and service. Many of the hypotheses derived from the theory-sketch had to do with accountability mechanisms including contract, law, regulation, and the norms of the private sector.

Contract. The privatization industry takes the view that a well-constructed contract increases public accountability because it places responsibility for wastewater treatment and facility operation unambiguously and enforceably on the privatizer. Privatization contracts show that this is not consistently so. Rather than leaving risk with the private sector, where it normally would be, the contracts tended to pass significant portions of it on to the public authorities. This passing on of risk is an example of the change of roles that the theory posits. Here the public authority takes on a characteristic of the private firm. Because the authority presumably gets a lower total cost in return for risk accepted, the redistribution of risk might be fine if (1) the extent to which this happened was clear to the parties and (2) corresponding accountability mechanisms were built into the contracts.

The evidence, however, suggests that the opposite was more nearly true. As the analysis in Chapter 7 concluded, several of the privatizing authorities would have difficulty exiting from the existing relationship. Furthermore, details gained in case study interviews suggest possible gaps in understanding of contract arrangements on the part of some privatizing authorities. In more than one case, it is not clear that the authority can determine just what the cost of the deal has been. In the same way, it is less than clear whether local officials in some cases have a grasp of the accountability mechanisms that are available to them.

The Legal Context. The context of national and state law is also a central element in the development and implementation of privatized projects. Clearly tax legislation is important for privatization. But beyond this fact, the context of national law, and of national policy more generally, is nearly nonexistent.

The situation is different at the level of the states, however, where great variety occurs in legal frameworks and the accountability structures they provide. The section of Chapter 5 dealing with state law provides a catalog of mechanisms through which state law can secure accountability as it changes the traditional roles of the parties in the process. An important part of the future politics of privatization will consist of the kinds of policies Congress and state legislatures enact to provide a positive network of accountability opportunities (as well as economic conditions) for private firms and public authorities at the local level.

The Regulatory Context. An additional element in the future politics of privatization is the manner in which national and state environmental regulatory agencies engage the privatization option. The record to this point is very thin, with the possible exception of the recent campaign for privatization sponsored by the U.S. EPA. This pattern may well be explainable in terms of bureaucratic politics. Federal and state regulatory agencies have done little or nothing to provide a foundation of support and guidance for local authorities interested in this option. While the

1972 Clean Water Act created a state-level institutional capacity for the administration of national water policy, specifically the WTW construction grant program, it did not create the state-level political and financial institutional capacity required to implement privatization. The resulting tension seems likely to increase as state agencies assume additional responsibility for clean water policy implementation and financing under the Water Quality Act of 1987 and as their role in the politics of privatization expands.

It was hypothesized that regulatory involvement in privatization projects would be low enough to permit savings in construction time and efficiency. The results here were mixed: it worked out this way in some states but not in others. Where the regulatory presence was slight, the explanation lay more in the limits of regulatory capacity than in the inherent dynamic of privatization. Thus the issue here is political: can state agencies be empowered and enabled to engage privatization in a manner sufficient to support the accountability requirements of local authorities?

The case studies, however, showed that high-level involvement of state agencies in enforcing national pollution standards contributed positively to privatization. That is, privatization was successful in those states in which compliance enforcement was high and regulatory involvement in privatization was low.

The Politics of the Private Sector. Privatization is essentially the combining of a public need with private capability and resources to create a market opportunity through which the public need is met and a profit is made. Again, several observations and conclusions come forward. The private sector companies that entered the WTW privatization market all did so on the basis of prior related experience and as a way to expand their own market. However, the specific motivation for market entrance ranged from short-term tax benefits and use of existing company capacity in an adverse economic situation to long-term interest in the WTW market. The organizational structure of the privatization components of those companies that entered the WTW market also varies substantially by type of company and motivation for market entrance. Furthermore, these organizational structures have varied substantially with changes in public policy and market conditions. The result is a significant degree of instability in private sector organizational structures with resultant implications for long-term contractual commitments and relationships with the public sector. This instability results in part from changes in the broader framework of national law and forms an integral part of the politics of privatization.

The companies with major and long-term interest in this service area remain committed to a public-private partnership structure and market. However, the majority of the companies report that further tax code revision for public infrastructure projects is warranted and needed, including revised depreciation schedules, arbitrage allowance, expanded bond capacity, and elimination or clarification of the buy-back requirement.

The industry role in privatization involves an element of politics at the level of personal relationships as well. A key element in the successful establishment of a public-private partnership in the WTW privatization area is the set of personal relationships that develop or fail to develop between the public and private sector organizations and personnel. This element is not unexpected, given that privatization to date is an informal process operating outside of any formal public policy structure. In this context, private sector organizational structures, marketing strategies, and personnel have a direct impact on the privatization process. In summary, the selection of a private sector partner is a critical public sector decision.

Changed Roles and Linking Mechanisms

In privatization the roles of the sectors change and linking mechanisms emerge to mesh the dynamics of the two sectors in their changed roles. A successful privatized project requires the establishment of a set of linking mechanisms between the public and private sectors. These mechanisms, once in place, constitute a new and different public-private structure that calls for new organizations, expectations and values, formal and informal rules, individual roles and routines, and management practices. The model of negotiated goals and continuing feedback mechanisms provides insights into how and why these mechanisms can work in support of partnership ventures.

Regression, Revolution, or Reform?

Privatization, in the worldwide and national context, is both a political strategy to alter public-private sector relationships and an economic adaptation to budget deficits, scarce resources, resistance to government growth, and increasing needs for public services. Its complexity permits multiple and sometimes conflicting interpretations. Inappropriately defined and implemented, it can be an unacceptable regression to unfettered private market competition for the provision and production of essential public services. The production of essential public services cannot depend on the forces of the private market. Appropriately understood and implemented, however, privatization can provide the accountability and stability needed to avoid such an outcome.

In its generic form, privatization is not a revolutionary concept. Multiple forms of public-private partnerships have existed throughout history. From time to time the dominant role or emphasis has shifted from the public to the private market or the private to the public. Clearly, the current and foreseeable future is a period of intense interest politically, ideologically, and economically in a strengthened role for the private sector. This period follows a decade or more of promotion of the public choice school of economics and politics and a growing distrust of or decline in confidence in the public sector.

If correctly defined and implemented, privatization constitutes a reformulated approach to conducting the public's business. Privatization is a new form of public-private partnership. It changes both the roles of and the relationships between them. By doing so, it calls for new organizational structures, management strategies, and forms of public accountability. Thus, some reformulation of traditional theory is needed. For instance, the premise of cost advantage is very much contextually influenced. Much more pointedly, the case studies offer a critical test that discredits some of the premises of private market competition. Many scores of interviews in dozens of locations have produced the firm conclusion that in this corner of public-private activity, the role of competition is far more complex and slippery than posited.

The premises concerning changed roles and linking mechanisms are confirmed. The data support an unmistakable pattern of changed roles reflected in linking arrangements. The reason why some of the most basic tenets of traditional privatization theory fall apart is precisely that, in privatization, the roles of the sectors do change, so that the traditional understanding of their dynamics is no longer applicable.

The implications of these changed roles are multiple. First, privatization does not mean the withering away of the state or even the reduction of the state, as called for by the President's Commission on Privatization. Rather, privatization requires the synthesis of the dynamics that govern and fuel each market—public and private. The provision of a vital public service, such as wastewater treatment, cannot be solely a decision of the private market. Further, its provision must be publicly accountable. Yet, the private sector, the data show, can produce and deliver this service in some cases more efficiently than can the public sector. Privatization can integrate the dynamic of each market into a new structure that capitalizes on the strengths of each.

To do so requires the creation of a new public-private structure, characterized by negotiated goals between the sectors and a continuing information and oversight role for each. This structure changes the role and dynamic for each market. The public sector becomes a provider and overseer rather than a producer and deliverer. The private market relinquishes some elements of competition and closed system in exchange for long-term partnership arrangements. If developed and implemented within this framework, privatization can be a viable option to meet some infrastructure needs.

This new structure calls for the development and implementation of revised management forms, organizational structures, and statutory and policy contexts. National and state policy needs to be enacted and implemented to provide structure and guidance for the continued development of privatization. Absent a policy framework with appropriate incentives—sanctions or rewards—states cannot implement privatization, on their own, as a national policy. National agencies could develop and implement a program of guidance, information, and education designed to assist state and local authorities in the development of privatization projects. National tax laws can be revised, where appropriate, to facilitate privatization, including depreciation schedule parity, expanded bond capacity for public works, and elimination of the WTW buy-back provision.

State policy and state agencies likewise could adopt and promulgate a clear policy on privatization. Appropriate state agencies could develop and implement a program of guidance, information, and education designed to assist local authorities in the development of privatization projects. A model state law for privatization could be developed in order for states to provide an adequate and uniform legal structure for privatization, including appropriate provisions for contracts, bidding, taxes, and accountability.

Local authorities can consider privatization as a viable option to meet some local infrastructure needs, specifically wastewater treatment needs. Inasmuch as privatization decisions are influenced at least as much by political and personal factors as by economic ones, local authorities need to establish well-defined processes to address both sets of issues.

Because local authority accountability and responsibility are defined in the privatization contract, it needs to include provisions to assure accountability and assign risk. For example, the provisions may address buy-back options, service fee schedules, O&M agent review, compliance responsibility, changes in circumstances, and related matters. These provisions take on special importance because they accommodate and link the changed roles of the two sectors. Most importantly, privatization must be considered and treated as a continuing public-private partnership rather than as a transfer of function. Thus, inclusion of continuing public oversight procedures is an essential element in the privatization contract.

The private sector must recognize and accept the importance of contract structures that provide public accountability and that incorporate a continuing public oversight role in the privatization structure. The privatization process itself needs to be simplified through the standardization of the contract process and the reduction of transaction costs. And, inasmuch as privatization requires the substitution of long-term contracts for short-term competitive processes, attention must be paid to methods and contract provisions that will assure stability and confidence in long-term service provision in privatization contracts.

These observations flow not only from the findings of this study but also from the context of contemporary public life in the United States. Two relevant facts of public life in the 1990s are that needs for infrastructure service development are enormous and that government cannot meet these needs by itself. The result is that an increased role of the private sector in meeting such needs appears highly likely, even inevitable. Attention will therefore turn to the requirements of public-private partnerships. However, a mechanical conception of these, including public accountability, will not be adequate nor will a mechanical conception of economic efficiency in the tradition of Adam Smith. Rather, a new normative fuel will be needed to drive the mechanisms that mesh the dynamics of the public and private sectors.

Appendix A
State Laws on Privatization

General Enabling Laws Authorizing Contracts with Private Entities for the Performance of Traditional Services

1. Alaska: (Franchise) *Alaska Stat.* § 29.35.060.
2. Colorado: *Colo. Rev. Stat. Ann.* § 30-11.101.
3. Florida: (General franchise) *Fla. Stat. Ann.* §§ 180.14–18.
4. Georgia: *Ga. Const.*, art. 9, § 2, ¶ 3.
5. Indiana: *Ind. Code* §§ 5-17-4-2, 36-4-8-12.
6. Minnesota: (General privatization law) *Minn. Stat. Ann.* §§ 471A.01–.12, 297a.258, 474.02–.03.
7. Missouri: *Mo. Stat. Ann.* § 70.220.
8. North Carolina: *N.C. Gen. Stat.* § 153A-449.
9. North Carolina: *N.C. Gen. Stat.* § 160A-20.1.
10. Oregon: (Franchises) *Or. Rev. Stat.* § 459.200.
11. Rhode Island: *R.I. Gen. Laws* § 45-2-4.
12. Utah: *Utah Code Ann.* § 73-10d-1 to -7.
13. Wisconsin: (Franchises) *Wis. Stat. Ann.* § 66.061.

Leasing or Financing

1. Colorado: (Lease-purchase) *Colo. Rev. Stat.* § 31-151-801 to -802.
2. Colorado: (Lease-purchase/corrections) *Colo. Rev. Stat.* § 30-11-104.1 to -104.2.
3. Florida: *Fla. Stat. Ann.* §§ 159.28(4), .285, .287.

4. Illinois: (Water & sewerage) *Ill. Rev. Stat.*, ch. 24, §§ 11-137-1, -2, -5.
5. Indiana: (Solid waste) *Ind. Code* §§ 36-9-30-5, -24 to -32.
6. Indiana: (Sewage) *Ind. Code Ann.* §§ 36-9-24-1 to -14.
7. Louisiana: (Corrections) *La. Rev. Stat. Ann.* § 39:1780–:1794 (1985).
8. Montana: (Solid waste) *Mont. Code Ann.* §§ 75-10-101 to -125.
9. South Carolina: (Industrial development projects) *S.C. Code Ann.* §§ 4-29-10 to -14-50.
10. Tennessee: *Tenn. Code Ann.* §§ 7-51-901 to -908.
11. Tennessee: *Tenn. Code Ann.* §§ 9-21-101 to -117.

Sewerage, Sewage Treatment, and Water Supply*

1. Alabama: (Sewage & water) *Ala. Code* §§ 11-97-1 to -27.
2. Arizona: (Sewage) *Ariz. Rev. Stat. Ann.* §§ 48-2001, -2011.
3. Arkansas: (Sewage) *Ark. Stat. Ann.* §§ 8-5-601 to -612.
4. California: (Sewage & sewerage) *Cal. Gov't Code* §§ 54250–256 (1986); *Cal. Pub. Util. Code* §§ 10013–14.
5. Delaware: (Water & sewer) *Del. Code Ann.*, Tit. 16, §§ 1401, 1406.
6. Georgia: (Industrial wastewater treatment) *Ga. Code Ann.* § 36-60-2.
7. Illinois: (Water & sewerage) *Ill. Rev. Stat.*, ch. 24, § 11-137-1, -2, -5.
8. Indiana: (Sewage) *Ind. Code Ann.* §§ 36-9-24-1 to -14.
10. Kentucky: (Water & sewage) *Ky. Rev. Stat.* §§ 107.700–.770.
11. Louisiana: (Sewage) *La. Rev. Stat. Ann.* §§ 33:4169–:4169.1.
12. Maryland: (Water, sewage, & solid waste) *Md. Health-Envtl. Code Ann.* § 9-905, -907, -945.
13. Maryland: (Water & sewage) *Md. Health-Envtl. Code Ann.* § 9-635.
15. Michigan: (Sewage) *Mich. Comp. Laws Ann.* § 123.245, .246.
16. Minnesota: (Sewage & water) *Minn. Stat. Ann.* §§ 471A.01, 297A.258, 474.02–.03.
17. Mississippi: (Sewage) *Miss. Code Ann.* §§ 21-27-161 to -191.
18. Mississippi: (Water & sewage) *Miss. Code Ann.* §§ 19-5-151, -175 to -179.
19. Nebraska: (Sewage franchises) *Neb. Rev. Stat.* § 14-365.05.

22. Nevada: *Nev. Rev. Stat.* §§ 269.129, 268.083. §§ 269.129(2) and 268.083(2).
23. New Jersey: (Sewage treatment) *N.J. Stat. Ann.* §§ 58:27-1–:27-18.
25. New York: *N.Y. Gen. Mun. Law* §§ 120-120(aa) (McKinney 1984).
26. South Dakota: *S.D. Comp. Laws Ann.* § 9-40-4.1.
28. Tennessee: *Tenn. Code Ann.* §§ 7-51-901 to -908.
33. Washington: *1986 Wash. Laws,* ch. 244.
34. West Virginia: *W.Va. Code* §§ 8-19-10, 8-20-9.

*Gaps in numbering of the list reflect omission of laws dealing only with water supply.

Source: From *Compendium of Privatization Laws,* compiled by Nutter, McLennan & Fish, Boston, Mass. Copyright 1986, 1990 by the Privatization Council.

Appendix B
Economic Model of Tax Incentives

The economic model used to analyze the impact of tax incentives on privatization considers the construction of a hypothetical wastewater treatment facility that cost $100,000 and will operate for twenty-five years regardless of whether it was municipally constructed or privatized. Despite the evidence that a privatized facility might cost less, the assumption of equal cost is made to focus exclusively on the tax differences. Three separate scenarios are compared. The municipally owned and operated plant is financed with tax-exempt bonds and pays no taxes. The early 1980s facility is owned and operated privately through a service contract with a municipality. This firm will be assumed to be operating under the provisions of the Economic Recovery Tax Act of 1981 but not under the provisions of the Deficit Reduction Act of 1984 or the Tax Reform Act of 1986. The late 1980s firm will operate a privatized facility under the 1986 provisions. In cases where there are transitional periods, the law after the transition is applied. The differences in each case are as follows.

Depreciation. From 1981 to 1986 ACRS depreciation was available. ACRS allowed some property to be depreciated over 5 years and other property to be depreciated over a 15-year period (Peat Marwick Mitchell and Co. 1985:II-3). After the Tax Reform Act of 1986 nonresidential property is depreciated using straight-line depreciation over 31.5 or 40 years, or for 125 percent of the lease time if the property is leased (Arthur Andersen and Co. 1986:252–53). In fact, municipal wastewater treatment plants have an average depreciation rate (ADR) midpoint of 25 years. Even if a facility were operated under a 25-year contract with a buy-back provision, 125 percent of 25 years is 31.25 years, so for purposes of this study a privatized facility will be assumed to be depreciated over 31.5 years.

Other features of the 1986 tax law affect depreciation as well, most notably the requirement that fewer construction costs are allowed to be expensed. Because of the complicated detail that these provisions would introduce, the model used compares a 15-year ACRS depreciation schedule for the entire facility with a 31.5-year straight-line schedule for the purpose of establishing the effects of tax reform. The most favorable 15-year ACRS schedule was used for the early 1980s scenario, while the 31.5-year straight-line depreciation was used for the late 1980s scenario. The amount to be depreciated in all cases assumes some salvage value that is not depreciated. The assumption is made that the firm has income from other sources against which any losses on this project can be taken for tax purposes.

Investment Tax Credit. Prior to 1986 a 10 percent investment tax credit was allowed but was repealed with the Tax Reform Act of 1986. In the model used, the investment tax credit reduces the cost to the local authority of a pre-1986 private facility by 10 percent when compared to a current project. The municipal facility and the late 1980s firm cannot take advantage of the investment tax credit.

Capital Gains. Prior to the Tax Reform Act of 1986 capital gains accruing to corporations were taxed at a maximum rate of 28 percent, compared with the prior maximum corporate tax rate of 46 percent. Capital gains after 1986 are taxed at the ordinary income corporate rate, which is a maximum of 34 percent (after a transitional year in 1987 when the rate was 40 percent). This change has the effect, first, of raising the tax rate on capital gains and, second, of reducing the advantage of taking income as a capital gain rather than as ordinary income.

At the end of the project all three scenarios in the study return the market value of the plant to the owner. Inasmuch as the market value at the end of the project does not necessarily equal the value to which the facility has been depreciated, the two privatized scenarios provide for the firm to pay capital gains taxation on the difference. While the tax rates for ordinary income and capital gains are now the same, the distinction remains between the two types of income. This distinction could be significant if at some time in the future capital gains are again taxed at a lower rate. While this distinction may be of interest, the model treats capital gains as being the same as ordinary income after 1986.

Tax-Exempt Bond Financing. One way to reduce the cost of a privatized facility is to finance it through tax-exempt industrial development bonds. The 1986 tax act restricts the types of activities that can be financed in this way. For example, convention centers, parking lots, and pollution control facilities may no longer be financed with tax-exempt bonds. Other types of activities have a cap on the amount of revenue that can be raised through industrial development bonds in each state. After 1987 the cap is $50 per capita or $150 million, whichever is greater.

Depending upon the circumstances in a particular state in a particular year, the cap may or may not be a constraint on a privatization effort. Quite clearly, the new law disallows this type of financing for privatized convention centers, but for wastewater treatment facilities the cap may or may not be a factor. The model considers this cap to preclude tax-exempt financing in the late 1980s scenario. Because the cap is state-wide, other interests in the state have an incentive to dissuade any particular municipality from engaging in tax-exempt financing for a privately owned facility because it could reduce their ability to raise tax-exempt funds. (See Levitan 1987 for a summary of the tax law changes as they affect municipal bonds.) Thus, both the early 1980s scenario and the municipally owned and operated scenario assume tax-exempt bond financing, while the late 1980s scenario requires private financing.

The assumption is made in the model that the difference in the market interest rate and the rate for tax-exempt bonds is equal to the tax savings accruing to the owners of the tax-exempt bonds. In the real world the actual tax savings will depend upon the particular tax situations of the owners of the bonds—which would be complicated to model accurately—but the simplifying assumption is justified because for identical projects with identical risk factors and repayment periods, the only reason why the taxed and tax-exempt interest rates should vary is due to the tax savings.

These assumptions in the model are made in order to compare the most favorable tax treatment possible, the early 1980s case, with the least favorable tax treatment possible, the late 1980s case. The municipal ownership case is used as a benchmark for both cases to see whether the federal treasury is subsidizing privatization efforts and, if so, to what degree.

The tax considerations in each scenario are important to three parties in the model: the municipality, the federal government, and the private firm in the privatization cases. Calculation of the net costs and benefits to each is a present value problem, but it is complicated by several factors: (1) the appropriate discount rate for the present value calculation, (2) the interest rate for both taxable and tax-exempt bonds, (3) the inflation rate, (4) the salvage value of the facility after twenty-five years, and (5) the taxable income that accrues to the private firm in the privatization cases. These factors are varied in the model to judge their effects.

In order to examine a wide variety of scenarios, the model was developed into a Pascal computer program. The model considers the net present value of the tax benefit for each type of arrangement for each of twenty-five years in the assumed life of the project. The tax factors in the model to be accounted for are depreciation, the investment tax credit, the treatment of capital gains, the use of tax-exempt bond financing, and the payment of income tax on the profits earned from the facility.

Depreciation. The municipally operated facility pays no taxes so does not take depreciation for tax purposes. The early 1980s firm takes ACRS depreciation while the late 1980s firm takes straight-line depreciation, which is 3.2 percent of the depreciable value of the project. The project is assumed to cost $100,000 and will have a salvage value, which is one of the variables in the model. The model assumes the same expected rate of inflation for each year of the project for the sake of simplicity.

Investment Tax Credit. The early 1980s firm is assumed to take a 10 percent investment tax credit in the initial year of operation. This credit is not available to either the municipal operation or the late 1980s scenario. Thus, for the $100,000 project, no inflation adjustment is made because the investment tax credit provides its benefits at the beginning of the project.

Capital Gains. At the end of the project all three scenarios return the market value of the plant to the owner. The municipality keeps this market value while the firms in both privatization scenarios are liable for capital gains taxation on the difference between the market value and the depreciated value. The depreciated value of the facility is equal to $100,000 minus the accumulated depreciation.

In the model, the depreciated value of the facility is in both cases adjusted for inflation. Inflation produces phantom capital gains that could be substantial after twenty-five years, so inflation can have a major effect on this component of the tax advantage, although in a present value setting anything happening twenty-five years in the future will have a relatively small effect on a present value calculation. The tax paid on the capital gain is 23 percent in the early 1980s scenario, or half the ordinary income tax rate, while in the late 1980s scenario the rate is the 34 percent ordinary income rate.

Tax-Exempt Financing. The municipal operation and the early 1980s scenario allow tax-exempt financing with the attendant lower interest costs and the lower federal tax collections. The late 1980s case is as-sumed to use taxable bonds. It is assumed that the difference in the rates is attributable to the tax savings to the owners of the bonds so that the tax advantage to the municipal bond issue equals the cost to the federal treasury of allowing tax-exempt financing.

The model assumes that twenty-five-year bonds are sold on which interest is paid for the life of the project. A sinking fund would need to be established to repay the principal, but the model does not include a provision for the disposition of the sinking fund. A municipal rate and a private market rate are parameters in the model, and the rate advantage to tax-exempt financing is the difference between the two rates. This rate advantage directly lowers the cost of the municipal and early 1980s proj-ects but must be adjusted for inflation to account for the lower real value that would be produced by inflation. No adjustment is made to the late 1980s privatization because it is assumed that municipal bond financing cannot be used either because of the tax-exempt debt limit imposed on the state or because the tax-exempt financing that was once allowed is no longer allowed under the current law.

Income Tax. The private firm would undertake the privatization effort because, presumably, there is a profit to be earned from the undertaking. The contract is assumed to be written so that the taxable income earned will not be affected by inflation, so no adjustment is made for inflation. Note that the contract will call for an exchange of a service for a price rather than for a particular profit rate, so the profit would only be known after the fact, although both the municipality and the firm would have a good estimate beforehand.

Value Problem. The model contains seven parameters that can be chosen to compare various scenarios. The six already discussed are (1) the market interest rate, (2) the municipal bond rate, (3) the inflation rate, (4) the salvage value of the facility for depreciation purposes, (5) the market value of the facility after twenty-five years, and (6) the profit accruing to a privatizing firm. The final variable is (7) the appropriate discount rate. A substantial literature exists on choosing the appropriate discount rate for public sector activity (see Holcombe 1988a:343–45 for an overview of the issues), but the model developed here allows several rates to be chosen to see what difference the choice of discount rates makes to the overall tax advantages to privatization. The final step in the model uses the present value formula to take the present value of each case so they can be compared.

Notes

1. The wastewater treatment deals lacked certain technical, political, and financial features that had made the comprehensive privatization of solid-waste facilities a plausible strategy even before tax law changes in 1981 and 1982 offered inducements for such deals. The technical difference was that solid-waste facilities required advanced, proprietary technology available only from a few firms that had an interest in building entire facilities. The political difference was that many cities had some form of wastewater treatment and had in place an established cadre of technicians and bureaucrats who claimed to be able, and were certainly willing, to assist in all phases of new sewage plant project work. On the other hand, few cities had existing solid-waste facilities or staff accustomed to dealing with them. Even where technical staffs were available, seldom did expertise exist to deal with the advanced technology of solid-waste combustion processes. The financial difference was that the solid-waste deals involved two cash streams not available in the case of wastewater treatment facilities. First, the solid-waste facility could charge tipping fees for waste brought to it. These were typically much more realistic than the nonexistent or highly subsidized fees usually charged for municipal wastewater treatment. Second, solid-waste combustion facilities were able to sell electricity they could produce through cogeneration.

2. One of the authors would be willing to expand the issue arena to suggest that the study of privatization and partnerships more generally can also serve as one (although only one) potentially useful "lens" (Allison 1971), or means of insight, into a complex of problems that nations now face. The idea is not that privatization should be seen as a splendid hammer that can be used to beat down or resolve a whole array of policy problems. But multiple recent and important contributions to the policy literature do point to a need for some new, and perhaps revolutionary, thinking about how the United States is organized to maintain a stable, productive, and competitive position in the world economy

and polity. This thinking will have to do with "interorganizational configurations" (Wise 1990). These configurations will need to cut across sectors to mesh and link economic productivity (Savas 1987) and development (Sharp 1990) with "synthetic innovation" (Kash 1989), effective administration (Kettl 1988), and effective government (Nelson 1987). The necessary thinking cannot be reactive or unidimensional: the results of president Ronald Reagan's decade of bashing government and its bureaucrats and invoking unrestrained reliance on the private sector have plainly been disastrous. At the same time, it would be counterproductive to reject the partnership movement by bashing the private sector for its insistence on profit. One proactive option is to explore and engage partnership experiences as one source of insights into "what actually happens" (Leopold von Ranke, quoted by Stern 1957:57), theoretically as well as empirically, when innovative and experimental interorganizational configurations are developed as means to serve both public and private ends in an era of global change.

3. The observations and work on which this study is based were conducted over a period of years. One of the authors became involved in 1983, as a private citizen, in the city of Auburn's review of privatization. Both authors were active in small projects supported by Metcalf & Eddy, Inc., an engineering company, and by the United States Environmental Protection Agency (U.S. EPA). From late 1986 to early 1989, the authors undertook a comprehensive national study with the support of Auburn University and the United States Geological Survey. This study is referred to below as "the project." Throughout this period, and especially during the project, a combination of research methods was used to address the question of the political and economic feasibility of the privatization of wastewater treatment works (WTWs). These methods included mail surveys and on-site interviews based on both structured and semistructured schedules; aggregate analysis of data generated by surveys and provided by other sources, including industry, state agencies, and the U.S. EPA; reviews of technical literature and legal materials; and economic modeling. Six different mail questionnaire or interview instruments were used to collect data from local authorities, state agencies, and firms in the financial, engineering, and construction industries. Twenty-nine case studies were conducted of municipal and other water authorities. The authorities were located in fifteen states in all regions of the country. The case studies included authorities that had privatized WTWs, authorities that had considered or were considering privatization, and authorities, chosen for comparative purposes, that had EPA-funded or self-financed WTWs. Case study data were compiled from surveys, telephone and on-site interviews, and aggregate data. In addition to the case study interviews, on-site interviews were conducted with more than fifty persons in municipal or other water authorities, state agencies, law firms, financial and accounting firms, banks, national interest group organizations, national government agencies, the Congress, and firms in the privatization business. In many cases multiple interviews

were conducted with individual persons or within individual organizations over the life of the project. Comments from these interviews are quoted throughout this book without specific attribution. Two separate surveys were conducted of fifteen privatization-related companies in the fields of engineering, construction, and operations and maintenance, with one survey conducted at the beginning of the project period and the second conducted at the end. All the companies have been involved in some way in privatization projects or in attempts to privatize. Aggregate data analyses were performed on data supplied by EPA in Washington, D.C., and by EPA regional offices. Economic models were developed and applied to these data as well.

4. The relationship between the public and private sectors varies substantially among nation-states. For an excellent review of the impact of these relationships on public-private partnerships see Brooks 1984 and Lindblom 1982.

5. In at least one important tradition of political and economic analysis, the role of capital immediately raises a host of ideological issues (see Marx 1965 and the preface to Marx 1981). While acknowledging the role and value of these issues in political analysis (Habermas 1973), we do not address them in depth.

6. A merchant facility is a speculative venture: a private sector firm builds it in the belief that demand for its services will occur.

7. Garcia, at 546, 83 L. Ed. 2d 1016, 105 S. Ct. 1005, quoting Gerhardt, 304 U.S., at 427, 82 L. Ed. 1427, 58 S. Ct. 969.

8. See, for example, Johnson and Heilman 1987b; Moe 1987; Sullivan 1987; and Zimmerman 1987. See also Morgan and England 1988.

9. See Goldman and Mokuvos 1984.

10. An excellent practitioner-oriented study of solid-waste facility privatization by Beck et al. (1988) suggests that despite the differences between solid-waste and wastewater facilities, many issues and relationships are common to the two kinds of cases.

11. This literature review, in substantial parts, appeared in a somewhat different version in Heilman and Johnson 1989.

12. AFSCME (1983) raises these questions pointedly. O'Toole (1988b) provides some tentative answers based on case study data organized to illuminate the interplay of multiple policy goals.

13. The notion of "systems" is particularly helpful because it illuminates the profound changes that public-private partnerships bring into play. In partnership arrangements, the private sector takes over one or more functions routinely performed by the public sector. For example, in privatization, the private firm develops, and in many cases contributes some of, the financing for public projects. In this process, it takes a shortcut through the cycle of activity in the political system, as commonly described by Easton (1965) and others. It brings the norms and processes of the market to bear on a problem of public finance driven by the political processes of the public sector. In this way, core political processes (in the functional areas of interest aggregation, articulation, and

conversion) are circumvented. Political and economic issues and norms are thrown together, absent the mediating effects of the input part of the political subsystem as commonly represented in the systems framework. In other words, when the private sector acts directly to contribute supports to meet demands in the public arena, the routine flow of activity, resources, and information through the political system is significantly interrupted and rearranged.

14. This section is based in part on an excellent critical review of E. S. Savas, *Privatization: The Key to Better Government*, prepared for a seminar in Public-Private Administration and Policy by John Morris, a doctoral student (Morris 1989).

15. The idea of a theory-sketch is suggested by Hempel's (1968:410) discussion of an explanation sketch. He described it as "presenting the general outlines of what might well be developed, by gradual elaboration and supplementation, into a more closely reasoned explanatory argument, based on hypotheses which are stated more fully and which permit a critical appraisal by reference to empirical evidence." Because the present sketch is used to generate hypotheses that later chapters test to varying degrees, the term used here is *theory-sketch*.

16. The hypotheses are phrased positively, rather than in the form of null hypotheses, because to use null hypotheses would obscure the joint, theoretically driven meaning the hypotheses intend to convey concerning how privatization may work. That is, this set of hypotheses is intended to serve heuristic as well as methodological purposes. The form of the null hypothesis assumes nothing happens or no differences are found. Such statements can have meaning, taken one at a time. but they cannot meaningfully reflect a theory of anything because they describe the absence of relationships rather than a coherent set of relationships. In other words, a story in which nothing happens is meaningless. This perspective draws on the "narrative" theory of explanation developed by Polkinghorne (1988).

17. In part, Chapter 2 is presented in the material in Johnson and Heilman, 1987a.

18. For brief historical accounts see EPA 1984; Illinois EPA 1987; Peat Marwick Main and Co. 1987; and Dilger 1986.

19. The policy literature has long included the notion of "unintended consequences" of policy. The concept applies to policy outcomes. In this case, however, the "opportunistic consequence" of policy is applied to the development, informally in the case of privatization, of new policy.

20. A detailed analysis of the diffusion of privatization is included in Johnson and Heilman 1990.

21. The authors extend appreciation to the many personnel who contributed to the Auburn case study. In particular, we thank Douglas J. Watson, city manager, Jan Dempsey, mayor of Auburn, and Dr. H. C. Morgan, of Auburn University, for their review of and comments on the study. The case study was

based in part on the master's thesis of Alfred Davis, a graduate research assistant at Auburn University.

22. The material in Chapter 4, in part, is presented in Heilman and Johnson 1989.

23. The decision to rely on case study data reflects both the nature of privatization and the small number of plants in existence. Hatry (1987:1) observes that "the appropriateness and usefulness of any method of privatization is highly situational. Success depends on many factors likely to be individual to the particular agency, at the particular location, and at the particular point in time." Netzer (1984) expresses a similar view. The design and construction of a WTW are complex activities that depend on the details of local geography, demography, water usage, stream characteristics, socioeconomic structure, political culture, and the role played by the state and federal environmental regulatory agencies. Thus, the case study approach, supplemented by summary quantitative data, was possible and appropriate.

24. Because some of the pre-1986 WTW privatization deals were undertaken by regional authorities rather than individual cities, the governmental units involved are referred to as *authorities* rather than as *cities*. The authorities involved are: Auburn, Alabama; Pelham, Alabama; Chandler, Arizona; Gilbert, Arizona; Downingtown, Pennsylvania; East Aurora, New York; Greenville, South Carolina (Gilder Creek plant); and Culpeper County, Virginia. The analysis in Chapter 4 reports on all except Culpeper County, which involves a small package plant for an airport industrial park. Its physical characteristics are so different from those of the other facilities that it would be misleading to include it in the analysis of system and process. (However, because a complete plant is involved, and because the service contract carries some highly interesting arrangements, it is referred to in some of the economic analyses in later chapters.)

For each of privatized cases the researchers contacted officials of engineering firms and the appropriate state regulatory agencies to identify a matching comparison facility. Selection criteria included facility size, type of sewage processed, permit limits, identity of the firms involved in design and construction, and the dates of project construction. The matching cases include Dothan, Alabama; Opelika, Alabama; Flagstaff, Arizona; Tolleson, Arizona; Lewiston, New York; Quakertown, Pennsylvania; and Greenville, South Carolina (Durbin plant). A southeastern city, to which we assign the pseudonym Blake, is used to provide a qualitative case study comparison with Auburn. All the comparison cases except one were financed in part by grants from EPA. The plant at Tolleson, Arizona, which served as a match on some measures of implementation for the Gilbert plant, was self-financed. The method of self-financing is an interesting sidelight because it points to the potential value of sewage plant effluent. The city of Tolleson sells its sewage plant effluent for use as a coolant by the nearby Diablo nuclear power plant. The income pays for not only the costs of sewage treatment but also a range of additional municipal service needs.

25. The National Pollutant Discharge Elimination System (NPDES) sets forth standards that wastewater treatment plants must meet. The standards refer to amounts of pollutants that are acceptable in the treated water discharged from the plant. The NPDES is central to the monitoring and enforcement program of the U.S. EPA. All wastewater treatment plants must submit samples for regular testing under NPDES standards and are subject to sanctions imposed by EPA or the state environmental regulatory agency in case they exceed acceptable limits of pollution.

26. Plant design may reflect unusual conditions (such as wastewater pollutants or special permit requirements); a plant location may have unusual aspects (such as limited space, adjacent residential neighborhoods, or rocky or swampy ground conditions); construction costs can be traded off against continuing O&M costs in many ways; labor and material costs vary from place to place; climatic conditions affect plant design and operation and vary from place to place; in some cases it is difficult at best to separate plant construction costs from other project costs, such as collector lines and pumping stations or even some engineering fees; the project may be an expansion and upgrading of an existing facility, some parts of which remain in use; in the privatized case part of the profits can accrue from arbitrage and from O&M over the span of twenty or twenty-five years; and the service contract may require the city to buy the plant back at the end of the contract period for "fair market value," an unpredictable quantity at best.

27. So defined, system and process are building blocks of political and administrative action. Reliance on these concepts in the study of urban politics is not new. In a much-cited comparison of "metropolitics and international politics," Holden (1964:633–34) calls for attention to "procedures of interaction." This term is an umbrella for matters including the number of players and the "frequencies and instrumentalities" of their "interaction." Calls for attention to these factors also appear in the literature on privatization. For instance, DeHoog (1984:35) states that it is "important to examine the contracting process and its procedures. The process itself will shape the results." The results reported here support the view that the same is true for the stages of project design and construction following contractual agreement.

28. O'Toole (1988a) develops and applies this distinction in terms of hierarchy and integration.

29. This outcome is not only vastly different from the norm on grant-funded projects but also highly anomalous when viewed from Marx's perspective on alienation (Ollman 1971). Marx argued that in capitalism wages replace the artisans' relationship to what they produce, thus leading to alienation. In this case, system and process in precisely that private sector context appeared to strengthen the workers' sense of satisfying personal relationship to what they were doing. It should be emphasized that "the workers" whose interview statements suggested this finding were hardly upper-level managers. For exam-

ple, one of the interviewees whose comments were very suggestive along these lines was in his early twenties and had no more than a high school education. He had just returned from manually cleaning the screens that filter the wastewater coming into the plant. This job is not very pleasant. He pointed out (and engineers confirmed) that virtually all grant-funded plants are designed with relatively expensive equipment to do this particular job automatically: it is difficult to get public employees to do this job. However, he continued, manual cleaning of the screens saves money and gets the job done at least as well.

30. For a more detailed review of tax issues in privatization with respect to the Tax Equity and Fiscal Responsibility Act of 1982 and the Deficit Reduction Act of 1984, see Quinn and Olstein 1984.

31. This discussion is based, in part, on Saltiel and Avruch 1986, which describes some of the major interests in state privatization laws.

32. The statistical analyses in this chapter were conducted by Dr. Randall G. Holcombe, professor of economics, Florida State University. Parts of the material have appeared in Holcombe 1990.

33. It is important to note that the cases in the Southeast study represent populations rather than samples. Because significance tests address inferences from samples to the populations from which they were drawn, the notion of statistical significance should be invoked in this case with caution.

34. The original Mount Vernon case study was conducted by Jean England, a graduate research assistant at Auburn University. The case study presented here is also based in part on Reinhardt 1988.

35. The WCRSA case study is based primarily on on-site interviews with WCRSA personnel, completed questionnaires, interviews with the privatizer, and a paper written by Charles R. Douglas, WCRSA director (see Douglas 1987).

References

AFSCME. 1983. *Passing the Bucks: The Contracting Out of Public Services.* Washington, D.C.: American Federation of State, County, and Municipal Employees.

Allison, Graham T. 1971. *Essence of Decision: Exploring the Cuban Missile Crisis.* Boston: Little, Brown.

American Federation of Government Employees. 1987. Statement of Robert E. Edzell, AFGE, before the Subcommittee on Antitrust, Impact of Deregulation, and Privatization. Committee on Small Business, U.S. House of Representatives, Washington, D.C.

Anderson, James E. 1984. *Public Policy-Making.* 3rd ed. New York: Holt, Rinehart and Winston.

Anthony Commission on Public Finance. 1989. *Preserving the Federal-State-Local Partnership: The Role of Tax-Exempt Financing.* Washington, D.C.: Government Finance Officers Association.

Armington, R. Q., and W. Ellis, 1984. *This Way Up: The Local Official's Handbook for Privatization and Contracting Out.* Chicago: Regnery Gateway.

Arthur Andersen and Co. 1986. *Tax Reform 1986.* New York: Arthur Andersen.

Babbie, Earl R. 1989. *The Practice of Social Research.* 5th ed. Belmont, Calif.: Wadsworth.

Beard, Charles A. 1913. *An Economic Interpretation of the Constitution of the United States.* New York: Macmillan.

Beck, R. W., and Associates, and Spiegel and McDiarmid. 1988. *Local Officials Guide—Municipal Incinerators: 50 Questions Every Local Government Should Ask.* Washington, D.C.: National League of Cities.

Birnbaum Jeffrey H., and Alan S. Murray. 1987. *Showdown at Gucci Gulch: Lawmakers, Lobbyists, and the Unlikely Triumph of Tax Reform.* New York: Random House.

Brooks, Harvey. 1984. "Seeking Equity and Efficiency: Public and Private Roles." In *Public-Private Partnership: New Opportunities for Meeting Social Needs,* edited by Harvey Brooks, Lance Liebman, and Corinne S. Schelling, pp. 3–29. Cambridge, Mass.: Ballinger.

Brooks, Harvey, Lance Liebman, and Corinne S. Schelling, eds. 1984. *Public-Private Partnership: New Opportunities for Meeting Social Needs.* Cambridge, Mass.: Ballinger.

Buchanan, James M., and Gordon Tullock. 1962. *The Calculus of Consent: Logical Foundations of Constitutional Democracy.* Ann Arbor: University of Michigan Press.

Butler, Stuart M., ed. 1985a. *The Privatization Option: A Strategy to Shrink the Size of Government.* Heritage Lectures No. 42. Washington, D.C.: Heritage Foundation.

―――. 1985b. *Privatizing Federal Spending: A Strategy to Eliminate the Deficit.* New York: Universe Books.

―――. 1987. "Privatization and the Management of Public Policy." Paper presented at the Annual Meetings of the American Political Science Association, Chicago, September 3–6.

Bynum, S. D. 1983. "Construction Management and Design-Build/Fast Track Construction from the Perspective of the General Contractor." *Law and Contemporary Problems* 46, no. 1 (Winter): 25–38.

Chandler, R. C. 1986. "The Myth of Private Sector Superiority in Personnel Administration." *Policy Studies Review* 5, no. 3 (February): 643–53.

Clark, R. C. 1984. "What Is the Proper Role of the Corporation?" In *Public-Private Partnership: New Opportunities for Meeting Social Needs,* edited by Harvey Brooks, Lance Liebman, and Corinne S. Schelling, pp. 195–220. Cambridge, Mass.: Ballinger.

Colman, William G. 1989. *State and Local Government and Public-Private Partnerships: A Policy-Issues Handbook.* New York: Greenwood.

DeHoog, Ruth H. 1984. *Contracting Out for Human Services: Economic, Political, and Organizational Perspectives.* Albany: State University of New York Press.

Denhardt, Robert B. 1984. *Theories of Public Organization.* Monterey, Calif.: Brooks/Cole.

Dilger, Robert Jay, ed. 1986. *American Inter-Governmental Relations Today.* Englewood Cliffs: Prentice-Hall.

Douglas, Charles R. 1987. "Using a Private Company to Provide a Public Wastewater Treatment Service." Paper presented to the Industrial Environmental Management Conference, Hilton Head, South Carolina.

Downs, Anthony. 1967. *Inside Bureaucracy.* Boston: Little, Brown.

Dror, Yehezkel. 1968. *Public Policymaking Reexamined.* Scranton, Pa.: Chandler.

Easton, David. 1965. *A Systems Analysis of Political Life.* New York: John Wiley and Sons.

EPA. 1984. *Study of the Future Federal Role in Municipal Wastewater Treatment.* Report to the Administrator, U.S. Environmental Protection Agency, Washington, D.C.

―――. 1987. *1986 Needs Survey Report to Congress: Assessment of Needed Publicly*

Owned Wastewater Treatment Facilities in the United States. EPA Doc. Washington, D.C.: U.S. Environmental Protection Agency, Office of Municipal Pollution Control.

―――. 1988. NMP Highlights. U.S. Environmental Protection Agency Enforcement Division, Office of Water Enforcements and Permits, Washington, D.C.

―――. 1989a. *1988 Needs Survey Report to Congress: Assessment of Needed Publicly Owned Wastewater Treatment Facilities in the United States.* EPA Doc. Washington, D.C.: U.S. Environmental Protection Agency, Office of Municipal Pollution Control.

―――. 1989b. *Public-Private Partnerships (P³) Strategy.* Washington, D.C.: U.S. Environmental Protection Agency, Administration and Resources Management (PM-225).

Executive Order 12615. 1987. "Performance of Commercial Activities." Washington, D.C.: The White House.

Feldman, Roger D. 1989a. "Can New Privatization Trend Save a Crumbling Infrastructure? *National Law Journal* 12, no. 1 (September 11): 1–4.

―――. 1989b. Comments made in a presentation on "Public-Private Partnerships for Infrastructure Finance" to the Conference on Making Ends Meet: Public-Private Partnerships in the 1990s, Washington, D.C.

Ferris, James M. 1986. "The Decision to Contract Out: An Empirical Analysis." *Urban Affairs Quarterly* 22:289–311.

Finley, Lawrence K., ed. 1989. *Public Sector Privatization: Alternative Approaches to Service Delivery.* New York: Quorum.

Fitzgerald, Michael R., and William Lyons. 1986. "The Promise and Performance of Privatization: The Knoxville Experience." *Policy Studies Review* 5, no. 3 (February): 606–13.

Foster, C. A. 1983. "Construction Management and Design-Build/Fast Track Construction: A Solution Which Uncovers a Problem for the Surety." *Law and Contemporary Problems* 46, no. 1 (Winter): 95–125.

Fraser, Robert, ed. 1988. *Privatization: The UK Experience and International Trends.* London: Longman, Keesings International Studies.

Fund for Renewable Energy and the Environment. 1988. *The State of the States—1988.* Washington, D.C.

Garcia, at 546, 83 L. Ed. 2d 1016, 105 S. Ct. 1005, quoting Gerhardt, 304 U.S., at 427, 82 L. Ed. 427, 58 S. Ct. 969.

Giantris, Philip D. 1989. "Business Perspectives—Environmental Infrastructure." In *Public Sector Privatization: Alternative Approaches to Service Delivery,* edited by Lawrence K. Finley, pp. 47–61. New York: Quorum.

Goggin, Malcolm L., Ann O. Bowman, James P. Lester, and Lawrence J. O'Toole, Jr. 1990. *Implementation Theory and Practice: Toward a Third Generation.* Glenview, Ill.: Scott, Foresman/Little, Brown.

Goldman, Harvey, and Sandra Mokuvos. 1984. *The Privatization Book.* New York: Arthur Young.

Goldman, Harvey, and Douglas J. Watson. 1985. "The Auburn Privatization Experience." Informational brochure. New York: Arthur Young.

Goodsell, Charles T. 1983. *The Case for Bureaucracy: A Public Administration Polemic.* Chatham, N.J.: Chatham House.

———. 1984. "The Grace Commission: Seeking Efficiency for the Whole People?" *Public Administration Review* 44, no. 3 (May/June): 196–204.

Habermas, Juergen. 1973. *Erkenntnis und Interesse.* Frankfurt am Main: Suhrkamp.

Hanke, Steve H. 1985. "Privatization: Theory, Evidence and Implementation." In *Control of Federal Spending. Proceedings of the Academy of Political Science,* edited by C. Lowell Harris, 35, no. 4:101–13. New York: Academy of Political Science.

———, ed. 1987. "Prospects for Privatization." *Proceedings of the Academy of Political Science* 36, no. 3. New York: Academy of Political Science.

Hardin, Garrett, 1968. "The Tragedy of the Commons." *Science* 162 (December 13): 1243–48.

Hatry, Harry R. 1987. "Problems and Concerns in the Use of the Private Sector for Delivering Government Services." Paper presented at the Annual Meetings of the American Political Science Association, Chicago, September 3–6.

Heilman, John G., and Gerald W. Johnson. 1989. "System and Process in Capital-Intensive Privatization: A Comparative Case Study of Municipal Wastewater Treatment Works." *Policy Studies Review* 8, no. 3 (Spring): 549–74.

Hempel, Carl G. 1968. "The Concepts of Covering-Law Explanation as Explicatory Model." In *Readings in the Philosophy of the Social Sciences,* edited by May Brodbeck, pp. 398–415. New York: Macmillan.

Henig, Jeffrey R., Chris Hamnett, and Harvey B. Feigenbaum. 1988. "The Politics of Privatization: A Comparative Perspective." *Governance: An International Journal of Policy and Administration* 1, no. 4 (October): 442–68.

Heritage Foundation. 1987. "Building Grass-Roots Support for Privatization." Presentation by Rep. Curt Weldon to the Heritage Foundation, May 19. Published in *Heritage Lectures,* no. 112. Washington, D.C.: Heritage Foundation.

Holcombe, Randall G. 1988a. *Public Sector Economics.* Belmont, Calif.: Wadsworth.

———. 1988b. "Tax Incentives for Privatization." Typescript provided to privatization research project. Department of Political Science, Auburn University.

———. 1988c. Personal communication to authors.

———. 1990. "The Tax Cost of Privatization." *Southern Economic Journal* 56, no. 3. (January): 732–42.

Holden, Matthew, Jr. 1964. "The Governance of the Metropolis as a Problem in Diplomacy." *Journal of Politics* 26, no. 3:627–47.

Hula, Richard C. 1986. "Introduction: Market Based Public Policy." *Policy Studies Review* 5, no. 3 (February): 583–87.

Illinois EPA. 1987. *State Revolving Loan Program for Financing Illinois Wastewater Treatment Needs.* IEPA, Division of Water Pollution Control, Springfield.

Jackson, John E. 1988. "The Battle of the Sectors." *Michigan Today* 20, no. 1 (February): 2–3.

Johnson, Gerald W., and John G. Heilman. 1987a. "Diffusion of Innovation: The Case of Privatization of Municipal Wastewater Treatment." Paper presented at the Annual Meetings of the American Political Science Association, Chicago, September 3–6.

———. 1987b. "Metapolicy Transition and Policy Implementation: New Federalism and Privatization." *Public Administration Review* 47, no. 6 (November/December): 468–78.

———. 1990. "Diffusion of Innovation: The Case of Capital-Intensive Privatization." Mimeograph.

Kash, Don E. 1989. *Perpetual Innovation: The New World of Competition.* New York: Basic Books.

Kay, John, Colin Mayer, and David Thompson, eds. 1986. *Privatization and Regulation: The UK Experience.* Oxford: Clarendon Press.

Kettl, Donald F. 1988. *Government by Proxy: (Mis?)Managing Federal Programs.* Washington, D.C.: CQ Press.

Kolderie, Ted. 1984. "Business Opportunities in the Changing Conceptions of the Public Sector Role." In *Public-Private Partnership: New Opportunities for Meeting Social Needs,* edited by Harvey Brooks, Lance Liebman, and Corinne S. Schelling, pp. 89–110. Cambridge, Mass.: Ballinger.

———. 1986. "The Two Different Concepts of Privatization." *Public Administration Review* 46, no. 4 (July/August): 283–91.

Kuttner, Robert. 1989. "The Perils of Privatization: False Profit." *Privatization Review* 4, no. 2 (Spring): 15–21.

Levitan, Donald. 1987. "Tax Reform: The Impact on Municipal Finance." *National Civic Review* 76, no. 1 (January/February): 71–74.

Lindblom, Charles E. 1982. "The Market as Prison." *Journal of Politics* 44, no. 2 (May): 324–37.

Longest, Henry. 1983. "The Federal Regulatory Perspective." Presentation at a Privatization Seminar sponsored by Arthur Young and the *Engineering News Record,* October, Washington, D.C.

McGarity, T. O. 1986. "Regulatory Reform and the Positive State: An Historical Overview." *Administrative Law Review* 38, no. 4:399–425.

Marx, Karl. 1965. *Capital.* Moscow: Progress Publications.

———. 1981. *Contribution to the Critique of Political Economy.* Moscow: Progress Publications.

Meier, Kenneth J. 1985. *Regulation: Politics, Bureaucracy, and Economics.* New York: St. Martin's.

Miller, Delbert Charles. 1970. *Handbook of Research Design and Social Measurement.* 2d ed. New York: McKay.

Moe, Ronald C. 1987. "Exploring the Limits of Privatization." *Public Administration Review* 47, no. 6 (November/December): 453–60.

Moe, Ronald C., and Thomas H. Stanton. 1989. "Government-Sponsored Enterprises as Federal Instrumentalities: Reconciling Private Management with Public Accountability." *Public Administration Review* 49, no. 4 (July/August): 321–29.

Montjoy, Robert S., and Laurence J. O'Toole, Jr. 1979. "Toward a Theory of Policy Implementation: An Organizational Perspective." *Public Administration Review* 39, no. 5 (September/October): 465–76.

Moore, Stephen, and Stuart M. Butler, eds. 1987. *Privatization: A Strategy for Taming the Federal Budget, 1988.* Washington, D.C.: Heritage Foundation.

Morgan, David R., and Robert E. England. 1988. "The Two Faces of Privatization." *Public Administration Review* 48, no. 6 (November/December): 979–87.

Morris, John. 1989. "Review of E. S. Savas, *Privatization: The Key to Better Government.*" Paper prepared for a seminar in Public-Private Administration and Policy, Department of Political Science, Auburn University.

Mosher, Alice. 1980. "The Relationship Between Personnel Ceilings and Contracting Out." Congressional Research Service briefing paper. Washington, D.C.

National Academy of Public Administration. 1989. *Privatization: The Challenge to Public Management.* A report by the academy's Panel on the Management of Privatization. Washington, D.C.

National Council on Public Works Improvement. 1988. *Fragile Foundations: A Report on America's Public Works.* Washington, D.C.

Nelson, Richard. 1987. "Roles of Government in a Mixed Economy." *Journal of Policy Analysis and Management* 6, no. 4 (Summer): 541–57.

Netzer, Dick. 1984. "Privatization." In *Setting Municipal Priorities,* edited by Charles Brecher and Raymond D. Horton, pp. 158–87. New York: New York University Press.

Niskanen, William A. 1971. *Bureaucracy and Representative Government.* Chicago: Aldine.

Ollman, Bertell. 1971. *Alienation: Marx's Conception of Man in Capitalist Society.* Cambridge: Cambridge University Press.

Ostrom, Vincent. 1974. *The Intellectual Crisis in American Public Administration.* Tuscaloosa: University of Alabama Press.

Ostrom, Vincent, and Elinor Ostrom. 1971. "Public Choice: A Different Approach to the Study of Public Administration." *Public Administration Review* 31, no. 2 (March/April): 203–16.

O'Toole, Laurence J., Jr., ed. 1985. *American Intergovernmental Relations.* Washington, D.C.: CQ Press.

———. 1988a. "Operating Costs and Performance in Municipal Wastewater Treatment: A Comparative Study of Public and Private Management." Auburn University Water Resources Research Institute Report.

———. 1988b. "Strategies for Intergovernmental Management: Implementing Programs in Interorganizational Networks." *International Journal of Public Administration* 11, no. 4 (April): 417–41.

Pagano, Michael A., and Richard J. T. Moore. 1985. *Cities and Fiscal Choices: A New Model of Urban Public Investment.* Durham, N.C.: Duke University Press.

Palmer, John L., and Isabel V. Sawhill, eds. 1984. *The Reagan Record: An Assessment of America's Changing Domestic Priorities.* Cambridge, Mass.: Ballinger.

Palumbo, Dennis J., and James R. Maupin. 1987. "The Political Side of Privatization." Paper presented at the Annual Meetings of the American Political Science Association, Chicago, September 3–6.

Peat Marwick Main and Co. 1987. *State Revolving Fund Training Course.* Manual and course presented by Peat Marwick Main and Co., the Ohio Company, and Squire, Sanders and Dempsey. Washington, D.C.

Peat Marwick Mitchell and Co. 1985. "Evaluation of Private Financing for Wastewater Treatment Facilities." Report to the U.S. Environmental Protection Agency.

Polkinghorne, Donald. 1988. *Narrative Knowing and the Human Sciences.* Albany: State University of New York Press.

Privatization Council. 1986. *Compendium of Privatization Laws.* New York.

Quinn, Kevin G., and Myron A. Olstein. 1984. "Privatization: Public/Private Partnerships Providing Essential Services." *Municipal Finance Journal* 5, no. 4 (Fall): 247–65.

Rehfuss, John A. 1989. *Contracting Out in Government: A Guide to Working with Outside Contractors to Supply Public Services.* San Francisco: Jossey-Bass.

Reinhardt, William G. 1988. "Public/Private Sewage Expansion: A Primer for Post-Tax-Act Deals." *Public Works Financing* (January): 7–12.

Report of the President's Commission on Privatization. 1988. *Privatization: Toward More Effective Government.* Washington, D.C.: President's Commission on Privatization.

Rogers, Everett M. 1983. *Diffusion of Innovation.* New York: Free Press of Glencoe.

Rosenbloom, David H. 1983. "Public Administration Theory and the Separation of Powers." *Public Administration Review* 43, no. 3 (May/June): 219–27.

Salamon, Lester M. 1981. "Rethinking Public Management: Third Party Government and the Changing Forms of Government Action." *Public Policy* 29, no. 3 (Summer): 255–75.

————, ed. 1989. *Beyond Privatization: The Tools of Government Action.* Washington, D.C.: Urban Institute Press.

Saltiel, David M., and Steven N. Avruch. 1986. "A Review of the State Privatization Statutes." *Privatization Review* 2, no. 4 (Fall): 30–47.

Savage, R. 1987. "National Clean Water Act Program Transitions into State Revolving Loan Funds." *Water Engineering and Management* 134, no. 6:24–25.

Savas, E. S. 1987. *Privatization: The Key to Better Government.* Chatham, N.J.: Chatham House.

————. 1989. "False Prophet: The Faulty Reasoning of a Privatization Foe." *Privatization Review* 4, no. 2 (Spring): 23–27.

Scully Capital Services. 1987. *Impact of the Tax Reform Act of 1986 on Privatization.*

Prepared for the National Council on Public Works Improvement. Washington, D.C.

Seidman, Harold, and Robert Gilmour. 1986. *Politics, Position, and Power: From the Positive to the Regulatory State.* 4th ed. New York: Oxford University Press.

Sharp, Elaine B. 1990. *Urban Politics and Administration: From Service Delivery to Economic Development.* New York: Longman.

Smith, Adam. 1937. *An Inquiry into the Nature and Causes of the Wealth of Nations.* New York: Random House.

Squires, Gregory D., ed. 1989. *Unequal Partnerships.* New Brunswick, N.J.: Rutgers University Press.

Stern, Fritz. 1957. *The Varieties of History: From Voltaire to the Present.* New York: Meridien Books.

Sullivan, Harold J. 1987. "Privatization of Public Services: A Growing Threat to Constitutional Rights." *Public Administration Review* 47, no. 6 (November/December): 461–67.

Sullivan, Ralph. 1986. "Effects of the 1986 Tax Reform Act on Privatization." Washington, D.C. Unpublished paper.

Sundquist, James L. 1984. "Privatization: No Panacea for What Ails Government." In *Public-Private Partnership: New Opportunities for Meeting Social Needs,* edited by Harvey Brooks, Lance Liebman, and Corinne S. Schelling, pp. 303–18. Cambridge, Mass.: Ballinger.

Tawney, R. H. 1926. *Religion and the Rise of Capitalism.* New York: Harcourt, Brace and World.

Tieder, J. B., and R. K. Cox. 1983. "Construction Management and the Specialty Trade (Prime) Contractors." *Law and Contemporary Problems* 46, no. 1 (Winter): 39–54.

Treiber, Hubert. 1985. "Crisis in Regulatory Reform: Remarks on a Topical Theme; or, Reflexive Rationality in the Shadow of Positive Law." *Contemporary Crises* 9, no. 3:255–80.

Tullock, Gordon. 1965. *The Politics of Bureaucracy.* Washington, D.C.: Public Affairs Press.

Waldo, Dwight. 1987. "A Theory of Public Administration Is a Theory of Politics Also." John Gaus lecture delivered at the Annual Meetings of the American Political Science Association, Chicago, September 3–6. Excerpted in *PS* 20 (Fall): 903–7.

Wartemberg, John P. 1989. Communication at the International Workshop on Urban Utilities and Infrastructure Management, Lyon, France, April 28.

Watson, Douglas J., and Thomas Vocino. 1990. "Changing Intergovernmental Fiscal Relationships: Impact of the 1986 Tax Reform Act on State and Local Governments." *Public Administration Review* 50, no. 4 (July/August): 427–34.

Wechsler, Louis F. 1982. "Public Choice: Methodological Individualism in Politics." *Public Administration Review* 42, no. 3 (May/June): 288–94.

Weimer, David L., and Aidan R. Vining. 1989. *Policy Analysis: Concepts and Practice.* Englewood Cliffs: Prentice-Hall.

Welch, Susan, and Kay Thompson. 1980. "The Impact of Federal Incentives on State Policy Implementation." *American Journal of Political Science* 24, no. 4 (November): 715–29.

Wiebe, Robert H. 1962. *Businessmen and Reform: A Study of the Progressive Movement.* Cambridge: Harvard University Press.

Wise, Charles R. 1990. "Public Service Configurations and Public Organizations: Public Organization Design in the Post-Privatization Era." *Public Administration Review* 50, no. 2 (March/April): 141–55.

Wittl, John F. 1985. *The Politics and Development of the Federal Income Tax.* Madison: University of Wisconsin Press.

Worthy, James C. 1984. "Managing the 'Social Markets' Business." In *Public-Private Partnership: New Opportunities for Meeting Social Needs,* edited by Harvey Brooks, Lance Liebman, and Corinne S. Schelling, pp. 221–40. Cambridge, Mass.: Ballinger.

Zimmerman, D. 1987. "Tax Reform and the State and Local Sector." *Public Administration Review* 47, no. 6 (November/December): 510–14.

Index

About the Authors

John G. Heilman and **Gerald W. Johnson** are Associate Professors of Political Science at Auburn University. Heilman received his doctorate from New York University, and Johnson holds a doctorate from the University of Tennessee.